SURVIVAL AND THE BOMB
Methods of Civil Defense

Survival and the Bomb
Methods of Civil Defense

Edited by

Eugene P. Wigner

Indiana University Press

Bloomington

London

Contents

v

Preface

Many books have already been written on civil defense and the reader may well ask why the writers thought this one to be necessary. The present preface will try to answer this question.

We felt that the books which are available fall into one of three classes. Those of the first class are fictionalized stories and depict mainly the horrors of nuclear war and the futility of civil defense. In a fictionalized story the writer is free to modify the actual facts and the writers of these books make ample use of this freedom. They strive for artistic rather than factual values, and the present writer would probably enjoy them if he had a liking for horror stories. There is no better subject for a horror story than nuclear war, and a nuclear war which finds the population wholly unprepared may be the most horrible war imaginable. However, whatever the artistic value of these books may be, they can hardly serve as rational guides when a decision concerning civil defense has to be made.

The books of the second class describe in some depth the drastic effects which nuclear war would have on our lives. The authors of these books start either with quite negative or with very positive attitudes toward civil defense and replace logical analysis with implicit emphasis on some values, complete disregard of others. This greatly oversimplifies the problems and permits the authors to arrive at their desired conclusions easily. The purpose of these books is to persuade rather than to inform. As a result, they fail to provide the reader with adequate information which would enable him to think rationally, and on his own terms, about civil defense.

The approach of the third group of books on civil defense is entirely pragmatic. They start from the possibility of a nuclear attack (which is undeniable), endeavor to describe its effects and to give rules for rational behavior which might mitigate the calamity. They do not explore the broader issues of civil defense preparations and they prove only that these preparations diminish the horrors of war and greatly increase the chances for survival. These are important points which we shall also discuss. However, they are inseparably related to other problems, such as the more lasting effects which a nuclear war would have on our way of life, on our physical surroundings, on our economy and social structure. Even the defense preparations themselves will have an effect on all these. These consequences of civil defense preparations appear to us to be almost as important as their effect on the physical survival of our people. Of similar significance is the effect of civil defense preparations on the likelihood of war. The omission of these questions is as little a fault of the pragmatic books as the lack of pragmatism is of the books striving for artistry. However, the omission of these questions convinced us of the need for a more comprehensive analysis, of the need for a book which tries to present the facts squarely yet does not disregard the problems which cannot be dealt with at the same level of precision as physical phenomena.

Several authors combined to write the present volume. This has, we fear, the consequence that it will not read as smoothly as a book written by a highly talented author. On the other hand, it has the advantage that the various subjects could be dealt with by authors with a long history of interest and competence in the subjects. It also has the advantage of not giving the impression that the views presented are those of a single individual who may well be isolated from the points of view of others and who might be unaware of some facts well known to others. Naturally, the book does not reproduce all the facts of the vast literature on the effects of a nuclear explosion or on the other subjects dealt with. It does endeavor to give a fair picture of the relevant facts, and it will have served its purpose if it contributes to the initiation of a rational discussion of civil defense.

I have written a short introduction before each chapter to help the reader relate it to the context of the book.

EUGENE P. WIGNER

Survival and the Bomb
Methods of Civil Defense

1

The Objectives
of Civil Defense

EUGENE P. WIGNER

¶ The first chapter is of an introductory nature. Whereas all later chapters deal with the technical problems, the limitations, and in particular the methods of the protection of people against the dangers precipitated by a nuclear war, this chapter is devoted to the rationale thereof. It tries to assess the effect of civil defense preparations on the likelihood of the outbreak of a war, on the social structure in peace time, and their effect on the morale and the confidence of the people in their government in case of a war.

Eugene P. Wigner

Thomas D. Jones Professor of Theoretical Physics, Princeton University

¶ Eugene Wigner was born in Hungary in 1902. He started his career as a chemical engineer, but his interests soon turned to theoretical physics. He taught this subject first at the Technische Hochschule Berlin, then at Princeton University and the University of Wisconsin. During the Second World War he was in charge of the group concerned with the theory of chain reaction and the basic design for the plutonium producing reactors at Hanford, Washington. He returned to Princeton University after the war but maintained his interest in nuclear energy and became a member of the General Advisory Committee to the U.S. Atomic Energy Commission. He acquired his interest in civil defense as a result of this membership and was commissioned by the National Academy of Sciences to be the director of the Harbor Project in the summer of 1963. This was a six-week study of

3

civil defense in which sixty-two natural and social scientists, engineers, and men of affairs participated. It was brought up to date a few months ago by a similar study. ¶ Wigner has published extensively on theoretical and nuclear physics.

T he subject of this book, beyond the present chapter, will be the physical, economic, and human factors related to the protection of people against the effects of nuclear war. Scientists versed in the various relevant disciplines will assess the problems of civil defense, try to evaluate its methods and limitations. This chapter, however, will deal with the rationale of civil defense, why, and to what extent, it is desirable to make every effort to protect people against the dangers of a war. It follows that it will be an "unscientific" one: it will not deal with the methods of, but the motivation for, a vigorous civil defense effort. It will try to articulate intentions, attitudes, and desires more than facts and procedures. Much of it will apply almost as well to active defense—that is, the destruction of the enemy's missiles and bombs—as it will to civil defense, which means protection of the population against the effects of the explosions of these bombs and missiles. The purpose of both defense systems is protection. In spite of its unscientific nature, we feel that the discussion will be useful if it succeeds in illuminating the political and emotional attitudes which are at the bottom of the civil defense controversy. As the reader well knows, this controversy has occasionally assumed a tone of stridency foreign to scientific discourse.

Civil defense is part of the total defense of the country. According to the preamble to the Constitution, one of the purposes of the Union was "to provide for the common defense." It seems difficult to think of defense without making every effort toward protecting what is most important: the lives of the people. It is, furthermore, difficult to avoid the conclusion that this defense is a federal responsibility. Why is it, then, that proposals to invigorate the civil defense effort have found so little response in the past? Is it that those who believe in the vital importance of civil defense do not make their voices heard because they are reluctant to espouse a cause for which others—the federal authorities—have been given responsibility? Is it that the federal authorities are reluctant to advocate a vigorous program which is passionately opposed by some, even though only a small minority? Do they, in particular, hope to be able to discharge their responsibilities without incurring the wrath of this minority? What motivates the opponents? Are they opposed only to civil defense, or to all defense of this country?

These are difficult questions, as are all questions concerning human motivation. Furthermore, the answers may, and in this case surely do, differ from person to person. Before trying to propose such answers, we shall give a very brief description of what civil defense means in terms of installations and arrangements; why such installations and arrangements appear desirable—in fact, necessary—to us; what the objections to civil defense are and to what extent they are valid. This description will then be followed by a discussion of the problems confronting civil defense and of the image of civil defense in our country. If an important decision has to be made, one should try to visualize the consequences of the various courses of action and choose the one with the most desirable consequences. I will try to analyze three such consequences: (a) the probable effect of civil defense preparations on the likelihood of war, (b) the effect of such preparations on the national morale in peace, and (c) their effect in the event of war.

What Is Civil Defense?

Before considering the question of how civil defense preparations, or the absence of such preparations, might affect our future, it is well to state in a few words what such preparations could consist of. Since much of the rest of this book is devoted to a more or less detailed description of civil defense, its purposes and functioning, I can be very brief at this point.

Three types of preparations can be distinguished: those which are intended to protect people and their livelihood during an enemy attack, those which render the postattack period easier by securing the availability of the physical necessities of life (principally food, shelter, and means of communication), and finally, those which should facilitate the preservation of our social institutions and of our government. Shelters—fallout shelters in rural areas and preferably blastproof shelters in cities and near military targets—form the principal means for protecting the lives of people from the attack itself. Safe and accessible storage of food, medicines, and of some other materials, such as tools and gasoline, could greatly abbreviate the period of severe privation and render the resumption of production faster and easier. Clear and well-thought-out plans for maintaining lines of communication and of succession, including the establishment of a chain of command for the postwar period, would reduce the confusion accompanying any catastrophe.

Clearly, the effectiveness of all these preparations would depend not only on their extent but also on a variety of other circumstances such as the magnitude of the enemy attack, the time of year, and many other factors. The remainder of this book will try to set limits on the effectiveness of the preparations. Even so, a large uncertainty is bound to remain. This uncertainty has been used as an argument against the preparations. This appears to me to be unjustified: even a somewhat uncertain future is preferable to a certain but entirely bleak one.

Civil Defense Preparations and the Likelihood of War: The Effect on Possible Causes

The effect of the civil defense posture on the likelihood of a war should be easiest to foresee. Nevertheless, it has been argued both that preparations to protect the people against the effects of a war render the war itself more likely and that they make it less likely. I shall first present the two views sharply formulated and then try to analyze them and the actual situation as objectively as I can.

Accepting the realistic point of view that conflicts of interest will inevitably arise in the future, the opponents of civil defense maintain that the U.S. Government would be more intransigent if it were assured that most of our people will survive a war than in the absence of such assurance. Such intransigence and lack of willingness to yield or compromise might well induce an exasperated opponent to mount an attack or at least to threaten one. The attack would trigger retaliation by the United States. Even the threat of it could precipitate a war with all the devastation that this would entail. Hence—to continue their argument—it is better if the U.S. Government is not in a position to be intransigent: we should have no civil defense. And the opponents go further:

Even the preparations themselves could precipitate the war. Should an inimical government view our civil defense effort as an indication that we are planning to attack, it could well "jump the gun" while our cities are still more vulnerable than his. At the very least, an inimical government may fear that its power to coerce the United States will diminish as a result of the defense efforts, and it may want to use its power while it is still unopposed.

The supporters of civil defense, on the other hand, believe that the protection of our civilian population afforded by shelters, and the other plans of civil and antiballistic defense, will decrease the danger of blackmail by possible antagonists, will contribute to the easing of tensions, will enable our government to negotiate slowly and calmly, and thus will decrease the possibility of war. They support this point of view by historical precedent, by studies of the temperament of nations, and by their greater faith in our own people and government.

It is in their faith in the United States that the two sides differ most markedly. Both agree that the power of the United States would be raised by civil defense, and admittedly power often leads to aggressiveness. However, the United States had a much more dominant power position in the years following 1945 when it alone possessed the atomic bomb, a superiority that no amount of civil defense would assure. Yet even under dire provocation such as the Berlin blockade, the occupation of Czechoslovakia, the breaking of the Hungarian peace treaty, it showed no tendency to exploit this power. It stood by while Russia annexed Estonia, Latvia, and Lithuania, yet pointedly refused to annex any people or territory for itself.

In fact, all the conflicts between East and West since the termination of the Second World War have been initiated by some move of the East toward an extension of its power. This has either been unopposed by the West as in the case of the occupation of Czechoslovakia, the breaking of the peace treaties with Hungary, Rumania, etc.—or has been resisted by the West, as in the case of the invasion of South Korea, the Berlin Blockade, etc. No conflict has been started by the West to extend its sphere of influence and there is no sign to indicate that the United States has any desire to extend its territory. It does wish to protect its own and that of its allies, and civil defense would greatly help this endeavor.

Civil Defense Preparations and the Likelihood of War: The Possibility of Nuclear Blackmail

A particular enemy tactic that may become very dangerous is called nuclear blackmail. If our people have little protection so that a hostile government could cause large losses of life in our population, this government might be tempted to make demands on us and to back them up by threats. They could demand that we evacuate Berlin, or that we withdraw our protection of the Philippine Islands—many similar demands are conceivable. Our present "defense" against such threats is the counterthreat of retaliation. This, however, seems a very fragile defense because no retaliation would bring back to life those who would die as a result of the enemy attack. Hence, our opponents may not take our counterthreat too seriously. They might figure, and perhaps rightly so, that we would, let us say, rather evacuate South Korea than exchange the lives of millions of Americans for the lives of any number of people of the hostile country. Let us assume, therefore, that the absence of protection of our people does induce us to yield and to do our opponent's bidding. If it does not, we may as well have protection for them—the enemy is less likely to attack protected than unprotected people and the protection would not increase the chances of war.

However, if we do give in to a threat, the opponent will have learned that he can impose his will on the United States by threats. He will be tempted to repeat the procedure, and every repetition, if successful, will make us weaker both physically and in our determination. In order to avoid foreign domination, we would be forced ultimately to fight[1]—and fight after having lost our allies and much of our vigor.[2]

The set of events just described, ending in war under very adverse conditions, need not come true even if the U.S. population is left unprotected. All of us hope that it would not. However, the grim possibility discussed above is not unlikely. World domination is a nearly irresistible temptation for some, especially rulers not bound by a tradition of accountability to their people.

If the United States made a vigorous effort to provide protection for its people against the dangers of a nuclear war, the course of events just described would become much less likely, if not impossible. The threat which a hostile country could pose would be much less severe physically and therefore would be less likely to succeed. Hence, the probability that it would be attempted would be reduced[3]—"Politics is the art of the possible." Not only the physical but also the emotional conditions for nuclear backmail would become less favorable. The defense preparations would make it clear that the United States is prepared to face threats.

The opponents of civil defense claim that, while civil defense would decrease the danger of nuclear blackmail being attempted against us, it would increase the chances that the United States might become too aggressive. This possibility appears to me to be remote. There is every reason to believe that the United States has no desire to impose its rule on other countries. In this regard, there is a great difference between the United States and the dictatorships. The contrast between the attitudes of the United States and the USSR at the conclusion of World War II was mentioned earlier. The USSR increased its territory by 266,000 square miles, extending its rule over 22,700,000 people—more than 10 percent of its prewar population. The United States granted independence to the Philippine Islands. The independence of the countries liberated by the United States is complete—those "liberated" by the USSR are still under tight rein.

It is in consonance with this difference that our government does not engage in hate propaganda against the East—it is by hatred that people can be motivated to a war of conquest.[4] If there is in our country an incitement to hate the opposite side, it is restricted to a small fringe, does not represent our government, and all of us have an opportunity (and hence an obligation) to counteract hate-mongering. A glance at the news media of communist countries shows the fundamental difference between the two sides in this regard. There is a similar difference between the treatment of those who want to leave the country: the contrast between our open borders and the six-mile-wide mined strips with barbed wire fences guarded by machine gunners could not be more obvious. The argument that assuring a reasonable chance for survival to our people would tempt our government to precipitate a nuclear war is far-fetched indeed.

Civil Defense Preparations and the Likelihood of War: The Accidental War

If no civil defense preparations have been made, a single enemy weapon can wreak tremendous damage and the report of an attack is likely to be answered with a heavy counterattack. This is the picture of accidental war which has often been projected. Similarly, in a very tense situation, people may start to flee from probable target areas, such as large cities, and thereby aggravate the tension. The enemy may feel compelled to act, lest his "hostages" disappear. These dangers are less grave if there is reasonable protection for the population. However, even if one does not consider specific contingencies, it is clear that the greater the danger which threatens the people, the more tense their leaders will become and the more likely they will be to make an error. The assurance, provided by civil defense preparations, that most of the people can find protection on short notice, would lessen this danger.[5]

In order to assure that the shelter taking—either haphazard or organized—does not increase tension, it is important that it does not worsen the opponent's strategic position. It is important, therefore, that the sheltering response time be short; that is, that people *can* take shelter even if they start to do so only when the attack is underway. In this case, the bargaining position of the opponent does not deteriorate even if some people do take shelter ahead of time and a spontaneous movement to shelter in a severe crisis—which may be unavoidable—would not induce the opponent to take precipitate action.

City evacuation has often been proposed as an effective way of reducing civilian casualties resulting from a nuclear war. Planning and organizing such evacuation would be significantly less costly than the building of shelters. However, city evacuation, though strongly advocated by the civil defense authorities of the USSR,[52] does have the disadvantage that it may aggravate the crisis—and an organized evacuation would aggravate it more than a spontaneous exodus of people from the cities.

In summary, I find little to support the facile conclusion that, if one makes preparations to decrease the effects of a war, one makes the war more likely. Least of all is this true if the preparations are made with due consideration for all their effects, in particular their effects to precipitate or aggravate a crisis. If this is done, the preparation will allay fears, ease tensions, and can become a powerful force for the preservation of peace.

Both civil and active defense—that is, antimissile missiles and other installations designed to destroy the enemy's antipopulation weapons—can decrease the effects of a nuclear attack. Hence, much that was said above about civil defense and about shelters, applies also to active defense. The relation and possible joint employment of active and passive defense will be discussed in Chapter 6.

Effect of Civil Defense Preparations on Our Society, Our Freedoms, and on the East

Since the effect of civil defense preparations on the likelihood of war led to widely divergent opinions, it is not surprising that their less clearly specifiable effects are also subject to controversy.

According to the anti–civil defense opinion, effective civil defense preparations would be accompanied by severe regimentation of the whole population and destroy our freedoms and our democratic way of life. This argument has been carried so far as to claim[6] that a truly adequate protection of the people (at a cost of about twice that of our space program) could be accomplished only at the expense of building programs for schools and hospitals. A second fear sometimes voiced is that the shelter program would evoke enmity toward the Soviet people and their form of government. Simply having to accept the idea that our freedom, our country's independence, must be defended might well hinder us in making genuine overtures toward peace and friendship. A third line of argument is that the daily sight of the grim reminders of war would insidiously affect people's peace of mind. They would become nervous and irritable, wanting perhaps to "get it over with," i.e., to attack the potential enemies now. Fourth and last, the proposed civil defense preparations would put the communist governments at a considerable disadvantage, consigning them to a permanently inferior and impotent position. They would feel, as Henry Wallace said, like a "caged lion" and would be inclined to act accordingly. This is not in the interest of anyone.

The large majority of people has little sympathy with the last two arguments. As to the fear of consigning communist governments to a feeling of impotency, most of us feel that their striving could be directed toward bettering the fate of the people under their care. As to the adverse effect of civil defense preparations on the attitudes of our own people, most of us believe that these are not children who should be kept happy by concealing from them the facts of life. Communist aggression will not go away if people close their eyes to it. If civil defense preparations remind them that our way of life is in danger, they should be reminded of it. The awareness that freedom sometimes has to be defended rather than simply taken for granted may even have the salutary effect of causing people to value it all the more.[7]

This last point also illuminates the different evaluations of the effect of civil defense preparations—and of defense preparations in general—on our democracy. The opponents of civil defense, particularly the extreme opponents, fear that, in order to conform with reasonable defense requirements, the average citizen would have to be strictly regimented. They do not describe the type of regimentation that would be necessary but propose, instead, that our fellow citizens be kept innocently oblivious of the dangers which may threaten their lives and also our democracy from the outside. Similarly, people must not be told that there are measures which would provide significant protection against nuclear weapons.[8] People may demand such protection. Those holding to these views set themselves up as seers and claim the privilege of determining what the people should; and what they should not, be told. Their ideal seems to me to be an elitist state—a system which I find repugnant.

Those holding the pro–civil defense point of view visualize an enlightened citizenry, well aware of the dangers to the nation and the cause of freedom, but courageously facing these dangers and willing to make the sacrifices which the defense of these freedoms requires. Surely, in peacetime, these sacrifices are not very grave, would be willingly made, and no regimentation would be necessary. The pro–civil defense view implies confidence in the sound judgment of most of our citizens and in their sober realism, even if most of the majority cannot articulate the basis of their judgment. If we refuse to make sacrifices for our ideals now, these ideals will be permanently discredited.[9]

Hand in hand with the different evalution of our fellow citizens, there is a difference in the evaluation of the probable behavior of communist governments. While those holding the anti–civil defense view do not go so far as to endorse the "dictatorship of the proletariat," many of them tend to forget recent history, greatly to magnify the benevolence of the Soviet leaders both toward the people at home and toward the foes of yesterday. The advocates of civil defense have a longer memory. They recall the extermination of conquered nations; the Katyn massacre; the fate of Nagy, betrayed to his death; the fate of Tibet; the economic exploitation of the conquered satellites. They may realize that these are transient phenomena and that the initial savagery of the conqueror is likely to subside later. However, they are determined to avoid the "period of transition." As Maynard Keynes said, "Things may adjust in the long run, but in the long run we are dead."

The point of the anti–civil defense opinion which surely has a certain validity is the second one, that if extensive preparations, visible to all, are used to resist the threat of aggression of the communist governments, this may make the transition to conciliation and friendship more difficult.[10] It is not easy to tell how large the effect of civil defense preparations would be in this regard —checking the account submitted to us by our bank, also an operation designed to prevent the infringement of our interests, fails to induce in most of us a permanent distrust or enmity toward the bank. But again there is an asymmetry, and I find it saddening not to be able to evoke, on the part of most advocates of this argument, any criticism of the hate propaganda fostered by the communist governments. Such hate propaganda surely prejudices conciliation and friendships much more than sober preparations against specific acts which are, furthermore, not directed against any particular government.

The two points of view regarding the effects of civil defense preparations on our society in peacetime which were described are extremes. This applies particularly to the picture given of the anti–civil defense point of view. Many shades of opinion between the two extremes exist, but the two extremes do illuminate the nature of the fundamental choice to be made.

Actually, it is quite possible, or even likely, that a modus operandi might be found which does not offend the sensibilities of either group. If shelters can be designed so that they are useful in peace and solve some of the emerging problems of urban life, they will not offend those who fear that the antagonism of people toward the communist governments will harden as a result of the daily awareness of defense installations. At the same time, the defense will be provided and this should not only reassure those of our citizens who feel the need for such defense, but should also give pause to the governments which might be tempted to abuse the "naked defenselessness" of our people. The most urgent problem of urban life with which the solution of the shelter system may be connected is the problem of transportation. The streets in cities are becoming ever more crowded and it is increasingly difficult to accommodate both vehicular and pedestrian traffic. If one of them could be shifted, at least in part, underground, the congestion could be relieved considerably. Some cities, such as Chicago, are planning underground passageways for pedestrians, others (such as Dallas) similar passageways for trucks and some (e.g., New York) for cross-city traffic. Several cities will install new subways. If the underground roadways can be made blast-proof, they can serve a double purpose.[11] Actually, there is every indication that the subways in the USSR are so designed as to be able to serve also as shelters; at least those in Moscow, Leningrad, and Kiev are about 120 feet underground and are provided with blast-proof doors 1½ feet thick. Here is an example well worth imitating by the West.

Effect of Morale During and after Hostilities

Opponents of civil defense rarely discuss the situation after the end of the war, except perhaps to make comments such as, "The living will envy the dead." Those favoring a vigorous defense program point to the enormous help which even modest preparations toward recovery can make. In particular, if food for a reasonable period were safely stored throughout the country, people would be relieved of the worry of the next day's bread and could devote their energy more completely to longer range plans for recovery. The same holds true for medicines. Recovery itself would be speeded enormously if key materials, such as gasoline and essential tools, were stored; and if people were kept in readiness to repair electric transmission lines, and for similar functions. All these questions will be discussed in more detail in the last part of this book (Chapters 11, 12, 13).

Even more important than the effect of preparations on economic recovery might be their effect on the morale of the people. Should disaster strike with no provision having been made to help the people recover, their faith in their leadership would be irrevocably shattered; they would feel betrayed, abandoned. (See in this connection particularly Chapter 13 by Peter G. Nordlie.) To restore the economy, the social system, and the unity of the country under these circumstances would be much more difficult not only because the situation would be so much worse physically, but also so much worse emotionally. "To a very large extent, the morale of the survivors of an atomic attack will be determined by the effectiveness of civil defense measures," as Irving Janis tells us in Chapter 3.

The Public Image of Civil Defense

I have attempted in the preceding discussion to give an appraisal of the effect of civil defense preparations on the likelihood of war, on the morale and attitude of the people in peacetime, and on the overall situation in the event of war. My approach is different from the highly dramatized discussions so prevalent in the literature.[12] These usually start with a description of the horrors of nuclear war, which are real indeed, and are based on the situation which would prevail in a country which entirely neglected its civil defense. This circumstance is, however, not pointed out,[13] and the reader is almost left with the impression that civil defense causes rather than mitigates the horrors of war. These articles show considerable artistic skill, but it is difficult to escape the conclusion that they intend to scare rather than to inform the public. The articles, essays, and speeches in question are not the only causes of the warped picture that much of the public has of civil defense. Those of us who advocate civil defense have to share some of the blame. Few technical problems proceed in a straight line from setting to solution. Errors and false starts accompany most overtures, a valid solution coming only after some paths are explored which do not lead to the goal. In most cases, the eventual user knows nothing about the unfertile attempts and sees only the success of the final effort. There are only a few cases, such as the history of the reciprocating engine,* in which the false starts are well recorded.

Civil defense preparations cannot be kept in the dark, and the public becomes aware of all the errors in judgment, all the false starts, that are made. This is unfortunate because it undermines the confidence of the people in the competence of those concerned with their protection. Even if the rocket designers did not have more technical insight into their problems than those working on civil defense, their competence would be more highly regarded by the public because their false starts are not subject to everyone's scrutiny. It is, however, appropriate to recall in this connection that the original errors in the design of the reciprocating engine—

* This is the old-fashioned steam engine, still in use in coal-fired locomotives.

attempting to use the boiler also as a cylinder—did not detract from the usefulness of the final product.

At present, there are several thorough and, we believe, unprejudiced studies on the technical feasibility and on the social impact of civil defense preparations. The purpose of the present book is to present an analysis of the problems involved: physical, economic, and social. Some of the older analyses—much more detailed and technical than the present one—are still classified. The conclusions of the Harbor Study, undertaken in the summer of 1963 and sponsored by the National Academy of Sciences, are available to the public and are still interesting reading.[14] So is the record of the hearings in the 88th Congress by a committee which actually held an adverse opinion toward civil defense when the hearings started. However, "a slow but easily perceptible change was evident in the attitude of the committee members. Opposition to the program melted and then hardened into an attitude of firm belief in the support of the fallout shelter program."[15] It should be noted, however, that the subject of the hearings (fallout shelters) was a more modest program than those which are primarily considered in the present book. We wish to quote, finally, from the report of the civil defense panel of the President's Science Advisory Committee: ". . . the possibility of survival and recovery may depend on the adequacy of civil defense."[16]

Summary

"The need for an effective system of civil defense is surely beyond dispute. No city, no family, nor any honorable man or woman can repudiate this duty." These words were spoken by Winston Churchill on March 1, 1955—more than ten years ago. His attitude was not the result of a careful analysis of the favorable and unfavorable consequences of a vigorous civil defense effort, but derived from his instinctive appreciation of the simple realities of life. Yet I believe that an analysis of the probable consequences of providing or of failing to provide protection for the people against the dangers of a war supports his conviction. In particular, it is difficult to avoid the conclusion that better protection would render the contingency against which we protect, that is, a war, less likely.

As to the effect of civil defense preparations on the structure of our society and on our democratic institutions, certain groups claim that such preparations are harmful, even destructive, but the reasons they cite differ greatly. The most extreme frankly want the United States to forfeit its present position of power, "to be shorn of discernible influence in international affairs, say, put in the position of Finland."[17] They seem to distrust any evidence of international goodwill ever shown by the United States. Fortunately, those who hold this view are as few in number as they are voluble in expressing themselves. I am opposed to these views and consider our present position of power as a responsibility and a privilege which we should cherish and use for the furtherance of international goodwill. We admit mistakes. However, on the whole, we trust our elected representatives and can cite much evidence to support our opinions. It is also good to remember that, had the United States in the past followed the policy now advocated by those who do not trust its present intentions, it would not have been able to offer effective help against national socialist Germany. These arguments do not convince those who view a courageous and self-assured United States with apprehension and of course, no country's attitude can be foretold with absolute certainty. What continually surprises me is that those who distrust the future intentions of the United States so often do not show similar distrust of the intentions of those governments whose professed purpose is the domination of the world.

There remains, of course, the argument that if one cannot foresee the results of a decision with certainty, one should refrain from making that decision. This argument has considerable emotional attractiveness. It should be remembered, though, that not making preparations for mitigating the effects of a dreadful danger is also a decision and a very grave one.

There is little question as to the effect of civil defense preparations on the suffering, and also on the morale, of people during and after a possible war. This point is disregarded by those who are opposed to civil defense because the war is too dreadful to contemplate. Nor is it one of the arguments particularly stressed by those who are in favor of civil defense because they consider the principal purpose and hoped-for effect of civil defense a decrease in the likelihood of war, not a decrease in the losses and suffering caused by a war. The difference between the lives lost without effective civil defense preparations, and the difference in the morale of the people who would feel forsaken and betrayed in one case, or resigned to the necessity of their suffering in the other case, is too great to be simply overlooked.

The reasons for the United States not having undertaken effective civil defense preparations in the past are difficult to assess. No matter what these reasons were, they should not prejudice the future. Rather, a fresh look should be taken at the problem, and the purpose of this book is to provide such a fresh look.

Notes

1 This is what actually happened to France and was one of the bases of Hitler's expectation that he would be victorious in the Second World War.

2 The alternative of complete surrender—though it has also been proposed as a choice to be considered seriously (cf. e.f., A. Rapoport, *Strategy and Conscience* [New York: Harper & Row, 1964], p. XX), and even advocated (e.g., Erich Fromm, *Daedalus*, 89, 1,015 [1960])—is not discussed here. It is questionable that it would bring peace to this country; more likely, the United States would become the staging area for a conflict between the conquering and another government. In addition, it is, of course, deeply repugnant to most of us to see the precedent established that the more humane governments are replaced by less humane ones because the former are unwilling to assert themselves.

3 Eugene Rabinowitch said in the *Bulletin of the Atomic Scientists* (VI, 266 [1950]) that "The fourth (i.e., civil defense) was—and re-

mains—the only fully effective means of reducing the consequences— and thus the likelihood—of an atomic attack if rational attempts to make it impossible prove futile," thus linking the unlikelihood of an attack to the reduction of its consequences.

4 It is not very pleasant to quote such statements nor it is easy to make a choice. The Sunday, June 27, 1965, New York *Times* describes the propaganda to which children in China are exposed. The article starts, "Recommended reading for children in Communist China today centers on stories stained with blood and tears." The article contains a lurid description of the kind of literature which Chinese children are given to read. The intensity of the hatred which shows in some of the Chinese propaganda is nearly incomprehensible to the average American. As compared with it, the USSR hate propaganda is relatively mild. For this writer, the most memorable remark dates from the zenith of coexistence. It is Khrushchev's praise of certain authors for their "irreconcilable hatred" of the West, ironically enough in his address on culture (see *Encounter* pamphlet 9; London: Society for Cultural Freedom, 1964). A more recent statement in a similar vein was made by Leonid I. Brezhnev on July 3, 1968: "The social and political order which engenders political banditry arouses contempt and revulsion throughout the world. The rotten society, the degrading society, the decomposing society—this is the United States called even by those who recently lauded the American way of life." However, one can also find much more conciliatory utterances. The pronouncements of the satellite regimes are somewhat in between those of the Chinese and USSR leaders. "Boundless hatred for the enemies of the German Democratic Republic is an indispensable qualification for the socialist soldier."—Admiral Verner, Deputy Minister of Defense of GDR (East Germany). "The mere existence of imperialist states is a menace to peace."—Czinege, Minister of Defense of Hungary. "Imperialist" in official pronouncements in communist countries means "Western." "The flame of retribution must not be limited to urban buildings and centers but the countryside must go up in smoke also. Remember the forests, the fields, the crops. Remember the pipelines and oil storage tanks."—Havana Radio.

This is not to say that the propaganda is fully effective—at least not yet—nor that the people of the East hate the West (some time ago a man, freshly arrived from Hungary, inquired whether there really had been a McCarthy). However, the propaganda does show what the leaders want their people to believe and the purpose, if possibly distant, is not really doubtful.

5a See J. Levey, *Survive,* Vol. 2, No. 2, (1969), 2.

 5 According to Thomas C. Schelling (*Daedalus* 89, 896 [1961]), "We both have—unless the Russians have already determined to launch an attack and are preparing for it—a common interest in reducing the advantage of striking first, simply because that very advantage, even if common to both sides, increases the likelihood of war." Civil defense decreases the disparity between offensive and defensive weapons and hence decreases the advantage of striking first.

It may be remarked that it also renders disarmament easier by the same token: the possession of a few nuclear weapons does not assure a dominant position. Hence, the control of the possession of such weapons need not be absolute.

 6 Dean D. F. Cavers of the Harvard Law School during the Panel Discussion on Civil Defense, organized by the American Nuclear Society. The verbatim report of the discussion appeared as a report (*Panel Discussion on Civil Defense* [ORNL—3865; Gatlinburg, Tenn., 1965], p. 34), issued by the Oak Ridge National Laboratory and obtainable from the Clearinghouse for Federal and Technical Information, U.S. Department of Commerce, Springfield, Va.

 7 This point of view has been eloquently stated in E. Teller's *The Reluctant Revolutionary* (University of Missouri Press, 1964).

 8 This point is well illustrated by the discussion about the effect of fires on shelters in connection with the Harbor Report (Publication 1237; Washington, D.C., National Research Council, National Academy of Sciences, 1964) conducted in *Scientist and Citizen* for May and August 1965, and February 1966. *Scientist and Citizen* is a publication of the St. Louis Citizens' Committee for Nuclear Information, an organization strongly opposed to civil defense. There are eight physicists on *Scientist and Citizen*'s Advisory Board who should be able to make calculations on heat conductivity. However, similarly erroneous views on technical questions, made in authoritative tone by nontechnical people, are too numerous to quote.

 9 It may be of some interest to note that there are conditions under which pacifist Einstein observed: "I consider military preparedness in these countries (the democracies) the most effective means, in times such as these, of making progress toward the goals of pacifism." (*Einstein on Peace; His Diaries and Letters,* eds. O. Nathan and H. Norden [New York: Simon & Shuster, 1960], p. 247.)

10 In a form which appears to me somewhat exaggerated, this argument was particularly espoused by L. Festinger, under the title, "Cognitive Dissonance." The dissonant elements are the defense against possible aggression and the striving for true friendship.

11 The dual uses of shelters are discussed in some detail in Chapter 9. Another "dual" use refers to the whole civil defense organization, not to the shelters. It is to cope with natural disasters, such as floods, earthquakes, etc. The civil defense organization has not always been successful in this regard. However, it has earned high praise for its activities during and after the earthquake in Alaska. During the Arizona flood, January 1966, the mayor of Phoenix (M. Graham) said: "Phoenix pays $29,000 per year for civil defense; it is worth $29,000 per hour today."

12 See, e.g., *On the Beach, Fail Safe, Seven Days in May*. These books depict the hopelessness of the survivors, their will power completely paralyzed. Actually, every evidence points in the opposite direction: adversities stimulate people to greater effort and inventiveness toward self-preservation. This was the experience also during the siege of Budapest, to be described in Chapter 4. There are, of course, also books depicting the terrible suffering of conquered people, for instance, John R. Hersey's *The White Lotus* (New York: A. A. Knopf, 1965).

13 See, e.g., "Medical Aspects of Civil Defense," Victor Sidel's contribution to the symposium sponsored by the American Association for the Advancement of Science in Berkeley, December 1965 (Publication 82; Washington, D.C.: AAAS, 1966).

14 *Civil Defense; Project Harbor Summary Report* (Publication 1237; Washington, D.C.: National Research Council, National Academy of Sciences, 1964). This report was updated recently. The "Little Harbor Report" is obtainable from the Division of Technical Information, U.S. Atomic Energy Commission, Washington, D.C.

15 88th Cong., 1st sess., House of Representatives Report 715, p. 3.

16 P. I–1 of the Report of the PSAC panel on civil defense.

17 A. Rapoport, Moderator's Remarks at the meeting on n. 13.

2

The American Public and Civil Defense

JIRI NEHNEVAJSA

¶ In a democracy civil defense depends on public opinion for two reasons. First, similar to all other measures of national importance, it requires the approval of the majority of the citizens. Second, in order to be effective civil defense requires the cooperation of large segments of the public, both at the time of its planning and installation, and also if the need to use it should arise. Chapters 3 and 4 will deal with the second question. As to the first question, there are several well-documented indications of public approval and willingness to cooperate. Thus, about 85 percent of those asked to provide rather detailed data from which the suitability of their basements as shelters could be determined did provide such data. A similar percentage of house-owners made the basements of their homes available for the storage of survival rations. However, the group of people involved in these activities do not represent the total population: they were house-owners or dwellers in one-family houses. ¶ Professor Nehnevajsa's study of opinions and attitudes on civil defense is based on a scientific selection of people; there is every reason to believe that the views obtained are representative of the views of the total population. In addition, his study describes not only the present attitudes but gives an insight also into the development of these attitudes. It contains much interesting material on public attitudes and opinions on many questions of war and peace. His findings may be an eye-opener for many.—E.P.W.

Jiri Nehnevajsa

Professor of Sociology, University of Pittsburgh

¶ Born in Czechoslovakia in 1925, Dr. Nehnevajsa was educated at the University of Masaryk (1945–48), University of Lausanne (1948–49), and University of Zurich (1949–50), and received his Ph.D. from the University of Zurich (1953). Prior to his appointment at Pittsburgh (1961), he was assistant professor of sociology at Columbia University (1956–61) and served as chairman of the Products Control Committee of the System Development Corporation in Paramus, New Jersey (1960–61). He was assistant professor (1952–56) and instructor in sociology (1951–52) at the University of Colorado. He is also associated, as principal research scientist, with the System Development Corporation. ¶ He has contributed chapters to the *Soziologen-Lexikon* (ed. Bernsdorf, F. Enke Verlag); *Handbuch der empirischen Sozialforschung* (ed. Koenig, F. Enke Verlag); *Automation and Society* (ed. Jacobsen, Philosophical Library); *Contemporary Sociology* (ed. Roucek, Philosophical Library); *Sociometry Reader* (ed. Morena, Free Press), a volume which he also co-edited. With Pearson and Elliott, he authored *Message Diffusion* (Univ. of Colorado Press), and others. ¶ Dr. Nehnevajsa is a Fellow of the American Sociological Association, member of the American Association for Public Opinion Research, American Institute for Astronautics and Aeronautics, and others. He is a member of the Civil Defense Committee of the National Academy of Sciences.

M 1. *Introduction*

More than fifteen years have elapsed since the first studies on national attitudes toward civil defense were undertaken. The present report tries to present a picture of the nation's images of, and attitudes toward, civil defense measures as gleaned from the studies of the past fifteen years. In order to include a broad range of results within the limited space of this paper, it has been necessary to sacrifice depth and detail of analysis contained in the original studies.

The studies in question are based on opinion polls; these give responses of Americans to questions of an interviewer. These responses are the data which, when analyzed, show certain patterns, and the studies endeavor to uncover these patterns. Some of the patterns are invariances; that is dispositions which have remained constant throughout time either for the population as a whole or for certain segments of the population. Other patterns are trends; that is, changes in the orientation of the public, which may be accounted for by shifts in the national or international environment or which, even if unaccounted for, appear to be important.

The "Americans" whose responses form the data furnished by the interviewers constitute a sample drawn from some appropriately defined "universe." The universe may consist of inhabitants, or households, of several specific cities. It may be a universe of community elites explicitly defined or empirically located for the purpose of an inquiry. It may be a universe consisting of the total national population beyond given age limits. The samples are selected by procedures which insure that the probability of selection for any element (individual, household, etc.) is known. This permits us to generalize from the sample to the underlying universe and establish a degree of confidence that the results based on the sample are not greatly at odds with the results we would obtain if we questioned every person in the universe.

The discussion which follows will be restricted to the consideration of those aspects of civil defense programs which pertain to the nation's defenses under conditions of enemy attack upon the United States. Hence, we will ignore any data that might be available on other disaster functions of civil defense.

2. *Opinions on the Likelihood of a Nuclear War and Its Probable Character*

World War III is believed to be less likely today than it was a few years ago or, in turn, a decade ago.[1] At the same time, the public views reflect increasing expectation of limited wars around the face of the globe. Should a central war occur at all, it is not expected to start from a sudden attack by the United States on the Soviet Union (or China). Nor is it, however, expected to start because of an accident. Rather, Americans feel that a major war might come about through escalation of more limited conflicts. This statement obscures the fact, of course, that many respondents consider a Soviet attack, or Soviet and Chinese attack, upon the United States a likely way in which the unlikely World War III might start, and that they also believe that full-scale fighting could break out after a period of deteriorating international relations but not, necessarily, preceded by more limited combat (Table 2.1).

Table 2.1. Which is the most likely way in which you think the World War will start, *if it should come?*[*]

		Percent 1963	*Percent 1966*
	World War III will never start.	14	1.0	1.1
A.	The war will start by accident.	174	12.4	7.6
B.	The war will start by smaller, more local wars becoming ever bigger until they change into a full-scale World War.	468	33.2	35.3
C.	The war will start with full-scale fighting after a period of worsening international relations.	224	15.9	13.7
D.	The war will start quite suddenly by a planned Russian, or Russian and Chinese attack on the United States.	309	21.9	18.1
E.	The war will start quite suddenly by a planned American attack.	10	.7	.9
F.	As additional nations will have nuclear weapons, some nation other than the United States, the Soviet Union, or China will start World War III.	192	13.6	8.4
	Other	17	1.2	.7
G.	The war will start through war between China and the Soviet Union.	26	no data	14.2
Total		1,434	99.9 (N = 1,408)	100.0 (N = 1,478)

[*] From the 1963 civil defense national probability sample, and from 1966 study.

Since limited warfare is expected, but a major war is anticipated to a substantially lesser degree (and the numbers of those who expect a central war has been dwindling), this means that our public does not believe that brushfire wars would, in fact, escalate. Should a central war break out, however, it is not thought to remain limited to the uses of conventional weapons. At the same time, the public does not expect such a war to be spasmodic in character either, that is, an all-out exchange of essentially all available thermonuclear devices in the earliest phases of the war.[2] The Soviets are seen assigning the highest priority to military targets in the United States and the next highest value to inflicting damage upon the nation's industrial complex. Population-centered attacks (that is, targeting to maximize casualties) are not believed to be a high priority goal in Soviet plans for waging a war.[3]

These are, indeed, interesting viewpoints of the general public which, admittedly, is not well versed in military doctrine, not knowledgeable in weaponry and weapons effects, not familiar with Soviet thinking apart from what it has learned from newspapers and other media of public information. Neither is it acquainted with most of the technical aspects of international violence of our time.

Small wars are expected, as is the basic maintenance of the status quo. These views are not incompatible with each other since the current state of affairs is already characterized by a localized conflict, that in Viet Nam. But the likely options involving limited wars and the basic continuation of the status quo are highly undesirable.[4]

Indeed, Americans would like to see the cold war terminated through arms control and disarmament measures. This alternative, however, is not believed very likely.[5] The lower likelihood of this most desired option may be, in part, accounted for quite readily. The public would like to see global disarmament under inspection and control of some kind of a United Nations police force. As a second alternative, Americans would like to see nuclear disarmament with provisions for inspection and control. At the same time, they believe that the Soviet Union is inclined to support nuclear disarmament without control and inspection provisions built into the agreement, or even a global disarmament without the enforcement measures to ensure its workability (Table 2.2).

Clearly, the public does not see the Soviet Union intent on having a major war. Americans do believe that Soviet statements re-

Table 2.2. Disarmament Situations by 1969*

	U.S. Public Expects Most		U.S. Public Desires Most		U.S. Public Thinks Russia Desires Most	
	1964	1966	1964	1966	1964	1966
Continuance of the current armament race	40.1%	43.4%	3.6%	2.8%	16.3%	15.3%
World disarmament with no control provisions	3.0	3.1	5.3	7.0	26.6	18.3
World disarmament with U.N. police force control	13.8	7.0	53.7	50.0	3.6	4.9
Disarmament of nations other than U.S. and Russia	2.6	5.4	2.3	2.3	16.7	22.8
Nuclear disarmament with no control	3.0	14.8	1.1	3.2	25.6	25.7
Nuclear disarmament with control	17.1	18.3	25.2	22.6	5.7	6.1
Major arms reduction	20.4	7.9	8.8	12.1	5.5	6.8
	100.0%	100.0%	100.0%	100.0%	100.0%	100.0%

* From the 1964 civil defense national probability sample and from 1966 corresponding study.

garding arms control and disarmament are largely serious; the bone of contention, of course, is the nature of inspection, control, and enforcement but not, it seems, the principle itself.

3. *General Dispositions Toward Civil Defense*

All major studies since 1950 reveal favorable attitudes toward civil defense. This may seem to contradict the tone of the articles in media of public information or, in particular, many lay publications of professionals who have addressed themselves to the subject.[6] Nonetheless, the results have been unequivocal in this regard. The data are consistent over time and across various national samples. Roughly, 2 out of 3 and perhaps even 3 in 4 Americans favor civil defense measures; perhaps 1 in 10, and as few as 1 in 20, are in consistent opposition. Most of our citizens would like to see further expansions in civil defense measures.[7] This attitude is found to be rather independent of the state of affairs current at the time of the interview and of the state of knowledge of the specific respondent.

Furthermore, the favorable evaluations of civil defense are not patterned in that they would characterize specific segments of our population. This is quite different from many opinions in which we are accustomed to find age, sex, race, religious, political, income, educational, regional, and class patterns. Both favorable and unfavorable sentiments cut across all these population groupings and categories in basically similar proportions so that the civil defense attitudes fail to be correlated with many salient characteristics of the populace. Within the fundamental pattern of favorableness, younger people are consistently even more favorable than are older people, women somewhat more than men—although women with very high educational achievements tend to be more prominent among the opponents of civil defense. Similarly, married people are more favorable than are single, separated, divorced, or widowed Americans but these segments, too, are highly positive in their responses. Couples with children are also even more favorable than are those without children, and respondents from larger households exceed in the strength of their endorsement the interviewees from small households or the positive attitudes of respondents who live alone. Finally, people from the largest metropolitan complexes (of 2 million inhabitants and more) and people from the countryside tend to be somewhat less inclined to be strongly positive than do Americans in middle-sized cities or other communities. People who worry more about the future are somewhat more favorable than those who appear less worried; but this is not worrying of the pessimistic variety because precisely the more pessimistic Americans are actually less favorable than are more optimistic respondents. The "worriers" seem to adopt a kind of insurance notion of civil defense, a concept adopted by the government for the past several years as central to the rationale for taking preventive measures; the "worriers" do not expect a major war more than do others but seem to express a desire to be ready for one if it should come. The "pessimists," on the other hand, tend to expect a major war more than do others, and believe that little, if anything at all, could be done to minimize its disastrous effect upon our nation. If proponents and antagonists of civil defense preparedness were drawn from somewhat distinct population segments—and this would be indicated by correlations of civil defense attitudes with other properties of the respondents—the national discourse about passive defenses might be conducive to the formation of new, or reinforcement of old, cleavages in the body politic. The absence of such associations coupled with the predominant positive assessment of the programs does not make civil defense a divisive issue although in a particular community at a particular time a specific local program might well become divisive.[8]

Instead, it places the problem into the context of issues on which there exists something like national consensus. This, of course, also has the effect of degrading the saliency or urgency of civil defense; the lack of built-in structural controversy throughout the nation also may help explain the low overt demand level, that is, the extent to which the population actually actively demands civil defense preparations. To the public, civil defense seems to be a routine and even self-evident undertaking.

We think that this explains the fact that civil defense issues have generally not been at stake in political campaigns for national or state office. There are no particular voting blocs to be gained or lost, except perhaps in the situation in which a candidate would make opposition to civil defense a major campaign issue. In this instance, we would expect this position to cost some votes, in fact, far in excess of the few votes such an issue might gain for a given candidate. While these statements hold in general, occasional local variations may exist.

Finally, some data are available on the manner in which Americans perceive their neighbors, the administration, their mayor (or equivalent), the Congress, their local clergy, their local newspaper editor, and such key groups and individuals in regard to civil defense. A summary of the findings is quite easy: the respondents do not identify any group or any influentials (in terms of position in the social system and not necessarily in terms of "real" influence) as opposed to civil defense programs.

An interesting result, in fact, obtains: respondents view themselves as somewhat less favorable to the programs than they consider the administration to be; and at the same time, they believe that people in their community are somewhat less favorably disposed than they are themselves. But these are differences within the context of overwhelming favorableness both of the respondents and of their attributions to the administration, their neighbors, Congress, and others.[9]

4. *Dispositions Toward Specific Programs*

Now, of course, people might be in favor of civil defense in general, but unwilling to accept specific programs which implement it. This is not the case. The least favored program is that of family shelters constructed at the expense of the individual American. Thus the actual program of some years ago has been least favored, and this may, in part, explain its less than spectacular success. Yet, the respondents claim (eight in ten and more) that they would be willing to have a family shelter if the government paid the expenses for it: far fewer would be willing, at least at the verbal level, to construct shelters if they were given the materials free of charge, or if the cost were tax deductible.

On the other end of the spectrum of desirability, measures for protecting school children are just about unanimously endorsed. School shelter programs are highly desirable, the allegations about their anxiety-engendering potential notwithstanding.[10] Whether this attitude has anything to do with shelters as such or whether it simply reflects the deep sentimentality of the public toward children (for whom thus any sacrifice is in order), we cannot say. Yet, this does not mean that specific school boards and people in particular communities, would be inclined to divert parts of school construction costs to sheltering provisions. The decision as to how scarce resources are to be allocated in the course of educational expansion programs is determined more by local conditions than by the general public desire to see the children protected against the hazards of a thermonuclear war.

Similarly, programs of shelter construction in industrial establishments and in shopping areas are highly desired. The marking and stocking program is also favorably evaluated, although by 1963 more than one-half of our citizens did not know that anything was being done in their communities in the way of surveying, marking, and stocking. The percentage of informed citizens increased by 1966, but not in any spectacular way. Not only is this a desired program, its implementation also has been considered quite probable (along with the school shelter concept).[11] Furthermore, there are more objective measures of its viability. The program has led to the marking and gradual stocking of millions of shelter spaces with some fallout protection capability; the owners of surveyed buildings have cooperated with the administration exceptionally well. Indeed, more than one-half of all the surveyed and technically effective facilities have become integrated into the program. The reason of the building owners for not joining the program was, as a rule, not opposition to civil defense (only about 1 in 10 of the non-participating owners were opposed and another 1 in 10 did not like the idea of the posting of a shelter sign), but the potential use of the sheltering areas for other purposes.[12]

Over the years there is evidence of increasing support for public shelters, and especially for programs which entail federal financing or federal financial support. More Americans prefer public shelters than would like private facilities (regardless of who pays for them); and most anticipate and want a mix of public and private shelters, which is the most logical program.[13]

Even hardened (that is, blast resistant) facilities are favored although we think that this is simply in the absence of any adequate knowledge on the part of the public about the difficulties attendant to constructing blast shelters, say, in Chicago or New York or for that matter in any major city in the nation.* What we are saying is that the public is receptive to blast shelters whether or not the concept itself is understood. Now it is essential to emphasize that various evacuation programs are also highly favored. This seems understandable. The earliest civil defense program, compatible with the age of long-range bombers and the warning time thus available before the ICBM era, stressed evacuation. Evacuation routes are still identified in many of our nation's communities. In other words, there is no clear dissociation of present civil defense thinking from its past—and it is largely a technical question whether the idea of evacuation should be totally abandoned.[14]

Furthermore, note that our citizens do not anticipate an accidental outbreak of a major war; by far more people expect some escalation effect leading to a war than expect that the conflict might begin "suddenly." We may argue that our people intuitively feel that strategic, rather than tactical, warning would most probably be available so that evacuation programs do not seem unreasonable. Finally, and this further points to an explanation for the apparent lack of urgency with which the public views the situation: if a major war would come about "gradually" rather than "suddenly," much could be done in the way of civil defense preparedness in

---

* EDITOR'S NOTE—Some of the contributors to this volume disagree with the assessment of difficulty here expressed.

the intervening period. The willingness to become informed, and to act, under acute crisis conditions is clearly shown by the events surrounding the Berlin wall or the Cuban quarantine tensions in which the escalation potential appeared, and possibly was, very real.[15]

The basic pattern indicates that the public essentially believes civil defense to be a government job which it approves of but which it does not want to manage. This may simply reflect a desire to avoid having to do anything, at least in the absence of an acute threat; it may mirror a public belief that the defense of the nation, after all, must be planned and implemented by the federal government and not by individual American families or even communities.

But this has not meant that even individual and family activities seen as reasonable would not find a great deal of public support. The 1966 data, for example, reveal high desirability of a program whereby private homes with basements would be surveyed, and the owners informed if their home qualifies as a shelter. Almost 9 in 10 Americans consider such an effort "desirable" and just about 6 in 10 believe it to be "highly desirable." It is then not surprising that, on balance, about 7 in 10 home-owners in those states in which the program was carried out actually responded to the Census Bureau request for information on a few key characteristics of their homes with the view of having their house evaluated for its sheltering potential.

Nor are Americans opposed to the idea of being provided with a definite (public or other) shelter assignment for themselves and their family members, that is, to be told which shelter facility they should use in the event of a nuclear attack upon the country. More than 95 percent of the 1966 respondents expressed themselves positively about such a program, and more than 2 out of every 3 respondents believed it to be "highly desirable." Corresponding government programs thus find a highly receptive climate, and there is little doubt about the nationwide feasibility of efforts based on such concepts.

5. *Shelter Effectiveness*

Whether or not particular protection facilities would do the job for which they were designed or designated is a technical question. Images which our people have of the possible effectiveness or ineffectiveness of shelters are not. These perceptions are highly salient in that people may not avail themselves even of existing structures if they should believe that they actually increase the danger to themselves and to their families, or if they have no significant effect on the chances for survival.

Substantial proportions of Americans do not, personally, expect to survive a thermonuclear war. In each community, with rare exceptions, people view themselves as more (or at least equally), likely targets than other cities and towns of the nation.[16] Even should they survive the initial attack because their particular area might not be subject to direct bombardment, most people feel that they could not survive the secondary effects of the weapons, that is, fallout. When fallout shelters are postulated, the number of Americans who think that they would have a very good or good chance of surviving increases sharply, and most respondents anticipate living through a thermonuclear war, if they were provided with shelters and not directly attacked.

Table 2.3. Shelter Effectiveness

| | 1964* | | 1962** |
Chances of Survival	Original Survival Estimate	Survival Estimate with Shelters	Survival Estimate with Shelters
Very good	4.7%	18.4%	21%
Fairly good	21.2	47.4	36
50–50 chance	11.3	13.6	—
Fairly bad	21.0	10.6	} 25
Very bad	34.7	8.0	
No chance at all	6.9	1.8	10
Don't know	—	—	8

   * *Perceived Effectiveness of America's Defenses*, pp. 105–106.
   ** *The Public's Opinions on Existing or Potential Federal Fallout Shelter Programs*, p. 9.

In this regard, the data indicate that shelters are believed to have a good deal of effectiveness; only about one in twenty respondents by 1964 think that their survival odds would be exceptionally poor with or without fallout shelters (Table 2.3).

In 1966 the distribution of responses concerning the "original survival estimate" (as in Table 2.3) remains just about the same as it was in 1964: survival estimates with shelters, if anything, indicate increased optimism in that some 23 percent of those interviewed thought that their chances were actually "very good," 47 percent rated them as "good," and 14 percent as just about 50–50.

6. *Costs of Civil Defense*

We may think of costs in two distinct, though related, ways. On one hand, civil defense programs entail particular price tags. On the other hand, there are social costs to be incurred in terms of possible or actual impacts of civil defense systems upon the national and international environment.

The shelter survey program and its attendant support systems cost a little less than 50 cents a person per year; a program to add federal funds for the inclusion of shelter spaces into existing buildings and into buildings under construction in particular, involves perhaps $1.60 per person. The development of a full fallout shelter system including the construction of shelters in the areas in which inadequate shelter spaces are available on the bases of past and expanded surveys might cost about $2.15 per person annually. The development and implementation of blast shelter programs in likely target areas along with fallout sheltering for the remainder of the population enhances the cost to about $21 per person a year or some $4 billion annually for the nation. A similar price tag is attached to some combination of fallout shelters and active defenses, the development of antiballistic missile defenses.

While in mid-1963 the nation was spending about 75 cents per person per year the public believes that actual civil defense costs have been about $4.60. The desired cost amounts to about $20.30. This means that Americans overestimate greatly the actual costs of current programs and that they believe much more ought to be spent in this area. In fact, the desired level of expenditures matches the most ambitious alternatives considered by the administration. thus far, and it far exceeds the cost of those options which have been actually proposed. This fact is further underscored by the observation that only about 1 in 70 respondents are convinced that the nation ought to be spending nothing on civil defense, whereas 6 in 10 respondents cite figures in excess of $10 per person annually.[17]

In the consideration of civil defense measures, problems associated with their effect upon the international environment are of great importance. The antagonists of passive defenses have tended to argue that civil defense systems, among other things, would enhance the chances of a major war. The proponents have occasionally asserted that civil defense programs would have the reverse impact because of their deterrent value. Right or wrong, Americans as a whole do not accept either argument. Nearly two-thirds of the respondents assert that civil defense programs are irrelevant with regard to chances for a major war; and as many individuals consider them irrelevant from the vantage point of added deterrent capabilities of the nation.[18]

Queried about conditions under which people might construct their own shelters, most respondents argue that they would do so if the chances of war were greatly increased. Coupled with the previous results, this suggests that sudden stepping up of civil defense activities, and particularly sudden decisions to move to programs of a major scope, might indeed be interpreted as indicators of deteriorating international conditions and convince quite a few Americans that the likelihood of war is greater than they may have thought it to be. But this is quite different from the proposition that the prospects for war would be actually increased. The actual danger of war has to do with an evaluation of Soviet intentions and

Soviet interpretations rather than with the possible, and perhaps even plausible, impact of rapid large-scale civil defense measures upon war expectations of our public. There is no evidence to suggest that gradual development of increased civil defense capabilities would have even this impact.

Shelter owners, the few there are, do not find that their relations with their neighbors have been negatively affected due to the precautionary measure they have taken. Nor do they find that they are laughed at or ostracized, and there is no evidence on the part of their neighbors to support a different conclusion. Most people, in fact, argue that they would grant access to their shelters to friends and neighbors as well as to strangers up to shelter saturation.[19] In a more general sense, two out of three Americans are convinced that people throughout the nation, and specifically in their neighborhoods, would help one another in the event of a thermonuclear war rather than merely look after their own interests.[20] Of course, this does not mean that about one in three Americans feel that people would not help one another and would look after only themselves and their family members.

Data of this nature cannot be construed as evidence of what would really happen under conditions of attack; but all disaster studies point to the cooperativeness and altruism of people affected by a disaster and of outsiders, the people from nonimpacted areas, who come to their aid. The shelter owners do not appear more aggressive, more bellicose, nor more complacent. Like other Americans, they would like to see the cold war end through reconciliation and disarmament; they find a major war equally unacceptable; they do not even expect it to happen any more than do others. They are, however, somewhat more worried in general and more concerned with the implication of the possible, if unlikely, war.[21]

7. *Consequences of Thermonuclear War*

No one can doubt the terrible effects which a major war would have upon our country and the world. This point seems beyond discussion, and there are no data to support the notion that the public might be blissfully unaware of the likely consequences.

While the public is fervently opposed to having a war, at the same time most Americans feel that their compatriots would make the best out of the bad situation should war take place. They are convinced that the nation could be rebuilt. They are convinced, as many as eight in ten, that such reconstruction would produce a country quite similar in its adherence to democratic values to the United States of today. They think that enough people would survive, even if they personally might not, to proceed with the job of reconstruction. And they do not believe that life would cease to be worth living.[22]

These are, of course, projections of sentiment into a world beyond one's comprehension or imagination. Yet, for what they are worth, they fail to suggest defeatism or pessimism or despair even should the unimaginable become reality. This relative optimism in face of a possible catastrophe may seem, and may actually be, quite naive and strained. But it is there and the tone it sets for the national climate of interpretations of world affairs cannot be lightly dismissed. It reflects a readiness, though perhaps only at the emotional and sentimental level, to cope with whatever may come. To students of American national character, past and present, these are not surprising features.

8. *Actions*

Some 2 percent of Americans claim to have constructed fallout shelters in their homes. For the past several years, and certainly since about 1961, this percentage seems to have remained stable. Whether such claims are valid, or whether the shelters to which the respondents refer are technically sound at all, we have no way of telling. But these are people who feel that they have done what had been suggested to them.[23]

About as many people argue that they plan to build fallout shelters. In an international environment in which the chances of a major war seem to have been declining, and in which people believe the likelihood has been decreasing indeed, the implementation of such plans does not appear probable. Furthermore, the national shift in emphasis from private to public facilities discourages even the extremely limited private activity which might otherwise exist.

Yet, one in four respondents state that they have taken some measures in their homes to provide a modicum of protection for their families.[24] These steps, if we accept the claims at their face value as we must, need not have been adequate or appropriate. Again, there is a feeling of having done something for one's family and the relevance of this cannot be ignored.

Throughout the years many Americans have volunteered their services to civil defense programs, and quite a few have actually participated. Many more express a willingness to volunteer and give some of their time to civil defense activities.[25] Those who are unwilling to work for civil defense rarely say that they are opposed to the program. As reasons, they suggest family and work obligations along with physical incapacitation of one kind or another: thus, the reasons for not being willing to participate are credible and they do not reveal objections to the program itself.

On the local level, carried out largely by volunteers to begin with, civil defense programs do not differ from most volunteer-based efforts throughout the country either in their difficulties of recruiting, or of sustaining, interested workers. Civil defense may not have been more successful than other efforts, but it would seem hard to show that it has been less so.

The various indices thus suggest more activity than appears on the surface. Whether much more public participation would not actually tax the system beyond its present limits of human and material resources and thus be conducive to major frustrations is not at all clear. We have already pointed to the greatly increased public activity level under acute crisis conditions: in large numbers, people seek information both from official sources and from each other; problems of civil defense become prominent in discussions with co-workers, friends, and neighbors, and particularly with family members; people make some minimum plans as to what they might do if war were to occur while they are separated from their families; they stock food and water above and beyond similar patterns of behavior in more "normal" circumstances; some additional shelter building occurs, considerably more is planned but never implemented. Thus when Americans say, as respondents to questionnaires, that imminence of war danger would, in fact, make them "build shelters" or "seek to be protected," the recent crises lend support to the notion that they really mean it.[26]

9. *Apathy*

The public has been frequently charged with being "apathetic" toward civil defense measures. Can lack of public clamor for active civil defense systems or for legislative action in this area be construed as evidence of apathy? This is, at best, highly doubtful. How many millions of Americans have rallied in some overtly known manner to demand the war on poverty—an unquestionably favored program? How many millions of Americans have demanded Medicare by triggering large-scale pressures on the President and the Congress? How many millions of Americans have similarly demanded the reduction of federal income taxes, a program which again has been welcomed by most (or all) citizens? How many millions of Americans have actively demanded foreign aid? How many have demanded the establishment, and continuation, of the Peace Corps?

Is it reasonable to conclude that the public has been apathetic to the war on poverty, Medicare, foreign aid, the Peace Corps, reduction in income taxes, or many other programs? These are the kinds of questions which need answering before the customary and superficial conclusion is drawn that the public has been apathetic toward civil defense or that it has been more apathetic to such programs than to other major governmental efforts. Of course, there is evidence of fairly low sense of urgency associated with measures of passive defense. But this would seem to make sense in face of the fact that the public does not expect a major war; that it believes that a major war, should it come, would start gradually and not unexpectedly so that there might be some (sufficient?) time to undertake various drastic steps and to implement various crash programs; that the nation's defense has been the task of the nation's government rather than of local organizations or of families; that the government has better information on which to base decisions about technical defense issues, and therefore, the government knows rather well when to initiate and implement various measures; that there exists national consensus regarding desirability of civil defense programs so that the issue is a routine one and does not call for organized public clamor.

Furthermore, even the most knowledgeable people must have something of a wait-and-see attitude with regard to civil defense systems above and beyond the wait-and-see evaluation of the international environment which accounts for the variable urgency of any program. Though intrinsically reasonable, but not fully explained, shifts from evacuation programs to family shelter systems and again to the utilization of existing public facilities raise questions as to the appropriateness of given measures in the light of possible policy changes in the future. We wish to underscore that even though such policy changes may well be dictated by sound technical considerations, their effect on the public initiative is bound to be adverse. Should individual families construct fallout shelters at their own expense if such shelters might be subsequently financed, in part or in toto, by the government? Should communities augment federal subsidies for public shelters in existing, or new, buildings if the decision-makers might hope that eventually the total cost will be absorbed by the federal government? Should fallout shelters be incorporated into existing structures if it may become desirable to provide for blast protection as well? Should protection capabilities in city areas be developed at all, regardless of who might be paying the bill, if programs of (strategic) evacuation to other protected areas may become feasible?

These are no easy questions. If the evidence fails to support the conclusion regarding public apathy or indifference, it also does not support the idea that the public is hyperactive. The nation's response has been a measured one. It has not been hysterically responsive to situational stimuli in the absence of longer-range implications. The public, however, will go along with just about any governmental program of civil defense. In large numbers, people would volunteer their time and effort if this were needed. If our people were told what to do, when and how and why, they would be likely to do it since in the enormously complex matters of political-military affairs of the world few Americans consider themselves more expert than they believe their administration and the Congress to be. In simple terms, Americans display basic confidence in their government even if, on occasions, specific policies do not meet with public approval.

10. *Uses of Public Opinion*

Results based on surveys of the public sentiment are not "votes" and should not be considered as such. They are expressions of viewpoint, disposition, attitude. As such, they provide the nation's policy-makers with advice on matters of policy which, in addition to the full spectrum of other technical and nontechnical information, is necessary for arriving at balanced decisions in exceptionally complex national and international circumstances and within the constraints of available resources. Public opinion establishes a climate in which certain policies may be easier to adopt and implement than others. Data on public attitudes also permit the identification of the sources of difficulty attendant to actual and prospective governmental actions: such difficulties may result from lack of knowledge, or unfavorable evaluation of a program, or fears regarding its potential social and monetary cost. The policy-makers, of course, sometimes may feel guided by the state of public opinion;

they may feel restricted or limited by it. Often, however, it is their obligation to guide public opinion. Even though this does not apply to an expanded civil defense program, it is well to point out that unpopular decisions may also have to be made for reasons which outweigh their lack of acceptability. In such instances, data from surveys point to areas in which the public needs to be enlightened, to ways of explaining policy, to the dynamics of implementation of policy in a less than receptive environment.

Thus the purpose of our discussion is not to advocate particular approaches to civil defense or to oppose them. This certainly cannot be done solely on the basis of public opinion data any more than the decisions themselves can be grounded solely in such considerations. Rather, we have sought to sketch out the main contours of the riverbed of public sentiment and some of the major characteristics of the prevailing climate as they bear upon the vexing problems of civil defense systems as tools of the total national capability to come to grips with the nightmare of thermonuclear warfare. And yet, the world is also pregnant with the promise of a great and ever-improving future. How to strike a balance?

Notes*

1 The percentage of Americans in national samples who think another world war is likely has dwindled since the early fifties. S. B. Withey of the Survey Research Center at the University of Michigan reports that in 1952, 53 percent thought a world war to be likely, 47 percent had this view in 1954, 38 percent in 1956, and 33 percent in 1961 (*The U.S. and the U.S.S.R.*, p. 36). D. K. Berlo in a 1962 sample found 33 percent thinking an attack likely (*The Public's Opinions on Existing or Potential Federal Fallout Shelter Programs*, p. 29). G. N. Levine and J. Modell report 35 percent of their 1963 nine-community sample thinking nuclear war likely (*The Threat of War and American Public Opinion*, p. 91). In 1964 the national Civil Defense Survey found 39 percent of its probability sample thinking

* Full citations appear in the list of references which follow the notes.

a nuclear World War III likely. Although these figures are not all directly comparable because of wording differences and the presence or absence of a middle (50–50) category, they do reflect an overall trend toward diminishing expectation of war. In the 1966 study we find some 31.8 percent of the respondents assigning World War III probabilities higher than 50–50.

2 Only 4.9 percent of the respondents in the 1964 Civil Defense Survey thought a world war would be fought with conventional weapons alone. An all-out immediate nuclear exchange was thought likely by only 23.0 percent. Of the remainder, 67.2 percent felt a world war would be fought via other strategies but would involve the use of thermonuclear weapons.

3 In the 1964 Civil Defense Survey 59.3 percent of the sample thought military targets would be assigned highest priority by an enemy, transportation centers by 29.2 percent, cities by 5.8 percent, and people by 5.9 percent.

4 When presented ten alternative "futures" of the Cold War, the respondents in the 1964 Civil Defense Survey found indefinite continuance the most likely alternative, but 71.2 percent found this highly undesirable.

Withey in late 1961 found 58 percent of a national sample thinking it likely that the United States would be involved in small wars within a two- to three-year period (*The U.S. and the U.S.S.R.*, p. 35). In the 1966 sample of the nation, we find that some 41 percent of the respondents consider smaller wars in the waning years of the decade rather likely, and an additional 48 percent assign such limited wars 50–50 odds. It is important to realize that the question explicitly postulated limited wars other than the struggle in Vietnam.

5 This outcome of the Cold War was found highly desirable by 71.6 percent of the 1964 Civil Defense Survey, and only 11.2 percent thought it undesirable in any degree. Better than a 50–50 chance of disarmament occurring in the sixties was given by only 39.8 percent, 20 percent thought it 50–50 and 40.2 percent less likely than that.

6 It is not surprising that a difference might exist between the national sentiment as expressed in carefully designed research studies and in the tone of mass media with regard to civil defense measures. The national dialectic about civil defense makes news to the extent to which provocative positions get presented: the simple and straightforward justifications for measures of civil defense do not have the

news value, we suspect, of a story quoting one or another more prominent American claiming that shelter programs would change our society into a garrison state, that civil defense might induce the Soviet Union to start a major war, or that civil defense systems would enhance general population anxiety.

Similarly, stories of thousands and thousands of shelters in which nothing at all happens does not make exciting reading. Alternatively, a report of a fallout shelter flooded following a rainstorm, or otherwise damaged under conditions considerably short in severity from nuclear warfare, makes news—as is entirely natural.

7 From 64.9 percent to 74.1 percent of the 1964 Civil Defense Survey found each of six different federal civil defense programs highly desirable. Five of these postures went far beyond the present program *(The 1964 Civil Defense Postures: Public Response, p. IV)*. In the same study 88.5 percent favored, rather than opposed, fallout shelters with 46.8 percent strongly in favor.

8 This discussion is based on the results of the 1963 and 1964 Civil Defense Surveys. More detailed presentations are available in the following:

Anderson, Martha Willis. *The 1964 Civil Defense Postures: Public Response.*

Kontos, Donna K. *Threat Perception and Civil Defense.*

Seldin, J. Elliott. *Attitudes Toward Civil Defense: An Examination of the Attribution of Maximum Approval.*

9 In the 1963 Civil Defense Survey respondents were asked to assess the level of support for civil defense among various groups of people. Those groups that might be commonly regarded as influential were generally regarded as most in favor of civil defense. The clergy, Congress, local mayors, and local editors were seen as opposed to civil defense by less than 5 percent, and usually about half the sample thought these groups found civil defense not only desirable but highly desirable. (J. Elliot Seldin, *Attitudes Toward Civil Defense: An Examination of the Attribution of Maximum Approval*, Appendix C.)

A similar question in the Levine-Modell nine-community study at the Bureau of Applied Social Research produced similar results and revealed that the group whose opinion counted most to the respondent concerning fallout shelters (scientists) was also the group seen most in favor thereof. (EDITOR'S NOTE—On this, the opinion of the general public appears to be borne out by the fact that the atomic cities, such as Oak Ridge, Los Alamos, are well ahead of the rest of the nation in civil defense preparations.)

10 The 1963 Civil Defense Survey found that 77.8 percent of the sample considered the provision of fallout shelters in schools to be highly desirable. Only 4.7 were opposed. Such a program was thought likely by 72.6 percent and practically certain to be implemented in the late sixties by 32.3 percent.

11 In both 1963 and 1964 the Civil Defense Surveys found that the marking and stocking program was highly desired by two-thirds of the samples and as likely to be implemented in the late sixties by two-thirds. One-fourth of each sample thought it practically certain. Yet, the 1963 survey found 54.4 percent thinking nothing had been done in their communities and only 11.0 percent thought that shelters had been stocked (*Some Public Views on Civil Defense Programs*, p. 63).

12 From the *License and Posting Summary* of the OCD National Fallout Shelter Survey Reports, July 10, 1963.

13 After being asked in the 1964 Civil Defense Survey how they favored fallout shelters, the respondents were asked what kind of shelter they had in mind when they answered. Family shelters were mentioned by 11.1 percent, community shelters by 30.7 percent, and both types by 58.2 percent. Those who thought of both types were also the group most strongly favoring shelters (52.1 percent strongly in favor compared to 21.8 percent strongly in favor for those who thought in terms of family shelters and 46.8 percent for those thinking only of community shelters). When the group which originally thought only of family shelters was asked about "the other kind of shelter," the percentage strongly favoring shelters rose to 25.8 percent.

Similar results were found by Levine and Modell (*The Threat of War and American Public Opinion*, pp. 146–48).

14 Both options were highly desired by two-thirds of respondents in the 1964 Civil Defense Survey and more respondents viewed them as likely than unlikely to be implemented by the late sixties (*The 1964 Civil Defense Postures*, p. 11).

15 *The U.S. and the U.S.S.R.*, p. 11.

16 Only one in four Americans in a national sample expected his area to be "better off" than the rest of the country in event of a nuclear war (*The U.S. and the U.S.S.R.*, p. 12).

17 *Some Public Views on Civil Defense*, pp. 15–16, 26.

18 The 1964 Civil Defense Survey found 78.6 percent thinking fallout shelters had no effect one way or the other on the likelihood of war and 80.0 percent thought shelters had no effect one way or the other on the difficulty of attaining disarmament. Over 85 percent of the 1966 respondents thought that fallout shelters have no effect on war probabilities. Over 63 percent were in disagreement (51 percent) or even strong disagreement (12 percent) with the idea that the American civil defense programs would be considered provocative by the Russians. Over 84 percent of the subjects thought that fallout shelter programs have no bearing on chances of successful arms control and disarmament negotiations.

S. B. Withey found that in late 1961, 63 percent regarded civil defense and shelters as irrelevant to the likelihood of war. Only 8 percent of this sample thought of shelters in terms of deterrence (*The U.S. and the U.S.S.R.*, p. 42).

19 Only one percent of a sample of shelter owners reported any change in their relationship with their neighbors and only one in seven would definitely refuse entry to others (*The Threat of War and American Public Opinion*, pp. 255–56).

20 The 1963 Civil Defense Survey found that 66.3 percent of the respondents thought that people in their neighborhood would help each other in event of a nuclear attack. (EDITOR'S NOTE—See in this connection also the next two chapters.)

21 From the 1964 Civil Defense Survey data and *The Threat of War and American Public Opinion*, pp. 239 ff.

22 The 1963 Civil Defense Survey found that 91.9 percent agreed that Americans will make the best of the situation if a nuclear war comes, 75.7 percent agree survival as a nation would be possible, and 67.4 agree that survivors of a nuclear war could rebuild a system which would maintain American values as we know them.

23 In mid-1963 2.2 percent of the Civil Defense Survey sample reported having some sort of shelter (*Some Public Views on Civil Defense*, p. 31). The Bureau of Applied Social Research, nine-community sample reported 2 percent having shelters in early 1962. Withey in late 1961 found some 2 percent claiming to have shelter space available to them (*The U.S. and the U.S.S.R.*, p. 25).

24 The 1963 Civil Defense Survey found that 24.9 percent claimed to be protected in some way from a nuclear attack even though they

did not have private fallout shelters (*Some Public Views on Civil Defense Programs*, p. 40).

25 When asked if they would contribute a weekend's labor for a community fallout shelter, 58 percent of a national sample were willing to do so and another 18 percent would donate the equivalent of their pay. Only 17 percent said they would flatly refuse to participate. (American Institute of Public Opinion Study No. 652, November 1961.)

The University of Michigan Survey Research Center Study No. 418 found 62 percent in 1956 willing to sign up for 2 to 3 hours a week for at least 6 months to learn about civil defense. Of the minority of respondents who were not unqualifiedly willing to sign up in 1954 (Study No. 408) 80 percent cited family or job responsibilities or health and age as reasons for not volunteering.

26 The 1963 Civil Defense Survey found that as a consequence of the Cuban crisis 30 percent of the sample had discussed with their families what might be done if a war started while they were separated. Provision for shelter was made by 15 percent and planning or building of shelters was carried on by 14 percent.

References

Documents

1 *Attitudes Toward Civil Defense: An Examination of the Attribution of Maximum Approval.* J. Elliot Seldin. Dept. of Sociology, Univ. of Pittsburgh, 1965.

2 *National Fallout Shelter Survey: Regional Distribution of Fallout Shelter License Refusals as of June 30, 1963.* Based on *License and Posting Summary.* OCD Shelter Survey Reports. Washington, D.C.: Office of Civil Defense, 1963.

3 *The 1964 Civil Defense Postures: Public Response.* Martha Willis Anderson. Dept. of Sociology, Univ. of Pittsburgh, 1965.

4 *Perceived Effectiveness of America's Defenses.* Dorothy V. Brodie. Dept. of Sociology, Univ. of Pittsburgh, 1965.

5 *The Public's Opinions on Existing or Potential Federal Fallout Shelter Programs.* Davis K. Berlo. East Lansing: Dept. of Communication. College of Communciation Arts, Michigan State Univ., 1962.

6 *Some Public Views on Civil Defense Programs.* Jiri Nehnevajsa,

Dorothy V. Brodie, Donna Krochmal, Richard Pomeroy. Dept. of Sociology, Univ. of Pittsburgh, 1964.

7 *The Threat of War and American Public Opinion.* Gene N. Levine and John Modell. New York: Bureau of Applied Social Research, Columbia Univ., 1964.

8 *Threat Perception and Civil Defense.* Donna K. Kontos, Dept. of Sociology, Univ. of Pittsburgh, 1965.

9 *The U.S. and the U.S.S.R.* Stephen B. Withey. Ann Arbor: Survey Research Center, Univ. of Michigan, 1962.

10 *Americans' Views on Civil Defense in the Cold War Context: 1966.* Jiri Nehnevajsa, Dept. of Sociology, Univ. of Pittsburgh, 1966.

Studies

A number of the references in this article are based on unpublished manuscripts and data tabulations obtained from the following studies:

AIPO No. 652—The American Institute of Public Opinion (Gallup) national poll of November 15, 1961, a national sample of 2,765.

Civil Defense Surveys—In the Study of Civil Defense and Cold War Attitudes, the Research Office of Sociology of the University of Pittsburgh (under this author's direction) carried out national probability surveys of American public opinion in the summers of 1963 and 1964, and again in 1966. The 1963 sample was of 1,434 Americans and the 1964 sample was of 1,464. In 1966, 1,478 Americans were included. The field work in these studies was carried out by the National Opinion Research Center of the University of Chicago.

Nine-Community Survey—In the Fallout Shelter Study, the Bureau of Applied Social Research interviewed respondents in January 1963 in nine northeastern communities. The representative cross-section subsample consisted of 1,382 respondents. The Levine-Modell report, *The Threat of War and American Public Opinion* is based on this study.

University of Michigan Survey Research Center—Study No. 418, a national sample of 1,643 Americans in 1956, and Study No. 408, a national sample of 1,611 in 1954.

3 Psychological Problems of A-Bomb Defense*

IRVING L. JANIS

¶ The question of how people would behave if the "sirens should sound," warning the people of imminent danger, has often been the subject of passionate debate. Some so strongly believe that people would panic in their flight toward the shelters, quite possibly trampling one another to death, that, for this reason, they are opposed to the installation of shelters. Professor Janis is one of the foremost students of human behavior under stress and his article throws considerable light on the probability of antisocial and maladaptive behavior if there is no shelter to turn to, or when seeking shelter, or while staying therein. ¶ It is remarkable how up to date this 1950 article is, and also how much of its message has been forgotten. It is reprinted here in its original form in order to demonstrate how certain insights and recommendations have remained valid after nearly twenty years. The principal point at which updating the article might make a difference is the recognition that an attack which is a complete surprise need not be possible and, most likely, the warning time would be hours if not longer. Certainly, a minimum warning time of about fifteen minutes could be guaranteed *under all conditions*. Missiles take about half an hour to reach the United States from the territory of any potential enemy, and the firing of rockets anywhere can be instantaneously detected. The present DEW line of radars pro-

---

* The following article consists of excerpts from a report prepared in 1950 for the RAND Corporation, Santa Monica, California, to which the author is a consultant. The report was designed to call attention to psychological problems arising from A-bomb attacks, which require intensive research. The material was included as part of a more detailed discussion in the author's subsequent book on the psychological impact of wartime disaster, Irving L. Janis, *Air War and Emotional Stress* (New York: McGraw-Hill, 1951).

vides only about ten or fifteen minutes' warning because it does not monitor the firing of the rockets but their passage over a line north of America, the DEW line. In addition, we have at present no means of conveying its message instantaneously to the public. ¶ Even though the possibility of a complete surprise attack is almost negligibly small under all conditions, and could be completely eliminated by suitable warning arrangements, the dire picture which Professor Janis paints of such an attack may retain some validity if a shelter collapses. Even the best shelter has only a limited blast resistance and even though the area in which a blast resistant shelter may collapse is very much smaller—perhaps 20 times smaller—than the fatal area would be without blast shelters, the destruction of some of the shelters by a determined enemy is possible. For the occupants of such shelters, the advice and warning, given by Professor Janis, may be pertinent. ¶ A relatively long warning time—at least of the order of one day—is likely because an enemy could gain no real advantage from destroying the lives of a large number of civilians: it is likely to threaten, rather than to carry out, an attack. However, a surprise cannot be threatened—the threat destroys the surprise. Even a fifteen-minute warning time would be of great benefit, particularly if supplemented by additional information given over the public address system immediately after the explosion, as recommended by Professor Janis. ¶ As far as evacuation is concerned, it may be mentioned that the tunnel-grid system, described in Chapter 9, unites the functions of shelter and evacuation systems. The reader will also note the similarity of this system to some recommendations of Professor Janis. ¶ The permission of the RAND Corporation and of the *Bulletin of the Atomic Scientists* to reprint the article is very much appreciated.—E.P.W.

Irving L. Janis
Professor of Psychology, Yale University

¶ Irving Janis was born in Buffalo, New York, in 1918. Before the Second World War he studied psychology at the University of Chicago and at Columbia University. He became a member of the Library of Congress' Experimental Division for the Study of Wartime Communications in 1941. During the war he served in the Department of Justice as a senior social science analyst of the Special War Policies Unit and in the War Department as military research psychologist. He returned to his studies at Columbia University in 1946, taking his Ph.D. in psychology in 1948 but was, concurrently, a research associate for the Social Science Research Council. He joined the Department of Psychology at Yale University in 1947 and since 1960 has been professor of psychology. ¶ Dr. Janis has received many honors, including the Hofheimer Prize of the American Psychiatric Association and the Socio-Psychological Prize from the American Association for the Advancement of Science for his research on psychological stress and fear. He has participated in many national activities. Perhaps most important from the point of view of his present article was his membership in the National Academy of Sciences' Committee on Disaster Studies. ¶ Dr. Janis has published extensively, particularly on psychological stress and on attitude change. His present research interests center on problems of decision-making, group influences on attitudes, and tolerance for deprivation. He is currently consulting editor of the *Journal of Experimental Social Psychology* and has served as consulting editor of several other leading research journals on personality and social psychology.

S udden awareness of immediate danger appears to have been the initial experience of almost all survivors of the atomic disasters at Hiroshima and Nagasaki. In the accounts given by those who lived through it, the atomic attack is described primarily as a personal catastrophe —a completely unexpected event during which there was a sharp realization of the threat of imminent annihilation.

Over one hundred of the survivors were interviewed several months after the atomic disasters by the Morale Division of the United States Strategic Bombing Survey (USSBS). The vast majority described exposure to extreme conditions of danger, especially the severe blast effects. Some spoke about the painful lacerations they suffered from missiles of flying glass. Others vaguely remembered having been knocked unconscious after being hurled through the air and then, in a semi-dazed and helpless condition, facing the harrowing dangers of a raging conflagration. A few alluded to themselves as being the sole survivors of a shattering blast that killed everyone else in the same room.

One of the obvious consequences of a "narrow escape" is extreme emotional excitement accompanied by temporarily impaired ego functioning. All available sources of information consistently indicate that acute anxiety was a dominant reaction to the atomic explosions. From statements made by survivors one is able to gain some inkling of the intensity of the emotional impact. The following spontaneous comments illustrate fairly severe terror states:

I became hysterical seeing my grandmother bleeding and we just ran around without knowing what to do. . . . After that atomic bomb I was constantly afraid.

(Domestic worker in Nagasaki)

After recovering from the concussion I got up and ran to the mountains where the good shelter was. I just ran like crazy. I stayed in the shelter for three days. . . .

(Office worker in Nagasaki)

My children were injured and I was in such emotional upset that I couldn't think straight.

(Factory worker in Hiroshima)

There are no words that can describe the terror it caused. . . . After our house was destroyed I took my children and fled to the woods. We were so scared that another would fall that we stayed in the woods for two days wondering what to do next.

(Housewife in Nagasaki)

Only a few respondents volunteered information of this kind. But it appears that at least in a small percentage of cases the emotional excitement reached such a level that there was temporary loss of inhibitory control over primitive, automatic manifestations of acute anxiety.

In other cases the acute emotional disturbance took the form of profound apathy and depression. John Hersey refers to several such cases in his report on Hiroshima. He describes one extreme case in detail: A fifty-year-old man, uninjured by the explosion, stood weeping at the window of a burning building. When an attempt was made to rescue him, his only response was "Leave me here to die." After being forcibly carried to safety he managed to break away and ran back into the fire.

Instances of less severe depressive reactions are to be found among the respondents in the USSBS survey. A Nagasaki housewife, for example, spoke about manifestly suicidal feelings:

> I carried my son on my back and we rushed toward the hills. It was very cold and the rain started to fall. At that time I wished we had died in the explosion of the bomb.

A few other respondents verbalized similar depressive tendencies which, from the context, do not appear to be mere expressions of conventional Japanese attitudes concerning the appropriateness of suicide.

In general, the quality and intensity of acute symptoms of anxiety and depression among the A-bombed survivors do not appear to differ in any unique way from those observed among the British and Germans who were subjected to exceptionally severe air attacks. As has been described in a separate report on civilian reactions to air raids during World War II, chronic psychopathological reactions (such as "traumatic neurosis") occurred very rarely as a result of bombing. Nevertheless, temporary emotional reactions to shock were quite frequent among those who barely escaped from immediate danger. From clinical observations in the European war, it appears that such experiences have the effect of temporarily shattering the individual's psychological defenses—defenses which had formerly prevented the outbreak of anxiety in the face of environmental threats by maintaining feelings of personal invulnerability. That the same psychodynamic processes were evoked by the overwhelming terror at Hiroshima and Nagasaki is suggested by certain of the interviews which indicate that intense emotional reactions were linked with subjective awareness of personal vulnerability. . . .

... On the basis of the available evidence on the conditions under which emotional shock occurs, it is possible to specify the types of events created by an atomic explosion that are likely to evoke acute symptoms. The most severe forms of emotional shock are to be expected among survivors who undergo experiences of the following sort:

a) being knocked down, violently shaken, buried beneath debris, or experiencing similar direct exposure to blast effects;

b) being injured by fire or by blast effects;

c) narrowly escaping from burning buildings;

d) witnessing the death of a member of the immediate family.

If the population of a target city is unprotected, the vast majority will probably undergo traumatic experiences of this kind in the event of an atom bomb attack. It should be recognized, therefore, that the adequacy of civil defense preparations designed to increase the physical safety of the population have a direct bearing on the emotional impact of an atomic disaster. If a target city cannot be warned and evacuated before an attack is launched and if the residents cannot reach adequate shelters, the devastating consequences cannot be counted solely in terms of the inordinate toll of dead and severely injured people. The less adequate the protection of the population from the physical impact of an atomic disaster, the higher the incidence of emotional shock and disorganized behavior. Such reactions, on a mass scale, would give rise to extremely critical problems of disaster control.

Maladaptive Behavior

In the event of an atomic disaster, even those survivors who are not casualties from emotional shock will be in an extremely aroused emotional state. The mere sight of the vast devastation and the hideous sights of the dead and dying will produce a terrifying effect upon almost everyone in the area of disaster. Those who escape any direct experience of the explosion in and around the target will be extremely disturbed not only by the appalling sights about them, but also by the intense suspense of not knowing the fate of their families and close friends. Many persons might also be extremely apprehensive about the possibility that they may have been exposed to lethal amounts of radiation. Such sources of emotional stress greatly increase the likelihood of excited, impulsive, and maladaptive behavior.

Under the disorganizing influence of acute anxiety, many uninjured survivors might fail to give essential aid to others who are in dire need of their help. There may be a widespread tendency to neglect the precautions necessary for avoiding exposure to contaminated supplies and lingering radioactivity. In attempting to escape from the raging fires, large crowds might congregate in areas which offer far less protection than other places of refuge which are just as accessible. In Hiroshima, according to Hersey, hundreds of people sought refuge in a park near a river, and, as the fire pressed closer, the crowd began to push toward the river. Those who were on the bank were forced into the water and many were drowned.

How can inappropriate, disorganized, and maladaptive responses be prevented? To some extent the prior training of the general population will be useful in preparing people to act intelligently in a disaster. (As is indicated in another section of the report, one of the major needs for adequate civilian defense preparation is a mass educational program that would reach the entire population of all potential target areas in the United States. The essential purpose would be to teach the most elementary knowledge necessary for appropriate behavior in an atomic disaster—with emphasis upon realistic information about *what the dangers are* and a corresponding set of *do's and don'ts*.) But such information is often forgotten at the very time when it is needed most, if people are highly aroused emotionally. Some special psychological devices are necessary to reduce emotional excitement promptly, to the point where people will make use of the preparation they have been given.

Perhaps the most effective device would be a calm, familiar, authoritative voice giving both reassurance and directions as to what should be done. Such a device might be readily available if there were an intact public address system in every major target area. An underground communication system might be installed which would be designed to withstand the damage from an atomic bomb explosion. Radio broadcasting units mounted on trucks might prove to be ineffectual because they could not reach the disaster area early enough to prevent confusion; mobile broadcasting units mounted on airplanes, on the other hand, might be a highly effective adjunct to the local broadcasting system and might even be a satisfactory substitute for it.

In any case, each potential disaster area probably could benefit considerably from having a public address system which could be put into operation immediately after an explosion. It could be a tremendous asset in a variety of ways. The survivors in each neighborhood could be given prompt instructions (based on information from air and ground observers) about appropriate actions to take. They could be told when to remain in their homes, when to evacuate, and where to go. They could be reminded of the precautions they had already been trained to take. In neighborhoods where there is little danger present, they could be urged to aid in rescue work and in other forms of disaster relief. But, above all, the calm, authoritative voice of a familiar radio announcer might be extremely effective in reducing confusion and emotional excitement, particularly if reassuring announcements are given about the arrival of rescue and relief teams.

There is probably very little danger that a metropolitan public address system of the kind suggested could be exploited by the enemy for purposes of psychological warfare. Appropriate code methods for putting the system into operation could easily limit its operation to designated civil defense officials who would be scattered among various communities in the defense region.

If engineering research solves the problem of devising a public broadcasting system that will remain fairly intact following an atomic bomb explosion, and if such a system becomes an integral part of the U.S. civil defense program, it will be worth while to investigate various means for insuring its maximum effectiveness. For example, it would probably be useful to give the metropolitan population some prior experience with it. The loudness, tonal quality, and location of the sound source should be familiar so that it will be readily recognizable in an emergency. If there are practice air raid alerts, it might be useful to employ the public broadcast system to announce the all-clear signal so that the radio voice will be expected following an air attack and will be associated with the emotional relief that accompanies termination of the threat. . . .

Emotional Responses of Relief Workers

One of the major goals of civil defense operations will be to give prompt aid to thousands of survivors within the A-bombed area. It will be necessary for medical first-aid units and many other types of civil defense teams to enter the disaster area as soon as it is reasonably safe to do so. The number of lives lost may be drastically increased if rescue workers are unable to carry out their assignments efficiently. Consequently, it is important to take account of emotional reactions which may seriously interfere with the performance of essential rescue and relief operations.

The tremendous devastation in the disaster area is likely to be a disturbing factor. Even more disturbing will be the sight of people who have been mutilated by the explosion. The USSBS report on the effects of the atom bomb on Hiroshima and Nagasaki asserts that many uninjured survivors were horrified and shocked by the sights about them. . . .

Many people when confronted by the appalling casualties may react so emotionally that they are unable to perform their assignments. Some special form of preparation—some kind of emotional inoculation—is necessary for the average civilian who is being trained to carry out an assignment in a disaster. Some of the devices which have been used on a limited scale in the psychological preparation of soldiers for combat—such as realistic sound films—may prove to be effective for this purpose, but a good deal of research will be needed in order to be sure that they do not do more harm than good.

It has been suggested that the device of using increasing doses of graphic sound films (preferably in technicolor) showing actual disasters should be investigated as a possible way of hardening people and preventing demoralization. This might also prove to be a useful screening method for eliminating from key positions those persons who become inordinately upset when exposed to disturbing stimuli.

The problem of the emotional reactions of medical aid personnel is an especially acute one, since there will probably be thousands of casualties whose life or death may depend upon the promptness and efficiency of the medical treatment they receive. John Hersey gives a graphic account of the experiences and behavior of a few survivors who set about the task of using their skills to aid the injured.

> . . . bewildered by the numbers (inside the hospital), staggered by so much raw flesh, Dr. Sasaki lost all sense of profession and stopped working as a skillful surgeon and a sympathetic man; he became an automaton, mechanically wiping, daubing, winding, wiping, daubing, winding.
>
> Near the entrance to the park, an Army doctor was working, but the only medicine he had was iodine, which he painted over cuts, bruises, slimy burns, everything—and by now everything that he painted had pus on it.

To avoid distraught and inept performances among civil defense workers, especially in rescue and medical aid units, it will be necessary to give them an opportunity to develop some degree of emotional adaptation to the job of handling large numbers of mutilated human beings. Perhaps the most useful method would be to introduce them gradually to the experience of working with patients in medical clinics and hospitals, ending, if possible, in the emergency room of a large metropolitan hospital. This type of participation in actual medical aid work has been suggested elsewhere in this report for other reasons as well.

Another type of problem which will confront many civil defense workers arises from the fact that they will be dealing with disaster victims who are in an extremely anxious or disturbed state. Quite aside from the cases of emotional shock who will require special psychiatric treatment, there may be large numbers of victims who will be in a severely apprehensive state about the realistic possibility that within a week or two they may die from radiation sickness. There will also be large numbers of persons, both among the sick and the well, who have been unable to locate members of their families. Knowing that there are huge numbers of unidentified dead and injured, they will be in an extremely agitated state. In addition to apprehensiveness about radiation sickness and anxious concern about missing loved ones, there will be other sources of emotional disturbance as well: bereavement, anxiety about disfigurement, jitteriness about the danger of another A-bomb attack.

There is a twofold problem here. First, the disaster victims will require calm, reassuring, patient handling during the days and weeks following the attack. Second, the civil defense workers who come in close contact with disaster victims must be able to withstand the emotional strain and demoralizing influence of working with large numbers of persons who are in an extremely anxious or depressed state of mind.

Such problems require careful consideration in planning the organization of medical and social services. For example, in setting up a system of sorting medical casualties so as to give priority to those who have the best chance of recovering, it may be desirable to arrange for segregating those radiation victims who are doomed to die, so that they will not have a demoralizing effect on a large number of medical aid personnel and on other patients. For the large number of patients who will be worried about epilation, ugly scar tissue, and other disfigurements, a special series of pamphlets and posters might be prepared in advance, containing reassuring information about treatment and the chances of recovery. These printed materials could be included in emergency supply kits and distributed at the appropriate time in disaster aid centers.

This problem should also be considered in the training of civil defense personnel. All those who are likely to deal with emotionally upset disaster victims might be given some instruction and practice in elementary psychotherapeutic principles. To the extent that defense workers are able to give appropriate help to disaster victims, the unfavorable effects of widespread emotional upset will be reduced within their own ranks as well as among the people they are trying to help. . . .

Psychiatric Casualties

The vast majority of cases suffering from acute anxiety and other symptoms of emotional shock will probably recover spontaneously shortly after the danger has subsided.

Nevertheless, there will probably be a sizeable minority who will not recover promptly from the harrowing, traumatic experiences of the disaster. Such persons will not be capable of productive work and will have a demoralizing effect upon others in the community. There is little likelihood that skilled psychiatric aid will be available for all of the temporarily maladjusted persons, but it may be possible to speed recovery by adopting sound policies of rehabilitation. This is a special problem which calls for planning in advance. For example, it might be possible to set up temporary rest camps in which a therapeutic atmosphere is maintained so that those who are too disturbed to return to productive activity will have an opportunity to recuperate. . . .

At present there are insufficient numbers of trained psychiatrists, psychotherapists, and psychiatric social workers to meet the current needs of the U.S. population. In fact, this is one of the most critical shortages of skilled personnel we face. As the armed forces are expanded, more and more psychiatrists will be drained from the civilian supply, making the shortage all the more acute. Obviously one of the essential needs of civil defense preparation is to increase greatly the number of skilled personnel capable of handling the emotional shock casualties to be expected in the case of A-bomb disasters. . . .

. . . Even with a greatly expanded professional training program, it will be necessary to have large numbers of nonprofessional civil defense workers trained in elementary psychotherapeutic techniques if cases of emotional shock are to be given the barest minimum of treatment. Considerable research effort is needed in order to develop effective psychiatric first-aid techniques and rapid therapy methods for handling large numbers of traumatized survivors.

It is possible that some special techniques of emotional inoculation will be discovered which might prove to be effective in reducing the incidence of emotional shock casualties among survivors of a disaster. It is unlikely, however, that any such devices will eliminate the need for psychiatric first-aid techniques. Nevertheless, there are marked individual differences with respect to ability to withstand traumatic events which could be taken into account. It should be feasible to improve methods of detecting the most vulnerable and the least vulnerable personalities for such purposes as selecting leaders and making evacuation plans.

General Effects on Morale of A-Bomb Attack

In general, a single atomic bomb disaster is not likely to produce any different kind of effects on morale than those produced by other types of heavy air attacks. This is the conclusion reached by USSBS investigators in Japan. *Only about one-fourth of the survivors of Hiroshima and Nagasaki asserted that they had felt that victory was impossible because of the atomic bombing.* The amount of

---

* Italics added.

defeatism was not greater than that in other Japanese cities. In fact, when the people of Hiroshima and Nagasaki were compared with those in all other cities in Japan, the morale of the former was found to resemble that of people in the lightly bombed and unbombed cities rather than in the heavily bombed cities. This has been explained as being due to the fact that morale was initially higher than average in the two cities because, prior to the A-bomb disasters, the populace had not been exposed to a series of heavy air attacks. Apparently a single A-bomb attack produced no greater drop in morale among the Japanese civilians than would be expected from a single saturation raid of incendiaries or of high explosive bombs.

An inordinately high degree of apathy was noted among the survivors in the A-bombed cities. The Medical Division of USSBS visited Hiroshima three months after the bombing and observed that the city had still not recovered to the point where adequate shelter and essential utilities were available: Only a few shacks had been constructed for homeless people; there was no garbage or sewage collection, etc. It is not likely, however, that the lack of organization and the absence of initiative found in Hiroshima was a unique effect of the A-bomb attack. Similar apathetic attitudes have been observed throughout Japan as a consequence of multiple sources of demoralization during the period immediately following the unexpected surrender.

It seems highly probable that the same factors found to be responsible for lowering morale among civilians exposed to the "traditional" type of air raids will be operative in the case of an A-bomb attack. Accordingly, a major source of information for predicting the effects of A-bombs on morale is the set of conclusions reached on the basis of studies of civilian reactions to air raids during World War II. . . .

Potential Sources of Demoralization

To a very large extent, the morale of the survivors of an atomic bomb attack will be determined by the effectiveness of civil defense measures. If aid and relief measures are not well planned or if they cannot be put into operation—owing to multiple A-bomb attacks—an extremely unfavorable situation is to be expected. Following the emergency evacuation of a bombed city, homeless survivors would be widely scattered over a large region. There would be frantic competition for the scarce quantities of food, water, and medical supplies available. Many groups of survivors who received no help from people in outlying communities might become extremely hostile and attempt to obtain shelter and supplies by force if necessary. Thousands of half-starved people would be wandering about for a long period, seeking for their lost families or friends.

Obviously, if this type of social disorganization occurs following an atomic disaster, a prolonged period of demoralization is to be expected. On the other hand, if the essential needs of the survivors are well provided for, and if there is sound community leadership, there is every reason to expect that within a short period the vast majority will willingly participate in reconstruction work and make a fairly adequate adjustment to the deprivational situation. . . .

In planning the organization of a community to function efficiently following a major disaster, it will be useful to know which types of persons can be relied on and which types are most likely to be uncooperative and demoralized. Field studies of current peacetime disasters in the U.S. might provide a rich source of empirical material for predicting *who* will be an asset or a liability during the reconstruction phase.

If the survivors cannot be permitted to return to the target city for a prolonged period because of the presence of lingering radio-activity, there are likely to be serious problems of social reorganization which may have an unfavorable effect upon morale. Deprived of the opportunity to return to their own community and to engage in its reconstruction, survivors are likely to become deeply pessimistic about the future. To meet this contingency, special plans are required to provide for either prompt relocation of the community on a new site or the absorption of survivors into other existing communities.

Morale in Unbombed Cities

The psychological effects of the bombs dropped on Hiroshima and Nagasaki were found by USSBS investigators to be much less marked in the rest of Japan than in the target areas. When the people in neighboring communities learned about the devastation produced by the bombs, their primary reaction was fear. But over the islands as a whole, the proportion who expressed a personal fear of being killed by an A-bomb was only half as great as that among persons who had been directly exposed to the bombing. The effect of the A-bombs on other attitudes which compose morale was also much less marked in the country as a whole. It was found that attitudes of defeatism and unwillingness to go on with the war because of the A-bomb varied inversely with the distance from the target cities. Only in the cities within a 40-mile range was there a definite effect on morale.

From the standpoint of predicting responses to subsequent A-bomb attacks, the findings on Japanese reactions are of very limited value because:

a) The vast majority of the population was already suffering severe wartime hardships, and among a substantial proportion defeatist attitudes had already developed owing to military losses, the food shortage, and the concentrated incendiary and high explosive attacks on Japanese cities;

b) The A-bomb was given almost no publicity within Japan prior to the surrender, and its existence remained unknown to the vast majority of the population;

c) The surrender followed very soon after the A-bomb attacks, obscuring whatever effect the latter might subsequently have had. (The surrender itself, according to USSBS investigators, was not largely attributable to the A-bomb attacks: a powerful faction of the Japanese government was already prepared to surrender unconditionally, and the A-bomb appears to have hastened this action by providing an obvious "face-saving" excuse.)

"Will There Be Widespread Panic?"

Prior to World War II, government circles in Britain believed that if their cities were subjected to heavy air raids a high percentage of the bombed civilian population would break down mentally and become chronically neurotic. This belief, based on predictions made by various specialists, proved to be a myth. Already there are some indications that a similar myth is beginning to develop with respect to future A-bomb attacks: the belief that the news of the first A-bomb attacks in this country will produce panic among the residents of unbombed metropolitan centers and industrial areas.

There is, of course, a serious danger that people who expect their city to be the next target might behave in an excited, socially disruptive fashion. But, for purposes of civil defense planning, it is not very useful to assume that "panic" will necessarily be the most probable response.

First of all, "panic" is an extremely ambiguous term. The image it usually brings to mind is that of a wildly excited crowd behaving in an impulsive and completely disorganized fashion, each person abandoning all social values in a desperate effort to save himself. From the available literature on extreme fear reactions, it appears that this sort of behavior very rarely occurs unless (a) there is an obvious physical danger which is immediately present (e.g., a raging fire only a few feet away), and (b) there are no apparent routes of escape.* Hence, "panic," in the limited sense of the term, is likely

---

* In a subsequent analysis of "the problem of panic" (Janis, Chapman, Gillin, and Spiegel, *Civil Defense Technical Bulletin TB–19–2*, June 1955) the author and his collaborators have reformulated the factors that create collective panic in a way that takes account of the conditions suggested by surveys of actual instances of mass panic:

. . . Many of the forecasts and discussions concerning panic which have

to be evoked by an A-bomb attack primarily in the area where the disaster actually occurs (e.g., among those who are trapped by the general conflagration within the city). In places which are not directly affected by the explosion (e.g., in cities which are likely targets for the next attack), there is far less danger of a serious outbreak of overt panic. That is to say, there is a strong likelihood that with appropriate preparation such reactions may be prevented.

---

received wide publicity assume that it will not be too difficult for an enemy nation to strike terror into the hearts of Americans—especially through the use of atomic and thermonuclear bombs. To the enormous loss of life and property—so runs the theme—panic or mass hysteria will add devastating disorganization and paralysis, a weapon more horrible in its effects than any known to man. . . .

An assessment of the facts shows that the existing evidence falls far short of supporting such vivid and dramatic prediction. The authenticated instances of mass panic known to have occurred in the last 50 years have been few in number and have been very restricted in their effect. . . .

The logical conclusion from the evidence, then, is that mass panic is a rare event which arises only under highly specialized circumstances. . . .

There are four main factors which are characteristic of the panic-producing situation.

1. *Partial entrapment.* There is only one, or, at best an extremely limited number of escape routes from a situation dominated by 2.

2. *A perceived threat.* The threat may be physical, or psychological, or a combination of both, and it is usually regarded as being so imminent that there is no time to do anything except to try to escape.

3. *Partial or complete breakdown of the escape route.* The escape route becomes blocked off, or jammed, or it is overlooked.

4. *Front to rear communication failure.* The false assumption that the exit is still open leads the people at the rear of the mass to exert strong physical or psychological pressure to advance toward it. It is this *pressure from the rear* that causes those at the front to be smothered, crushed, or trampled. In instances where people are trampled to death, as in the Cocoanut Grove fire, this is usually the single, most important factor.

When a mass panic occurs, it usually happens that people do not actually see the "escape hatch," whatever its nature may be, but infer its existence from the fact that other people are moving in a specific direction. This inference made by the individual is reinforced by statements of people in the immediate vicinity. None of these communications, however, is based on realistic information about the actual conditions at the "escape hatch." The people at the rear of the mass, especially, are too far away from the exit to be able to obtain accurate information about its actual state. Thus, when the exit becomes blocked or jammed, the people at the rear behave as if it were still open.

"Panic" is often used by both popular writers and social scientists as a colorful term to designate a wide variety of activities which are judged to be inappropriate to the situation. . . . For purposes of analyzing and predicting social responses it is preferable to avoid using a term which connotes the sort of behavior that occurred in the Cocoanut Grove fire when referring to other less extreme sorts of action motivated by fear. In order to avoid ambiguity it is necessary to reformulate the question with which this discussion began; instead of asking, "Will there be widespread panic?" our inquiry should be centered upon: (*a*) What forms of overt behavior are likely to occur under various conditions of A-bomb attack? and (*b*) By what means can the more extreme forms of personal disorganization and inappropriate action be prevented? The discussion which follows will be limited to some of the more general considerations.

One of the major conditions under which extreme emotional reactions are likely to occur is a very sudden, unexpected confrontation of the threat. . . . In a sense, almost all of the points discussed in this report are tied up with the problem of providing adequate psychological preparation for the U.S. public so as to prevent the occurrence of excited, disorganized, and maladaptive behavior. To the extent that the public is informed about ways and means of coping with the dangers and trained to participate in civil defense operations, disruptive fear reactions will be minimized. The educational program for the general public—as well as for the other features of an adequate defense program to be discussed later—should have the effect of building up realistic expectations and of counteracting feelings of helplessness when the danger becomes imminent.

It cannot be assumed, however, that a successful program of preparation will eliminate subjective feelings of fear. No matter how well they are prepared, the residents of all potential target areas will become extremely apprehensive as soon as they learn that the first A-bomb attack has occurred in this country. The preparation they have been given, however, should serve to *channelize* their overt reactions: If the population does not feel utterly helpless, and if emergency measures have been well planned and organized in advance, there will probably be a high degree of conformity to the regulations issued by the civil defense authorities. . . .

Unauthorized Evacuation

Obviously, there will be a strong urge to get away from threatened target areas. This will be an asset or a liability from the government's point of view, depending upon whether or not its defense calls for prompt evacuation of metropolitan targets. A number of social scientists have strongly recommended that if mass dispersal is not carried out in advance, the government should make plans to minimize casualties by evacuating the population of metropolitan areas rapidly, as soon as the first atomic bomb attack is launched against the United States. If this policy is adopted by the government, and if plans have been worked out for orderly and controlled migration to dispersed assembly centers, there is likely to be a fairly high degree of conformity to the evacuation plan. The strong drive to leave the target area will motivate the population to respond to official evacuation orders. While there is always a possibility of spontaneous, disorganized flight or of disruptive competition to reach the most advantageously located safety zones first, such tendencies can be minimized by preparing the public in advance. Such preparation might include:

1. Informing the residents of each city about the local evacuation plan, and perhaps also assigning most adult members of the community to a "battle station" in specified evacuation localities where it is one's "duty" to be present;

2. Emphasizing the benefits (for oneself, one's family, and the entire community) to be derived from strict conformity to the local evacuation plan, along with emphasis on the theme that nonconformity is socially irresponsible behavior;

3. Notifying the public of special sanctions to be applied against nonconformists in the event of an evacuation crisis.

If the government's defense plan requires residents of an obvious target area to remain there, considerable public resistance is to be expected immediately following the first A-bomb attack. The degree to which there is spontaneous, unauthorized evacuation from cities and reduced productive efficiency among essential industrial workers will depend upon a variety of factors. Obviously, one of the most important factors will be the amount of public confidence in the civil defense organization. . . .

. . . If the initial attack occurs without any warning before war has been declared, the spontaneous tendency of the majority of the population in unbombed metropolitan areas will be to evacuate the city immediately, whether that action is authorized or not. The most critical factor in preventing this form of action—short of a convincing official announcement to the effect that no further attacks are possible—will be the availability of adequate shelters. If the shelters are regarded as inadequate, a sizeable proportion of the urban population may be expected to pack up and leave unless they are prevented from doing so by coercive force—in which case there is likely to be considerable resentment as well as a marked deterioration in job performance. Hence, in avoiding widespread confusion and nonconformity to official demands during the period immediately following the initial A-bomb attack, the key problems are: (a) to develop a feasible plan for an organized emergency evacuation of those who will not be needed in the target area; and (b) to supply adequate shelters for those who will be required to remain.

Emergency evacuation on a mass scale will be a considerable undertaking requiring detailed plans not only for the orderly migration from threatened areas but also for the social organization of the evacuation centers. If large numbers of people are to remain in evacuation centers for a prolonged period, many social and psychological problems may be expected to arise. In this connection, social science research should be directed toward obtaining essential information for the planning of sound evacuation policies.

Population Dispersal

A number of writers have urged that the entire urban population of the United States be widely dispersed so as to reduce the effectiveness of atomic bomb attacks. For example, Edward Teller, in an article in the *Bulletin of the Atomic Scientists*,[1] claims that the enormous effort involved in large-scale dispersal would be rewarded by a high degree of safety: "Then a few thousand Hiroshima bombs could kill only one per cent of our population." Although many scientists agree that in all likelihood we shall be attacked by large numbers of atomic bombs if there is another war, very few share the optimistic expectation of achieving such a high degree of safety by means of mass dispersal. Moreover, it has been pointed out that a dispersed population would be just as vulnerable to bacteriological warfare as people in cities, if not more so; this might also hold true for radiation poisons and other unconventional weapons as well.

From the many estimates which have appeared on the staggering economic costs involved, the length of time this dispersal would take, and the tremendous social and political consequences it would entail, it appears to be highly improbable that a mass dispersal program will be adopted in this country. Nevertheless, some limited degree of dispersal is to be expected. According to some reports, relocation of industrial plants has already begun on a very small scale; it is likely that decentralization of industry will be increasingly encouraged, if not demanded, by the government. In numerous articles attention has been called to the vulnerability of centralized administrative agencies of the government, and it is not improbable that these, also, will be subject to dispersal. Consequently, it appears safe to assume that at least a small segment of the U.S. population will be affected by a limited dispersal program.

So long as the dispersal program is kept down to a small scale, little resistance is likely to occur. But if large-scale industrial units are removed from areas in which they employ a large percentage of the resident population, considerable protest and resistance is to be expected.

Such resistance may be overcome by offering attractive inducements to those affected, to encourage and facilitate their moving along with the industrial organization that has been employing them. But, if the problem occurs on a sufficiently wide scale, it is likely that a major psychological problem of national scope may arise.

One of the obvious ways of attempting to convince dissident industrial workers that they should accept relocation is to arouse their anxiety. Strong emphasis upon the dangers of atomic bomb attacks and on the avoidance of this danger by taking advantage of the opportunity to move to a less vulnerable section of the country may appear to be a successful way to overcome resistance to dispersal. But it may also be effective among broad sections of the population for whom no relocation plans are intended. Instead of the problem of resistance to the limited dispersal program, the government may be faced with public clamor for far more extensive dispersal plans; at the same time there may be a considerable amount of spontaneous, unplanned relocation. The possibility of such boomerang effects calls attention once again to the need for public opinion and attitude research on the predispositional tendencies of the American population, in order to gauge the probable impact of alternative policies in communication.

The Problem of Shelters

It is likely that an important feature of the national defense program will be a priority system in the construction of shelters, underground installations, and other protective sites. If a large proportion of the available manpower and raw materials of the country are devoted to building up offensive weapons and well-protected retaliatory installations, the construction of shelters in urban areas will undoubtedly be limited to the barest essentials. Underground shelters and installations may be constructed for key industrial and administrative personnel; for critical supplies; for irreplaceable libraries of blueprints, maps, industrial, and military data. Some provisions may also be made for workers in essential industries. But it is highly unlikely that there will be sufficient manpower to construct adequate shelters for the majority of the population, even in the most vulnerable urban centers.

Noting the ever increasing signs of hectic preparation, seeing and sometimes participating in the construction of shelters for others, urban residents are likely to become increasingly alarmed by the fact that no attempt is being made to provide them with protection from direct exposure to an atomic bomb attack. If the potential danger of such attack becomes more and more apparent, the demands for public shelters may become a critical political issue.

This anticipated social problem might be easily solved by a single technological advance. An effective, inexpensive, radioactive-absorbent material is needed which would reduce the costliness of the construction now required when earth, concrete, or lead is used. If a new substance were invented which could be readily manufactured in mass quantities from raw materials in plentiful supply, it might be possible to furnish a large proportion of the urban population with prefabricated shelters. . . .

If physical scientists are able to solve the technological problem of providing the American people with the materials for constructing adequate physical protection against A-bomb explosions, many of the social and psychological problems to be discussed in the remainder of this section and in some of the other portions of this report will be eliminated.

Assuming that the only substances available are concrete, earth, and bricks, the critical factor preventing construction of adequate public shelters will most probably be the manpower shortage. If this should prove to be the case, there is a partial solution to the problem which may prove to be both feasible and psychologically sound: the policy of encouraging people to build their own shelters. If the public is told how to build private shelters, and if there is high anxiety about the danger of an atomic bomb attack, it is probable that a fairly large proportion of the urban population would contribute their spare time to providing this measure of security for themselves and their families.[2]

From the available information, it would appear that there is nothing unusually complicated about the construction of home shelters of a type which would give a fair degree of protection in an atomic bomb attack. According to some experts, it would be difficult to build a shelter that gives close to 100 percent protection because it would have to be blast-proof and airtight, with an oxygen supply that would last for many hours or even days without becoming contaminated by radioactive particles from the outside. But in an atomic disaster tens of thousands of lives might be saved even by shelters which are only partially effective.

Front-line combat troops are encouraged to dig foxholes even though this form of shelter offers no protection against a direct hit. If the urban populations are exposed to the threat of an atomic bomb attack, they will probably feel that they are in comparable danger, and they could be encouraged to provide themselves with something equivalent to a foxhole if nothing better can be provided. For example, by lining the walls of the basement of a private dwelling or of an apartment house with concrete or bricks, one can make a fairly adequate shelter. If entered before the detonation occurs, it might provide excellent protection against heat blasts and flying glass, and—depending upon the distance from the explosion—some degree of protection against gamma rays.

The problem of what *kind* of shelters people could build for themselves is one that should be tackled by practical engineering technicians, who would take into account the nature of the materials that are most likely to be available. A set of specifications could be drawn up ranging from complicated structures that are highly protective to simple ones which provide a slight amount of protection. These specifications could be made available to the public, together with full details about how to carry out each step, where to get the materials, and so on.

Additional information on the possible uses of caves and other special features of the terrain might be provided for those who live in towns near mountains or hills. Details could also be given on the probable amount of time there will be between a warning signal and the atomic bomb explosion, along with some advice about how close the shelters should be to one's own home. In some neighborhoods, for example, the residents might wish to build community shelters if they could expect to have sufficient time to get to them. . . .

If specifications for various kinds of homemade shelters are drawn up, the information could be incorporated into the public education program. The government might be able to give additional encouragement to the homemade shelter program by providing certain types of available materials free or at a nominal cost and by setting up in each community (perhaps as one part of the civil defense organization) a board of local construction experts who would be able to give advice to those in need of it and to inspect homemade shelters for the purpose of suggesting simple ways of improving them.

One of the major drawbacks of such a program is that it may arouse acute social resentments among those classes of the population which are not in a position to acquire or build adequate private shelters. To prevent disruptive social antagonisms from arising it would probably be necessary to resort to careful rationing procedures of available materials and to provide some form of government subsidy to equalize the opportunity for constructing shelters among all economic classes.

If the problem of class differences in safety can be solved, the homemade shelter program might be extremely successful at a time when there are strong feelings of insecurity about impending atomic bomb attacks. First of all, participation in this form of self-protective activity would contribute to the feeling that "I am really able to do something about it." When danger is anticipated, feelings of anxiety are most intense if a person feels that he is helpless, that he is unable to do anything to ward off the impending danger. Such feelings are counteracted by engaging in constructive activity. Second, if personal responsibility for providing one's own shelter is accepted, there is less of a tendency to place full reliance for one's protection upon the authority figures of the government. Consequently, there would be less likelihood of reacting to apparent "neglect" on the part of the government with anxiety and resentment. Third, after the homemade shelters are constructed, they may become an important source of reassurance. Awareness of their real protective value as well as non-rational factors (e.g., "I made it myself") may invest them with considerable symbolic value as an anxiety-reducing feature of the environment. Hence, even though surprise attacks may preclude the usefulness of shelters for some people, they will, nevertheless, be psychologically advantageous. So long as people do not expect all atomic bomb attacks to be surprise attacks, homemade shelters may be expected to serve this function. And, if our population is ever exposed to atomic bomb attacks which are not surprise attacks, the feelings of security provided by the shelters will prove to have been highly realistic.

Notes

1 *Bulletin,* III (February 1947), 35.
2 EDITOR'S NOTE—Concerning some of the problems here touched upon, see the more technical discussions in Chapters 8 and 9.

4

Human Behavior in Disaster: The Siege of Budapest

FRANCIS S. WAGNER

¶ Like Irving Janis's article, Dr. Wagner's chapter deals with the behavior of man under heavy stress, when his relations with others are influenced by constant fear of death. However, whereas Janis's article is based on an overall study of tragic events as well as on the general principles of psychology, Dr. Wagner's relates his and his co-sufferers' experience in a single event: the seven-week siege of Budapest which was spent, by most of the inhabitants of the city, as well as by himself, in underground shelters. His article throws some light also on the medical problems of shelter living, and is a vivid testimony of the willingness of people to restore productive capacity and to start a new life again after an extended sheltering period and, in this case, under very adverse external and political conditions.—E.P.W.

Francis S. Wagner

Staff Member, Library of Congress

¶ Francis Wagner was born in Hungary—the scene of this narrative of his own experiences. He studied at the University of Szeged and earned his Ph.D. in history, philosophy, and literature summa cum laude in 1940. He taught at the colleges of Szeged and Budapest and served as a Slavic specialist in the ministries of Public Education and of Foreign Affairs of Hungary. Between 1946 and 1948 he was head of the Hungarian Consulate General in Bratislava, Czechoslovakia. Since 1953 he has been on the staff of the Library of Congress. ¶ Dr. Wagner's interests center on the nationality problem of central and eastern Europe, the diplomatic history of World War II, and on the theory and history of the doctrine of dialectical materialism. He has published several books on these subjects. He is also a regular contributor to *Studies for a New Central Europe*, to *Historiography*, to the *American Historical Review*, the *Journal of Central European Affairs*, the *American Quarterly*, *Revue de'Histoire Comparee*, the *Hungarian Quarterly*, and *Free World Review*. He has also written for other journals and prepared chapters of other books.

Part I. Prehistory of the Siege

From early Roman times, from the Mongol and Turkish invasions up to the end of World War II, Budapest has caught the covetous eye of would-be possessors. This "Pearl of the Danube," inhabited by well over a million people, contains not only two-thirds of Hungary's manufacturing industry and over sixty percent of its skilled manpower but also a network of internationally significant routes which have made it the geographical center of Southeast Europe as well as a gateway to Vienna, Czechoslovakia, and Southern Germany. Little wonder that Budapest with its strategic position and economic and political importance should have made the city a prime target for German and Soviet troops or that these troops were willing—particularly in the closing phases of the last war—to exert a major effort, sacrifices notwithstanding, to obtain it. Yet the true heroes of the street and house-to-house fights were the beleaguered city's unarmed population, the valiant citizens who found their physical, mental, and moral strength severely taxed in the dragging months of ordeal.

Credit must also be given to the government, which did much to create and maintain a panic-proof atmosphere by its foresighted provisions for the nation's defense needs. The first law to this effect was passed as early as 1935 (Law No. 12). This law was thoroughly amended in 1939 (Law No. 2) and implemented through numerous decrees by central and local authorities prior to and during the war. It is significant to note that through Law No. 2 the cellars of Hungary, particularly those of her capital, were converted into an effective network of air raid shelters well before the long series of bombardments started in the spring of 1944.

The 1939 revised edition of the Budapest Building Code (Budapesti Építésügyi Szabályzat) was well updated and could form a solid basis for the shelter policies of the succeeding years. Owners were required by law to protect their homes and families. A typical air raid shelter consisted of a fore part and an inner part. Situated below street level almost without exception, shelters were equipped for blackout, reinforced to make them gasproof and splinterproof, and fully protected against debris. The ceiling of each shelter had to be reinforced to withstand the weight of falling rubble and even the collapse of the entire building, should this occur. In addition, special steel doors and shutters were installed and fitted with rubber gaskets, making them completely airtight.[1]

Time and again the public was reminded to store water, sand, and other fire-extinguishing materials, including chemicals, various digging implements, first-aid kits, etc., in the shelters.[2] All shelters located in the same block were interconnected by holes of about 4 feet by 4 feet, dug at the base of the partition walls in the cellar. Several ministerial decrees insured uniformity in the location, design, construction, and equipment, as well as in the technical quality of shelters.[3]

The number of family shelters was quite insignificant in the capital. Most shelters were situated in public and industrial buildings and in particular in apartment houses. German-type public communal shelters (bunkers) designed to afford complete physical protection for tens of thousands and to safeguard buildings against "Volltreffers," i.e., bombs hitting the shelters themselves, were virtually nonexistent. The great majority of inhabitants used cellars of apartment houses rebuilt for this purpose. The bomb shelters in the city of Budapest were designed by registered architects and engineers, trained in special courses.[4]

The Battle of Budapest convincingly proved that its population could be protected from air strikes and other gunfire with the aid of expertly designed, constructed, and equipped air raid shelters. Simple wooden posts and girders, closed or battened openings, and elementary hygienic provisions saved the lives of many tens of thousands in World War II.

The civil defense training program somewhat preceded the execution of shelter construction policies. As early as 1938 (through Decree No. 167,710/1938 B.M.) the Minister of Interior had approved the bylaws of the newly founded National Air Raid Protection League which were, in turn, modernized in September 1942 (Decree No. 138,383/eln.35) by the Minister of Defense.[5] This leading government-controlled social organization for civil defense established central, intermediate, and local branches for the education and training of the masses. To provide the latest techniques of air raid protection, its headquarters distributed monographs and periodical literature; assumed the responsibility for lectures, meetings, and activities in schools of all levels; promoted information campaigns through the radio and the newspapers, and sponsored puppet shows and exhibitions. In 1939, during the month of May alone, one million copies of an air raid protection pamphlet (A.B.C.) were prepared and distributed free of charge by the League, which also published its monthly *Riadó* (Alarm) as well as its supplement *Légoltalmi Közlemények* (Air Raid Protection Communications), a technical and scientific review. From about 1940 on, civil defense topics became regular, full-fledged subjects in the school curricula, with special regard to the problems of large cities.[6]

Centrally guided public drills were held frequently, in some places almost biweekly, in apartment houses, industrial, public, and school buildings years before the bombardment of the city began.

During this period of practice the public became so well trained and disciplined that its unquestioning obedience to air raid control organs was apparent even during the heaviest bombings. Moreover, there were no signs of widespread panic. Instructions on correct behavior in air raids were printed and posted in each shelter. Among them, the simplest but most significant were those which stressed the application of the following rules: "Maintain your composure," "Do not start or spread rumors," "Do not smoke," "Do not ignite an open flame," etc. In order to encourage shelter occupants to do their best to obey these rules, a special air raid protection medal (légoltalmi jelvény) was established and awarded to those who excelled in this field.[7] House and block wardens, along with their deputies, attended special eight-hour courses every year. These were designed to improve their theoretical and practical knowledge.[8]

A highly effective warning system was operated in the city by the Army and by specially educated squads with main headquarters in Castle Hill, where cellars and tunnels bored into the rocks offered complete protection against air attacks.

The cooperation among the various participating agencies (the Army specialists, police, fire-fighting volunteer troops, medical corps, transport companies, and the capital city authorities) was brilliant.[9]

But by far the most significant factor in this cooperative effort was the attitude of the well-trained Hungarian people, who willingly gave full support to the theoretical and practical measures designed for their protection, and also took an active part in them.

Early April of 1944 saw the beginning of the long era when air raids became part of the city's daily life. For many months the air strikes were carried out by Anglo-American air forces. The civilian population's first performance indeed proved exemplary, mainly because of the shelter construction and air raid protection training policies of the government. Within minutes following the warning signal, the citizens marched down into the shelters under the deserted town. There they impressively maintained their composure and refrained from spreading disquieting rumors, cooperating fully with the defense organizations. Yet the air strikes caused great shock and confusion in their minds. Up to now they had believed—wishfully—in the widespread rumor that a tacit agreement existed between the Kállay Government and the Western Powers not to bomb Hungary and its capital city.

When German troops first occupied Hungary on March 19, 1944, friends and relatives half-heartedly tried to convince one another that their situation had in no way deteriorated. But it was not long before they were forced to face the alarming truth about their position—that their own small country was fast becoming a target for all the great powers, German and non-German alike, that they stood at the center of a world crisis, surrounded by formidable foes, and that they had no strong allies to turn to. People began to sense that the concept of collective responsibility, which had served in the past to justify awful inequities perpetrated in the alleged interest of the Hungarian people, would now be applied to them. Moreover, the long anticipated threat that the front would advance to their homes began to materialize. Pro-Anglo-Americanism, on the increase until this time, came to a sudden halt, declining steadily with the intensity of the bombings and reaching an all-time low during the summer months. In some circles a modest revival of sympathy for Germany, in others for Russia, took place. But by far the greatest majority of the people grew suspicious of all foreign influences, turning their attention inward upon themselves. The government reflected these isolationist sentiments in a decree making even the act of listening to all foreign radio broadcasts punishable by internment.[10]

Despite the severity of the regulation, more and more people listened to foreign newscasts, all the while evaluating them solely in the light of their local relevance. Neither the history-making Normandy invasion nor the operation in the Pacific Theater could compete in interest with local events. To be sure, the bombardment of the city resulted in some shifting of allegiance: a few who were disillusioned with the West at least outwardly accepted Communism or Nazism. But this attitude was not widespread. The common reaction to recurrent bombings was rather a transference of interest from the world around them to their own immediate situation, a concern with their own future, which strongly stiffened their resistance during the darkest hours of the siege. The air raids aroused the natural instinct of self-preservation, which overshadowed all political affiliations.

On October 15, 1944, the national state of turmoil was aggravated by the failure of the decade-old, feeble Horthy regime to put its poorly planned cease-fire into effect. Instead, the Hitler-backed Szálasi government assumed power. Yet the situation remained confused. People, growing accustomed to living without leadership in the present, or political faith in the future, intensified their efforts for self-preservation. Impetus in this direction was furthered by the knowledge that the Red Army land forces were speeding toward Budapest on a 300-mile-wide front line. By November 10 Soviet tanks suddenly advanced and reached the metropolitan area ten miles south of the capital. Between this date and February 13, 1945, the end of the siege, the bombing and flash of cannons became part of the everyday experience of the citizenry. And on November 10 traditional joke-making, so characteristic of peacetime Budapest, came to an abrupt halt. Thoughts of the ever-advancing front filled the minds of all. But, characteristically, even these substantially worsened conditions could not destroy the optimism of the general public. While the impending storm was the focal point of daily talks, not a single person believed the siege would last longer than three or four days. Some even dreamed of the possibility that Budapest would be declared an open city. Partly for this reason, no extensive preparations for the storing of foodstuffs or any other useful articles were made. Moreover, since large quantities of food reserves had already been confiscated and transported into Germany, the food ration card system could no longer operate satisfactorily except in the case of a single item, the daily ration of 150 grams (5½ ounces) of bread per person. Fortunately, leguminous plants (beans, peas, and lentils), plentiful in most households, saved Budapest from starvation.

Contemporary closeups of city life showed great inner restlessness: capacity crowds in restaurants, night clubs, cinemas, and theaters; slow-down and sabotage in industrial establishments and transport agencies; hundreds of thousands, partly from the already Russian-occupied countryside, migrated across the city toward the West. At the same time, tens of thousands of army deserters, draft dodgers, and fugitive Jews remained in the city and defied martial law.

The ghetto was a special feature in the heart of the besieged metropolis. According to the Jewish Council, 69,000 Jews were liberated from the ghetto; 25,000 were found in the so-called protective houses; and 25,000 were hidden in houses occupied by non-Jewish Hungarians. Metropolitan authorities started to supply the ghetto on December 8. According to their report, only a minimum food reserve was available, with the exception of dry soups of low calorie value. One day there was "pea soup," the next "bean soup," then mashed carrots, and from time to time noodles. Nazi Party shock detachments in charge of supervising the enforcement of the often conflicting military orders acted ruthlessly against the Jewry.[11]

Two measures which considerably affected living conditions and brought much abuse in their wake were Decree No. 100,482/eln. (November 28, 1944) issued by the Minister of Defense, founding the special military police, and Decree No. 100/1944.T.M.H.M. (December 10, 1944) issued by the Minister of Total Mobilization, drafting all citizens between the ages of fourteen and seventy. On the ground of these and some other decrees, shock detachments were authorized and even compelled to execute by shooting all army deserters, stragglers, draft dodgers, and people who disobeyed evacuation orders. The same applied to those who failed to deliver stocks of flour at the official collection points, gave refuge to fugitives (especially Jews) and immediate relatives, all emergency law violators, etc. The barbarously severe application of these emergency measures brought the reign of terror into being weeks before the siege began. The emotional climate of these historic days was given expression by the performing arts of Budapest in a moving refrain, which spread from tongue to tongue: "Egy nap a világ!" (The world lasts but a day.) This truly reflected the general mood of the citizenry who already had one foot on the battlefield as Christmastide approached.

Part II. A Brief Military History of the Siege

Shortly before and after the memorable events of October 15, 1944, Hitler notified the Hungarian government, through his Chief of Staff, Colonel General Guderian, that Budapest would be "defended" by German troops and that German generals would assume supreme command over the Hungarian armed forces. The Führer, recognizing in advance the far-reaching consequences of the forthcoming battle, transferred several of his elite divisions from Poland, France, Italy, and the Balkans to the Budapest theater of operations. These divisions participated in the unsuccessful breakthrough attempts. The German-Hungarian joint forces operated under the command of Colonel General Pfeffer-Wildenbruch. The Second and Third Ukrainian Army groups were under Marshals Malinovsky and Tolbukhin. All divisions were equipped with modern weapons.[12]

On Christmas Eve 1944 the thunder of cannon and of explosions shook the capital, thus marking the launching of the direct siege. Red Army units poured through a gap in the German-Hungarian line, and on December 26 Budapest was completely surrounded. Meanwhile, the civilian population moved into underground shelters for permanent protection against air attacks and ground fire. According to the *Pravda* editorial of February 15, 1945, if fierceness of fighting and some other aspects of the siege are taken into consideration, the Battle of Budapest should be regarded as an extraordinary episode in modern warfare. This point of view is shared by most military experts. Let us make a brief survey of the abnormal conditions menacing the city's population. Immediately after the siege, on March 25, 1945, an official census was to show the extent of damage to dwelling houses as follows:

Table 4.1. Extent of Damage

	Number	Percent
Slightly damaged (windows, plastering)	10,323	26.0%
Damaged	18,686	47.1
Seriously damaged	9,140	23.1
Completely destroyed	1,494	3.8
	39,643	100.0%

None of the buildings escaped unscathed.[13] This means that 13,588 dwelling units (flats) were completely destroyed, 18,755 became uninhabitable, and nearly 48,000 were partially damaged and unfit to live in.[14] Living conditions were severely affected and 300,000 persons left homeless. The area of roofing totally demolished amounted to approximately 26 million square meters (280 million square feet) and affected 24,000 buildings.[15]

The capital lay in a ravaged, paralyzed state, with all of its bridges destroyed. Only four motor buses remained in usable condition, and the few undamaged streetcars could not operate after the siege either because tracks were heavily damaged or because only 44 miles of the city's 267 miles of overhead electric lines functioned adequately.[16] Only 6 percent of the 1,808 large-scale industrial establishments were undamaged, and local industry lost 90 percent of its production capacity.[17]

In April 1944 Budapest first experienced destructive air raids. On Christmas Eve of the same year, the city was already the scene of ground fighting. Many civilians lost their lives as a direct result of war injuries; great numbers died from mental and emotional agitations of the siege as well as from severe physical privations, such as deficient nourishment, unhygienic conditions in dark, cold shelters, and lack of proper ventilation. Table 4.2 shows the monthly distribution of civilian deaths on a comparative basis.[18]

Table 4.2. Number of Deaths (includes nonresidents)

	1944		1945	
		Yearly Rate° Per 1,000 People		*Yearly Rate° Per 1,000 People*
January	1,782	17.3	11,995	172.8
February	1,832	17.8	7,723	111.3
March	1,847	18.0	5,081	73.2

° These rates are calculated under the assumption that the death rate remained the same throughout the year as it was during the month in question. This applies also to later tables.

The mortality rate in January 1945 was almost ten times that of the monthly average (1,300) of the peacetime years. More than 12,000 civilians lost their lives as a direct result of war injuries; 15,700 died from consequences of the unsanitary conditions up to June 1945.[19]

The self-sacrificing behavior of the municipal public health service reduced the number of fatalities considerably, even though not more than 4 of the 45 major hospital buildings remained undamaged; none of the 7,567 beds (in 860 ward rooms) was left in usable condition after the siege; and practically nothing was left of the 86 operating rooms and 87 laboratories.[20] It should also be noted that 60 percent of the medical instruments of Budapest's clinics was destroyed and that medicines were practically unavailable for a prolonged period.[21]

In the category of deaths from natural causes the rate of certain diseases increased tremendously, as Table 4.3 illustrates:

Table 4.3. Chief Causes of Natural Deaths (January–September)[22]

	1938	1944	1945
Infectious diseases (including tuberculosis)	1,937	2,273	4,180
Tuberculosis	1,374	1,725	2,188
Cancer	1,174	1,393	1,148
Cerebral hemorrhage	619	789	1,073
Heart disease	2,574	2,922	5,565
Respiratory disease	1,306	1,580	2,571
Digestive diseases	871	886	4,293
Congenital diseases	403	642	1,148
Old age	246	424	5,291

Part III. Human Behavior

By Christmas Eve 1944 the people of Budapest cared only about what was going on in the capital. Neither national nor world affairs occupied their attention. In fact, from the moment that they moved underground their thoughts focused solely on their immediate surroundings, their lives becoming increasingly passive and vegetative. Although the majority of the shelters were interconnected, the inhabitants imposed a kind of isolation on themselves, breaking off communications with even the adjoining shelter dwellers. Such isolated communities in Budapest consisted of small groups averaging from sixty to eighty persons per shelter, each group living in absolute seclusion and displaying a marked lack of interest in affairs which were not somehow connected with its own daily routine. Consequently, shelter dwellers reacted with extreme hostility to any outside interference aimed at strengthening the city's defense line.

A particular set of circumstances made Budapest unique among other besieged cities of World War II and served to heighten the already intense psychological conflict of the populace. First, there was no civilian government which the people could rely on in time of crisis. Only the right-wing totalitarian party leadership and its brutal executive organs functioned regularly. These organs were not only extremely hostile to the population, endlessly molesting it, but were in frequent conflict even with German and Hungarian military authorities. Amid the misery and confusion stemming from the complex relations of the beleaguered city, law enforcement agents of the gendarmery, the police, and the military also became hostile toward the civilians. Their antipathy was based on the fact that people sabotaged all official orders on total mobilization, especially those drafting into active military service all citizens between fourteen and seventy years of age and ordering the construction of tank traps and street barricades. Yet it would be a mistake to believe that the people looked to the fast-approaching Soviet troops with any feeling other than anguish. Their exposure to anti-Communist propaganda over the decades, together with the bad reputation of the Red Army, instilled fear in their hearts even before this army arrived. Thus, the people found themselves harassed by both contending parties, Soviet and German alike.

Because of the food shortage weeks before the battle on December 9, 1944, the system of the one-course meal was introduced by Decree No. 118,500/1944 K.M., issued by the Minister of Food. The daily bread ration per capita had been only 200 grams (7 ounces) since October 18, 1944 (see Decree No. 116,610/1944 K.M.). Beans, peas, and lentils, which constituted the basic diet, saved tens of thousands from starvation. Immediately after the siege, medical authorities issued several warnings against this one-sided diet because of its many harmful effects. The suffering of the inhabitants was greatly aggravated during the siege and the subsequent months by the almost complete failure of services. To provide the daily supply of water, a number of shelter dwellers had to venture into the streets, usually in a hail of falling bombs and shells, to reach the emergency wells drilled throughout the city by the municipal authorities. As could be expected, there were many casualties among those who left the shelters.

Likewise, small power plants were installed in several huge blocks as a substitute for gas pipelines and electric networks destroyed in the course of the fighting. As a result of the air raids and the land war, the main and auxiliary channels of the drainage system broke in many places and endangered public hygiene. The lack of telecommunication services (telephone, radio) also aggravated the psychological atmosphere and intensified the feeling of isolation.

Day-by-day deterioration in conditions substantially increased public antagonism against the defense forces in the belief that the latter's staunch resistance needlessly prolonged the torment of the population. In the interest of historical truth, it should be noted that the terroristic actions of the Hungarians who belonged to the Communist Party provoked much deeper and more bitter antagonism than the emergency measures taken by German troops. This situation was partly responsible for the failure to develop a resistance movement against German forces. However, some other reasons should also be noted, such as Order No. 144,770/eln.VIII.Csf.– 1944, issued by the Minister of Defense on November 2, 1944, which compelled citizens to surrender all arms, ammunition, and equipment. This order was severely enforced—the penalty for disobedience was death. In spite of intense disaffection toward both Germans and Russians, there was no guerilla warfare since it had no tradition in the country. In addition, when the Soviet Army entered Hungarian territory (September 28, 1944), society was in a state of intense disorganization. Because of the war, the whole social structure had already disintegrated. On the other hand, the Hungarian masses nourished a historically evolved resentment against the Russian and the Bolshevik way of life; they felt that Communism deprived them of all vestiges of human dignity. It is quite probable that in the case of a Western occupation, a much stronger anti-German and anti-Fascist popular feeling and movement would have arisen all over the country.

In the final analysis, it was the instinct of self-preservation—the craving to insure their own physical survival—that determined the attitudes and behavior of the people and that saw them through the mental and physical trials that they were called upon to endure. Perhaps the most conspicuous effect of these long-lasting hardships was the prevalence of a permanent atmosphere of tension, a psychological climate that favored morbid nervousness, extreme irritability, and egocentric behavior. Profane language, spoken in a highly agitated manner, typified the shelters having a cross section of society. Only in shelters where people of the same class gathered did a higher degree of discipline prevail, especially in those of the educated classes. Judging from a series of on-the-spot observations, as well as from data collected subsequently, it seems safe to say that most of the profanity and similar signs of emotional unrest occurred during the short-lived cessations of military hostilities.

Yet there were many exceptions. From the moment the first bomb exploded some people put concern for their fellows above and beyond concern for themselves. There were bakery workers who, despite the danger to their lives, walked ten or more blocks to distribute daily bread free among their starving fellow citizens; there were public utility service men, physicians, priests, and people from all walks of life who could think beyond what was happening to themselves and could overlook the hardships they had to undergo. The exemplary behavior of these heroic groups prevented an even greater deterioration of the general atmosphere. It is remarkable perhaps that no physical fights between individuals took place, no serious or even less serious crimes were committed against either persons or property. And even the later very active group of informers did little harm to others until after the first weeks of Red Army liberation. The community feeling was strong enough to ensure that persons and families bombed out of other shelters were readily accepted, and there were always some individuals prepared to share their food, clothing, and other belongings with needy newcomers. These acts of kindness, widespread at a time when most people were concerned with their own condition of darkness, hunger, cold, and uncertainty about the future, were truly heroic.

Significantly, the number of deaths from infectious diseases, respiratory diseases, and heart diseases doubled that of peacetime years. Doubtless, crowded, unhealthful shelter conditions were responsible for the increased death rate from infectious and respiratory diseases, while the agitations of war were to blame for the increase in deaths from heart disease. Among the deaths from natural causes, those due to disease of the digestive organs—principally enteritis—occupied a prominent place.[23] Of particular significance is the number of deaths from old age, a figure twenty times higher than that of peacetime years.[24]

It was not difficult to conclude from outward signs and on-the-spot conversations with fellow shelter dwellers that a kind of emotional pattern recurred daily. Each day they experienced a two-way reaction to what they were undergoing: feelings of gloom and depression in regard to their personal and national situations on the one hand, and feelings of optimism and hope on the other. In the early morning after a relatively comfortable rest, the typical reaction was that of semiconscious depression. This mood, though fought off by a consciously induced mental resistance, nonetheless reached its climax in the evening hours. Interestingly enough, the two daily stress-induced phases had their counterpart in the siege itself. The first phase (corresponding to the early morning depression) lasted until December 30, 1944, the day that the shelter dwellers first realized that after the killing of the Soviet white flag–bearing parliamentarians by the Germans, a long and merciless battle had begun.

Between the morning and evening periods was the midday lethargy which corresponded to the long middle part of the siege.

The daily evening phase was paralleled by the last days of the siege when most people foresaw the end of street fighting and tried to view their present and future life through rose-colored glasses, hoping for a new, secure system of living. A third, or final, stage of stress did not materialize either in daily or in general relations, except in some cases of mental and physical exhaustion. The relatively small group of citizens who experienced this phase could endure the long-lasting, excessive tensions neither physically nor mentally. The thousands suffering from senility, which in most instances developed overnight during the last days of the siege or afterwards, were all well over sixty. But even the sorely trying circumstances failed to exhaust the staying power of the vast majority of the people. The overwhelming part of the population did in fact preserve its mental and physical fitness and, according to the reports of public health authorities, no symptoms of diseases of the nervous system could be detected at any time. On the contrary, convincing signs of a spiritual renewal were noticed by observers throughout the city. This fact is amazing in view of the fact that neither central nor local government existed during the siege or for weeks thereafter. Under the horrible conditions in the war-torn city, a virtual Red Army–made jungle, the miraculous work of spiritual and material reconstruction began through the spontaneous voluntary efforts of the masses. Indeed, the moment the siege ended, an optimism excited the population to rebuild their city on the material as well as the political ruins of the past.

Let us now consider the morale of the masses. The February 28, 1945, appeal by the newly formed Budapest National Council to the people of Hungary made an accurate report on the mutilated capital:

> The people of Budapest are in a situation of extreme need. We are barely subsisting among the ruins, with no water or electricity in houses with no windows. Yesterday it was war, today it is starvation, tomorrow it might be an epidemic decimating our ranks. Women and

children are dying of hunger; men are collapsing at their jobs. The people of Budapest want to live. We are doing everything we can. We are working to rebuild the transportation and communications systems. And we cultivate every single foot of ground for food. . . .

The story of the dead Budapest rising like the phoenix from its ashes can best be told by some selected facts and data on its spontaneous postsiege redevelopment.

Neither the terrors of the long-lasting battle nor the heavy economic losses could crush the spirit of the population. When Budapest was finally captured by the Red Army (January 18, Pest; February 13, Buda), shelter dwellers were climbing up through the ruins, and upon reaching the open air—almost without exception—they made some remark about their first breath of fresh air. Destruction was everywhere, but they had prepared themselves during their underground life, which had been full of unchecked, never-ending, disquieting rumors, for an even worse situation.[25]

On December 23, 1944, 12,084 employees still worked in the Weiss Manfred Works, the country's largest heavy industry concern. This number gradually fell to 120 on January 9, 1945 (Tuesday), the date of the Soviet occupation. By Friday this number had risen to 1,163 and on the next day to 3,684, though a few miles away heavy street fighting continued for weeks to come.[26]

Because of the lack of electric current, the workers of the Ganz Shipyard, in January 1945, operated hand-driven machines.[27] Likewise, while the war in Buda still raged, on the Pest side workers of several industrial establishments, hospitals, spas, and tenants of apartment houses earnestly initiated the reconstruction.[28]

On January 18, a few hours after the Pest side had been captured by the Russians, a group of fifteen men, comprising thirteen old-time social democrats and only two Communists, reestablished the Central Council of Hungarian Trade Unions.[29] On the same day, January 18, a few people established a trade union organization for technical intelligentsia of the kind which was not permitted to organize or to function in prewar years. Its membership rose to 250 by the end of the month, while on the other bank of the Danube the siege was still on.[30]

The war inflicted heavy losses on the whole transportation system. It destroyed, for example almost all the highway, river, and railroad bridges, and 90 percent of the motor vehicle stock.[31] Nevertheless, the newly constructed Kossuth Bridge opened on February 1, 1946. It was the first permanent bridge built on the Danube between Regensburg and the Black Sea in the postwar period.[32] Though only eight motor vehicles remained in operable condition in the whole country and all of them were in the possession of the Provisional Government in Debrecen, the Hungarian Automobile-Motorcycle-Motorboat Association was reorganized in Pest in January 1945. Only months after the siege, the Association arranged three international (Grand Prix) motorcycle and car races with several Hungarian competitors, who had withstood the siege, winning several gold medals on their self-repaired cars.[33]

The desire to marry and to start a family has often been considered as an indicator of the morale of the people and of their faith in the future. Table 4.4 compares the monthly marriage rates in the early months of 1944, of the last year before the war, i.e., 1938, and of the year of the siege, 1945.

Table 4.4. Marriages

	In Absolute Numbers			Yearly Rates per 1,000 People		
	1938	1944	1945	1938	1944	1945
January	696	746	144	7.7	7.3	2.1
February	809	914	933	8.9	8.9	14.3
March	736	1,105	1,205	8.1	10.7	17.4

In the first month of 1945 only 144 marriages were concluded in Budapest, a figure unprecedented in the annals of the city. However, the months immediately following the siege showed a revived inclination toward marriage, a fact accounted for partly by restored confidence in a happier future.[34]

Table 4.5 may prove the preceding statement even more convincingly.

Table 4.5. Development of the Number and Ratio
of Marriages in Budapest

	In Absolute Numbers			*Yearly Rates per 1,000 People*		
	1929–38 AVERAGE	1945	1946	1929–38 AVERAGE	1945	1946
First half year	5,245	5,528	6,122	10.4	12.8	11.9
Second half year	6,203	6,453		13.0	13.1	
Total	11,448	11,981		11.7	13.0	

Undoubtedly, the hardships and excitements of the siege had considerable effect on the suicide rate. Many persons committed suicide. Yet, hard to believe as it may seem, more people in Budapest committed suicide during the months of political crisis in 1944 than during the actual siege itself.[35]

Table 4.6. Suicides Committed in Budapest

	1938	1944	1945	1946
First quarter	111	130	222	43
Second quarter	139	489	128	63
Third quarter	104	148	117	
Fourth quarter	96	496	161	
Total	450	1,263	628	

The number of suicides reached a first peak after the German occupation (March 19, 1944) and a second peak at the end of the same year, during the Arrow-Cross Regime. It would require a psychological investigation to reveal and compare the motives for suicide during these two periods.[36]

On the whole, the civilian population emerged from the siege remarkably free of drastic ill effects of either a physical or a psychological nature. It can be argued that the fundamentally decent behavior of the people stemmed from well-established, traditional moral principles. Indeed, all things considered, Budapest stands out as a shining example of how people in time of disaster can demonstrate the essential nobility and dignity of the human spirit through concern for their fellow sufferers.

Notes

1 See Decree No. 88,008/eln.lgv.–1939 issued by the Minister of Defense. Unless otherwise stated, the decrees referred to in this section were issued by the Minister of Defense and published in *Budapesti Közlöny*, the official gazette of the Hungarian government.
2 Decree No. 161,300/eln.35–1943 and Decree No. 119,800/eln.35–1944.
3 See, for example, instructions *Lego ut. VIII–1*, and Decree No. 141,400/eln.35–1942.
4 The list of names of these architects was published by the Minister of Defense in Decree No. 162,490/eln.35–1943 and 162,491/eln.35–1943. One of the architects, Dr. László Ácsay, now lives in New York City, and I am greatly indebted to him for his description and evaluation of the air raid shelter system of wartime Budapest.
5 For a description of the organization and network of the National Air Raid Protection League, see *Budapesti Közlöny*, No. 207, Sept. 13, 1942.
6 *Légoltalmi ABC; a Légoltalmi Liga ingyenes tájékoztatója* (Budapest: Légoltalmi Liga Elnöksége, 1939), 64 pp.
7 See the long list of medal winners on the eve of battle in *Budapesti Közlöny*, No. 235, Oct. 15, 1944, 2–10, in Decree No. 125,000/eln. 35–1944, issued by the Minister of Defense, Aug. 16, 1944.
8 For their curriculum, see Decree No. 137,193/eln.35–1942, issued by the Minister of Defense, in *Budapesti Közlöny*, No. 208, Sept. 12, 1942.
9 Phases of development in the warning system are described in the following decrees: 88,001/eln.lgv.–1939 H.M.; 124,300/eln.35–1944; and 126,700/eln.36–1944, all issued by the Minister of Defense.
10 1,310/1944.M.E., published in *Budapesti Közlöny*, No. 75, April 2, 1944.

11 For further details, see Eugene Lévai, *Black Book on the Martyr-dom of Hungarian Jewry,* ed. Lawrence P. Davis (Zurich: Central European Times, and Vienna: Panorama, 1948), 475 pp.

12 To quote S. Smirnov, the "Encirclement of Hitler troops in Budapest was called by the Germans *Budapest pocket.* This pocket contained an enormous grouping of enemy amounting to more than 170,000 soldiers and officers. Several hundred tanks and self-propelled guns, about 2,000 guns and mortars, over 5,000 motor vehicles constituted the armaments of the encircled Germans . . . it can be said certainly that the encircled Hungarian capital held high possibilities for a prolonged resistance." (*V boyakh za Budapesht* [Moskva: Voennoe izdatel' stvo Ministervstva vooruzhennykh sil Soyuza SSR, 1947], p. 52). Communist historians agree that 50,000 Germans and an unknown number of Hungarians defended the city, and 110,000 prisoners were taken. On the other side, Ferenc Adonyi states that Budapest was defended by 6 divisions against 16 to 20 Soviet ones. (See F. Adonyi, *The Hungarian Soldier in the Second World War, 1941–1945* [Klagenfurt: Ferd. Kleinmayer, 1954], p. 169.)

13 See Központi Statisztikai Hivatal Budapest Városi Igazgatósága, *A felszabadult Budapest tizenöt éve 1945–1959* (Budapest: Közgazdasági és Jogi Könyvkiadó, 1959), p. 78.

14 Lajos Bene, ed., *Budapest on the Road to Revival: Report on General Conditions in the Year 1946* (Budapest: Institute of Letters, Arts of the City of Budapest, 1946), p. 9.
Excerpts (paraphrased):
   Repair of buildings (p. 101). Most of the reconstruction done in 1945–46 was mere repair work. Minor repairs were simply reported at the District Engineers Office, while more substantial reconstruction work required permits from the Engineering Department at City Hall. . . . In 1945 requests for 32 permits for reconstruction of dwelling houses and 130 for alteration resulted in 546 rehabilitated homes. In the first 9 months of 1946, 521 permits for reconstruction and 107 for alteration of houses were issued. Hence about 2,000 flats were repaired according to the district engineering offices. These figures are actually below the true figures because a number of minor jobs, particularly after the siege, went unreported. The number of new-building permits between January and September 1946—more than double the number for all of 1945—is indicative of the recovery of the building trades.
   The Gasworks (p. 19). Reconstruction was started at the main

plant at Óbuda immediately after the siege. This was followed by the clearing away of debris and by salvage work at the other plants. Private homes were first supplied with gas in March 1945, but only in Buda (west side of the Danube). As repair work on mains, etc., continued, the supply of gas was improved, and by the end of 1945 it was extended to the whole city and to the suburbs. Less than a year after the termination of the siege, gas production reached the peacetime average.

Electricity (p. 21). At the beginning of the reconstruction following the siege, the one small auxiliary power station in operation could supply barely a fraction of the electricity needed by the capital. Only the most important institutions, military commands, etc., were supplied with electricity. Electricity was not available to private consumers until three months later when the Kelenföld power station, which produces the greatest part of current consumed in Budapest, was repaired. Meanwhile, the restoration of high tension wire connections between the Bánhida power station and Budapest facilitated repairs of the wiring in Budapest. The town's supply of electricity was nearly normal by May 1945, about three months after the end of the fighting. Later, in the winter of 1945–46, shortage of coal forced the government to order a partial cut in the capital's current consumption. The replacement of burned out and destroyed cables was particularly difficult because production in Hungarian cable factories had completely stopped.

15 Antal Fabriczky, ed., *The Ruins Come to Life: Budapest's Struggle to Rebuild, 1945–1947.* (Budapest: Légrády Testvérek Rt. 1947, p. 4; and Oszkár Lehoczky, "A Full-Scale House-Building Drive," *Hungarian Trade Union News,* No. 2, Feb. 1965, p. 9.)
Excerpts from Antal Fabriczky, ed. (paraphrased):

After the siege, the most important job was to clear away those ruins which constituted a hazard to life. Next came the repair of roofs (p. 3). After these, our most urgent tasks, we drew up a city plan to determine which jobs should be given first priority (p. 4).

One of the foremost tasks was to build a bridge between the two parts of the city separated by the Danube River. Within a five-month period, the Petöfi Bridge, a temporary pontoon bridge 350 meters long, was completed; 350 tons of iron (mostly from ruins) went into its construction.

During the siege a few engineers worked in the shelter of the City Hall (Központi Városháza) on plans for the reconstruction of Budapest. They contributed substantially to the reconstruction as well as to the extinguishing of fires in City Hall during the siege (p. 9).

January 22, 1945, marks the liberation of Pest. Our engineers went by boat to parts of Buda where fighting was still going on and organized the reconstruction of the large St. John Hospital. In spite of the fighting, this was the day that they started reconstruction work on the Rókus Hospital, the Municipal Bread Factory, and the Central City Hall in Pest (p. 9).

During the siege, except for a twenty-four hour period, the city's public health service worked continuously in shelters. They soon reorganized the public health service system after first issuing orders to bury the thousands of dead lying in the streets, to remove garbage, and to reconstruct hospitals . . . (18).

The City Hall was almost ruined. There were no contractors, no skilled labor, no proper equipment, and no building materials. Yet a start on reconstruction had to be made. . . . Primitive methods had to be used to restore parts of this huge building. Because of the shortage of glass, windows and doors were covered with paper. Employees and unskilled labor participated in this reconstruction in the beginning (p. 29).

We have to acknowledge that the personnel of the Budapest Waterworks did a heroic job during the siege. They repaired damage done by the bombings immediately, enabling the water service to function at full pressure two weeks after the siege. On the second day, after the liberation of the Waterworks, most of the employees resumed their functions there (p. 38).

Already in January 1945, when the siege was still going on in Buda, the workers of the Széchényi Bath in Pest started reconstructing it. Thus, on March 15, 1945, a part of the bathing institution was open to the public, and during the year of 1945 more than 800,000 persons visited the Széchényi Bath. (Few private baths existed in the city; fewer were usable [p. 47].)

16 Budapest Directorate of the Central Statistical Bureau: *Fifteen Years of Budapest After the Liberation (1945–1959)* (Budapest: Közgazdasági és Jogi Könyvkiadó, 1959).

17 Budapest, Statisztikai Hivatal, *Budapest on the Threshold of the Winter 1945–1946* (Budapest, Institute of Letters, Arts, and Sciences, 1946), p. 65.

18 Ibid., pp. 16–17. In addition, well over 10,000 German and Hungarian soldiers and more than twice as many Russian soldiers died.

Note that the population of Budapest was well over a million in 1944 but dropped to about 830,000 as a result of a large-scale exodus from the capital before and perhaps also during the siege. The time and mode of departure is not entirely clear. See Lajos Bene, ed., *Budapest on the Road to Revival: Report on General Conditions in the Year 1946* (Institute of Letters and Arts of the City of Budapest, 1946), p. 40.

19 Budapest, Statisztikai Hivatal, *Budapest on the Threshold of the Winter 1945–1946*, pp. 16–17, 20; and Bene, pp. 47–48.

20 Bene, p. 14.

21 Budapest Directorate of the Central Statistical Bureau, *Fifteen Years of Budapest After the Liberation (1945–1959)*; and Budapest, Statisztikai Hivatal, *Budapest on the Threshold of the Winter 1945–1946*, p. 18.

22 Budapest, Statisztikai Hivatal, *Budapest on the Threshold of the Winter 1945–1946*, p. 20.

23 Budapest, Statisztikai Hivatal, *Budapest Statistics: Compendium of the Municipal Statistical Bureau* (Budapest, 1945), p. 45.

24 See Központi Statisztikai Hivatal Budapest Városi Igazgatósága, *A felszabadult Budapest tizenöt éve;* and Bene, pp. 56–57.

25 See also some diaries kept on related events: Mária Galántai, *The Changing of the Guard; the Siege of Budapest 1944–45* (London and Dunmow: Pall Mall Press, 1961), 224 pp.; Miksa Fenyö, *Az elsodort ország; naplójegyzetek 1944–1945–böl* (Budapest: Révai, 1946), 637 pp.

26 Béla Kirschner and Béla Rácz, "Adalékok a Felszabadult Csepeli WM elsö Négy hónapjának Történetéhez," *Párttörténeti Közlemények*, Vol. 7, No. 3 (Aug. 1961), 124–52.

27 János Kende, "Budapest Felszabadulása," *Munka*, Vol. 15, No. 2 (Feb. 1965), p. 19.

28 Fabriczky, p. 51.

29 Magyar Munkásmozgalmi Intézet MTA Történettudományi Intézete, *Felszabadulás; 1944 szeptember 26–1945, április 4.Dokumentumok* (Budapest: Szikra, 1955), 313 pp.; and "Mozgalmunk Húsz Esztendeje," *Munka*, Vol. 15, No. 4 (April 1965), 1–7.

30 Miklós Philip, "Igy Kezdödött," *Müszaki Élet*, Vol. 20, No. 7 (April 8, 1965), 5.

31 György Csanádi, "A magyar közlekedés húsz éve," *Közlekedéstudományi Szemle*, Vol. 15, No. 4 (April 1965), 137–39; and Lajos

Tölgyes, "Emlékezzünk, 1945-1956," *Vasút,* Vol. 15, No. 3 (March 1965), 1–5.

32 *Uj Magyar Lexikon,* Vol. 1, p. 382.

33 See contemporary dailies and "Emlékeztetö," *Autó Motor,* Vol. 18, No. 6 (March 21, 1965), 3–11; and "A Millenaris pincéjében kezdödött," *Autó Motor,* Vol. 18, No. 6 (March 21, 1965), 29–30.

34 Budapest, Statisztikai Hivatal, *Budapest on the Threshold of the Winter 1945–1946,* p. 11.

35 Bene, pp. 42–43.

36 See Bene, p. 5.

References

1 Afonyin, I. M. "The Liberation of Budapest," *Népszabadság,* Feb. 14, 1965, p. 3.

2 Borus, J. "The Significance of the Military Operations in Hungary in the History of the Second World War," *Hadtörténeti Közlemények,* Vol. 11, 1964, 422–48.

3 "Military Operations Around Budapest," *Népszabadság,* April 4, 1965.

4 Friessner, Hans. *Betrayed Battles; The Tragedy of the German Army in Rumania and Hungary.* Hamburg: Holsten-Verlag, 1956, 267 pp.

5 *Military Operations in 1944–45 for the Liberation of Hungary. Selections from History of the Great Patriotic War 1941–1945.* Budapest: Zrinyi Kiadó, 1964. Pp. 1–140.

6 Malahov, M. A. "The Military Operations of the Soviet Army during the Liberation of Hungary," *Hadtörténeti Közlemények,* Vol. 11, 1964, 563–97.

7 Nemes, D. *The Liberation of Hungary.* Budapest: Szikra, 1955. Pp. 256 ff. (Chapter on military operations near Budapest, pp. 98–109, and the Liberation of Budapest and its rescue from hunger, pp. 165–83.)

8 Paal, J., and A. Rado, eds. *The Coming to Life in Debrecen: Narrative of the Birth of the Democratic Hungary.* 1st ed. Debrecen, 1947, 384 pp.

9 Razso, Gy. "From the Late Harvest to the Devil of the Forest," *Élet és Tudomány,* Vol. 20, No. 7 (Feb. 19, 1965), 291–96.

10 Samsonov, Aleksandr Mikhailovich, ed. *Osvobozhdenie Vengrii ot fashizma.* Moskva: Nauka, 1965, 262 pp.

5

Offensive Weapons
and Their Effectiveness[*]

HAROLD L. BRODE
and JOHN S. NEWMAN

¶ The effectiveness of civil defense installations, and their limitations, cannot be assessed without understanding the most important effects of nuclear explosions—the blast wave spreading in all directions from the explosion, the intense heat radiation emanating therefrom, the gamma radiation produced by the nuclear process (prompt gammas), and the radioactive fission fragments resulting therefrom. These latter attach themselves to dust and temporarily vaporized soil and come down as radioactive fallout. This chapter surveys these effects of nuclear explosions, giving quantitative evaluations of the magnitude of each effect, under a variety of conditions. It also reviews briefly the effectiveness of nonnuclear and of "exotic" nuclear weapons.—E.P.W.

Harold L. Brode
Staff Member, the RAND Corporation

¶ Harold L. Brode, born in the state of Washington (1923), the son of a school teacher and administrator, spent his childhood years in Oregon and California. He was in military service in the Air Corps from 1943 through 1946. His Bachelor of Arts degree was conferred with honors by UCLA in 1947 (in physics) and a Ph.D. (in theoretical physics) by Cornell University under Professor H. A. Bethe in 1951. He was a President White Fellow at Cornell in 1948. Since

---

[*] This chapter does not represent an official position of any agency of the United States Government.

1951 Brode has been a member of the Physics Department at the RAND Corporation, Santa Monica, California. For fifteen years he has worked on the effects of nuclear explosions, contributing to the theory of the blast, fireball, thermal, ground shock, and cratering phenomena. He has been active in nuclear effects test and research planning as an advisor to the Defense Atomic Support Agency and to the Office of the Director of Research and Engineering in the Defense Department. He has long been an Air Force advisor on protective construction and system hardening. He is a member of the National Academy of Sciences Civil Defense Advisory Committee, and participated as a group leader in the Project Harbor summer study on civil defense. He is a member of the White House Engineering Advisory Board, and has been a lecturer in UCLA engineering extension courses since 1960. He has participated in international conferences dealing with weapons effects, protective construction, and civil defense. ¶ Brode is the author of several papers on nuclear explosion phenomena and weapons effects and a contributor to several books concerned with or using such information. He has published over fifty technical papers dealing with specific weapon effects. ¶ Dr. Brode was married in 1951, has six sons, is active in Boy Scouts, and is a member of Optimists International.

John S. Newman

*Associate Professor of Chemical Engineering,
University of California at Berkeley*

¶ A native of Richmond, Virginia, and a graduate of Northwestern University and the University of California (Berkeley), John Newman received his M.S. degree at Berkeley in 1962 and was immediately appointed to the chemical engineering faculty as acting instructor. He became an assistant professor the following year after completing the Ph.D. requirements, and is now an associate professor. He has been a principal investigator with the Inorganic Materials Research Division of the Lawrence Radiation Laboratory since 1963 and spent the summers of 1965 and 1966 with the Civil Defense Research Project at Oak Ridge National Laboratory. ¶ Newman's research at Berkeley has been mainly in the fields of fluid flow and electrochemical transport, with emphasis on the solution of practical electrochemical problems involving transport properties. He received the Young Author's Prize for 1966 offered by the Electrochemical Society for the paper, "Current

Distribution on a Rotating Disk below the Limiting Current." His research at Oak Ridge has included shock wave propagation, fallout contamination, and thermal effects in shelter habitability.

T 1. *Introduction*

This chapter treats the effects of offensive weapons with special concern for possible large-scale attacks on a civilian population.

Offensive weapons can be classified as follows:

1. Conventional high explosives as in general purpose bombs and shells.

2. Burning devices such as flamethrowers, napalm bombs, and incendiary bombs.

3. Pathogenic (disease inducing) microorganisms including a wide variety of lethal and incapacitating viruses and bacteria.

4. Toxic chemicals, that is, poisons, such as mustard gas as well as nerve gases and toxins.

5. Nuclear weapons including fission and fusion devices as well as some exotic variants.

Of these, nuclear weapons constitute the most serious potential threat to the civilian population of the United States. High explosives, flame devices, and toxic chemicals could be a hazard to the populations of some nations, but not of the United States because there is no potential enemy with a foreseeable capability of delivering such weapons in significant amounts. Biological agents could be a more serious threat, but they are easier to defend against than nuclear weapons and do not destroy property.

The factor determining the relative importance of the various types of weapons is the compactness of the destructive ability. This is important because it would be difficult to deliver a large amount of any material to a distant and widely dispersed target such as the U.S. population. If severe and extensive damage is to be caused with small amounts of the delivered material, that material must have great effectiveness. Consequently, after a brief consideration of the possibilities of toxic biological agents, the bulk of this chapter deals with nuclear weapons.

2. *Biological Weapons*

Biological warfare utilizes pathogenic (disease producing) organisms found in nature. While the development of entirely new organisms is highly improbable, selective growth does lead to more virulent or resistant strains of existing organisms.

Against unprotected populations the effectiveness of these weapons may be comparable to that of nuclear weapons on a cost basis and perhaps also on a weight basis. However, shelter and simple preventive measures such as masks, inoculations, and shelters equipped with air filters can be quite effective against biological agents. These air filters are installed at the air intakes of the shelters and they eliminate any germs that may be in the air outside. The uncertainties of weather and biological agent distribution mechanisms, together with the ease and effectiveness of countermeasures, makes unlikely the use of biological weapons on a wholesale basis against a nation.

In addition to agents which are incapacitating or lethal for humans, there are agents which attack crops and livestock. Against these, a large storable food surplus would be an invaluable asset. The vulnerability of the United States to anticrop warfare is substantially reduced by current excess food production capacity and by the diversity of our agriculture. In the future, as our food surpluses shrink and our population swells, the nation may become more vulnerable to crop disruption attacks.

Most biological agents are inexpensive to produce, and they can be effectively disseminated over thousands of square miles by a single aircraft. Agents vary widely in virulence and in their biological decay rate. This is illustrated in Table 5.1.

Table 5.1. Lifetimes of Biological Agents in Air

	Spores	*Active Cells*
In darkness	several days	5 to 12 hours
Overcast day	several days	minutes to hours
Clear day	hours	a few minutes

3. *Nuclear Weapons*

Nuclear weapons release a large amount of energy per unit weight and thus have the compactness necessary for a large-scale attack on a widely dispersed population. Part of the nuclear energy is released by the fission of heavy elements (uranium and plutonium). For thermonuclear weapons, about half of the released energy comes from the fusion of the isotopes of hydrogen, but this fraction can be varied between rather wide limits.

The effects of a nuclear device are described in the next two sections, first for an air burst and then for a surface or subsurface burst.

4. *Effects of an Air Burst*

a. *Blast Waves*

The release of a large amount of energy in a small space creates a very high temperature, that is, "a fireball," which in turn leads to thermal radiation from the fireball as long as it is hot. The sustained temperatures in the fireball also result in high pressure and an expansion of the air with the consequent formation of a blast or shock wave. This blast wave consists of a sudden pressure jump followed by a pressure drop below the initial pressure (Fig. 5.1). The pressure wave propagates outward from the blast center at a rate comparable to, but somewhat greater than, the speed of sound in

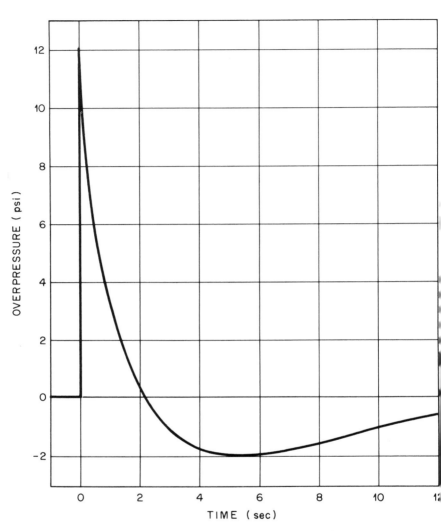

Fig. 5.1. Transient Overpressure, as a Function of Time, at a
Distance of 1.8 Miles from a 1-Megaton Surface Burst

The time is counted from the arrival of the shock wave, actually about
3½ seconds after the explosion. At that time the pressure suddenly increases to about 12 psi, stays above normal for about 2 seconds then
drops below normal. Most of the damage is done by the high pressure,
particularly the sudden increase of pressure at the arrival of the shock
wave.

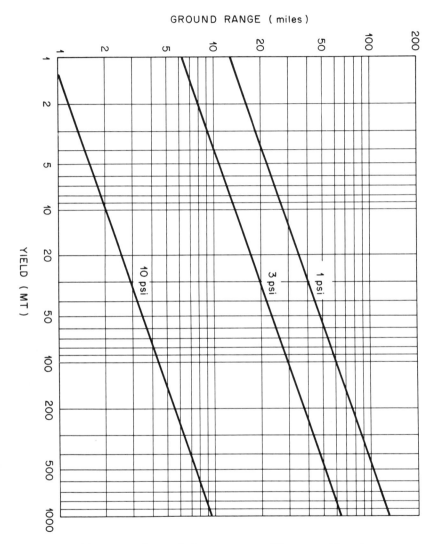

Fig. 5.2. Range for Peak Overpressures (Bursts at Altitudes to Maximize Range for 3-PSI Overpressure)

air (1,100 feet per second). Its intensity, that is, the maximum pressure of the blast, decreases as it moves away from the explosion center. The sudden pressure rise or shock wave is followed by a strong wind blowing in the direction of the propagation of the shock wave. Thermal radiation and blast waves accompany any explosion. A nuclear explosion also releases neutrons and prompt gamma radiation resulting from the nuclear reactions. It also creates large quantities of radioactive materials which contribute to fallout or what is also termed delayed gamma radiation.

It should be useful to indicate the relative protection provided by hardened shelters (Fig. 5.2). For unprotected buildings and people in such buildings a 3-psi (pounds per square inch) blast wave can be very dangerous. For a megaton burst, such overpressures can extend to a range of 34,000 feet, or 6.4 miles. Against targets resistant to 30-psi overpressures, the lethal radius is reduced to 6,600 feet, or 20 percent of the 3-psi range. At 100 psi the distance is 3,900 feet. The effective area of a weapon against a 30-psi target is thus less than 4 percent of the effective area against a 3-psi target; against a 100-psi target the area is less than 1½ percent. For weapons larger than 1 megaton, the ratios would still be the same.

b. *Thermal Radiation*

Figure 5.3 shows the range for thermal ignition of fine kindling under various weather conditions as a function of yield. The effectiveness of the thermal radiation depends upon the burst height; there is a burst height at which the thermal effects are largest. This is somewhat different from the height for greatest blast effectiveness. A higher fireball can shine down better on a larger area, but at too great a distance the radiation intensity again becomes low.

The data summarized in Figure 5.3 show that the transmission of thermal energy depends strongly on the weather, and a comparison with Figure 5.2 shows that thermal effects increase in importance relative to blast effects for the larger weapons. This increased effectiveness of the thermal radiation applies only to unprotected targets,

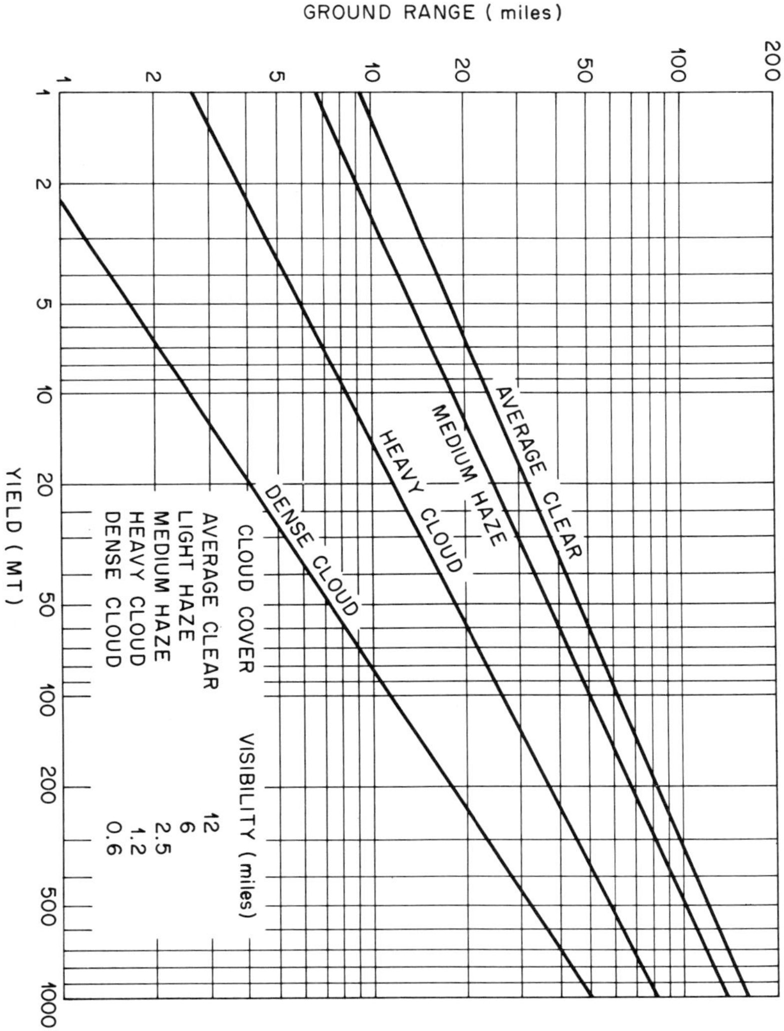

GROUND RANGE (miles)

Fig. 5.3. Ignition Range for Fine Kindling (Bursts at Altitudes to Maximize Range for 3-PSI Overpressure)

since people can be more easily protected against thermal radiation than against blast waves.

However, it is difficult to obtain reliable predictions of the overall effectiveness of thermal radiation since there are uncertainties in the amount of combustible material available, in its ignitability, and in many other factors which will determine whether the initial small fires can grow to form large-scale conflagrations or firestorms. Nevertheless, if the magnitude of the nuclear explosions and the weather conditions are given, it is possible to estimate the fire hazard as accurately as blast effects can be estimated and more accurately than fallout radiation can be predicted.

As far as materials are concerned, the susceptibility to ignition by thermal flash is mainly limited to thin, kindling fuels, such as dry newspaper, dry grass or leaves, some drapery and upholstery materials, broken wood, shingles, shavings, or paper trash. With a concerted effort to eliminate these materials, it would be possible to reduce significantly the susceptibility to fires resulting from the thermal radiation of a nuclear explosion. Also, a small amount of light material, even if it catches fire, will not always start a large conflagration. However, large fires can be started if there is a great deal of easily combustible material around; at shorter distances from the explosion less easily combustible material also catches fire.

c. *Fallout*

For an air burst the fireball is formed high in the air and rises so that the radioactive products of the nuclear reactions enter the stratosphere in a finely divided form. These decay to a considerable extent before they drop to the earth's surface. Under these conditions fallout is not a significant immediate hazard. If the radioactive materials remain in the stratosphere for an average of five months, less than 5 percent of the radioactivity ever reaches the ground, and that which does is by then widely dispersed around the world.

d. *Prompt Radiation*

Generally, for large-yield (multimegaton) explosions, the prompt radiations cannot penetrate the surrounding air in sufficient intensity to be a serious hazard in areas not covered by very heavy blast pressures also. Shelters designed to furnish protection above about 20 psi from a 1-MT (megaton) explosion require additional shielding. Thus, if the shelter can withstand 100 psi, it will be safe from the blast of an explosion more than 4,000 feet away. In order to assure the safety of those inside the shelter also from prompt radiation, the shelter should have the equivalent of the radiation protection of 5 feet of earth. In order to provide protection from the prompt radiation of a 100-MT explosion at the distance at which the blast pressure is 100 psi—that is, a distance of 18,000 feet—very little earth cover is needed because the intervening air provides radiation protection. However, most shelters with 10-psi blast resistance would naturally be under at least 5 feet of earth cover.

5. *Effects of a Surface or Subsurface Burst*

Surface or contact bursts are required to produce cratering, ground shock, local fallout, and very high blast damage. Such a burst might be used in order to knock out a hardened missile site. Figs. 5.4, 5.5, and 5.7 illustrate some of the effects of a surface burst.

a. *Blast Waves*

For a surface burst Fig. 5.4 shows ranges versus yield for overpressures of 1, 3, 10, 30, and 100 psi. The blast wave characteristics are similar to those for air bursts except that the ranges are smaller for low overpressures (compare 1 and 3 psi with Fig. 5.1) and larger for extremely high overpressures.

b. *Thermal Radiation*

Ranges for thermal ignition are indicated on Figure 5.5. The fireball from a surface burst is a less efficient source of radiation than

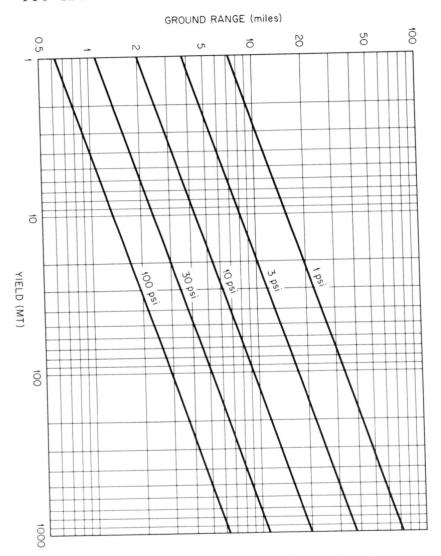

Fig. 5.4. Range for Peak Overpressures (Surface Bursts)

that from an air burst because the radiation is incident at a lower angle and must penetrate a more dense atmosphere and because the earth and debris drawn up into the fireball absorb the radiation somewhat. They also obscure and distort the radiating surface of the rising fireball.

c. *Fallout*

A surface or subsurface burst picks up large amounts of earth and other material, and some of these become contaminated with radioactive fission products. The heat resulting from the explosion creates a strong upward draft and this carries the contaminated materials up in the atmosphere. They are then carried downwind for distances up to hundreds of miles before the contaminated material settles as dust to the earth's surface, bringing with it the radioactive particles.

Particles of fallout can be regarded as having diameters mostly in the 50 to 500 micron size range (0.002 to 0.02 inches). Of course, larger particles settle sooner and nearer the burst point, and smaller particles are carried longer and farther downwind. The radiation intensity of fallout decreases with time after the burst roughly as shown in Fig. 5.6. The intensity of the fallout one hour after the burst is used as a reference value, measured in roentgens per hour, although most fallout does not reach the ground by the end of the first hour. The total accumulated dose from one hour on, measured in roentgens, is about four times the one-hour reference dose rate, measured in roentgens per hour. In most areas subject to dangerous fallout, however, the actual accumulated dose on the ground will be much less than four times the one-hour reference dose rate, because the fallout does not reach the ground until several hours after the explosion.

The vagaries of winds at high altitudes leave considerable uncertainty in the direction and precise distribution of the fallout, but large-yield weapons will lay down a dust plume several hundred

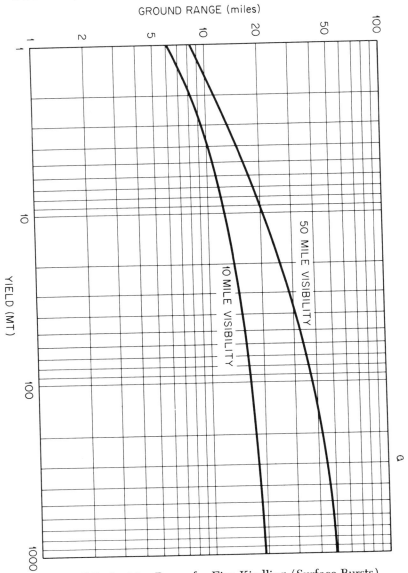

Fig. 5.5. Ignition Range for Fine Kindling (Surface Bursts)

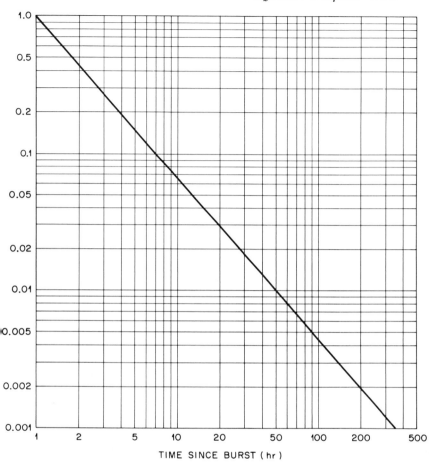

TIME SINCE BURST (hr)

Fig. 5.6. Decay of Radioactive Fission Products

miles long. In areas where the fallout comes down one hour after the explosion, the initial radiation dose may be as high as 3,000 roentgens per hour. In areas reached at later times, it will be lower, following roughly Fig. 5.6.

d. Prompt Radiation

The ranges for various prompt radiation doses from surface bursts are indicated on Fig. 5.7. Doses up to 100 roentgens produce no obvious short-term biological effects; the mean lethal dose is about 400 roentgens. Shielding will reduce the dose relative to that for unshielded objects. The shielding properties of earth are summarized in Table 5.2.

Table 5.2. Attenuation of Gamma Radiation by Earth
(density 100 lb/ft^3)

Earth Thickness (ft.)	Attenuation Factors	
	PROMPT γ ($\sim$ 6 MEV.)	FALLOUT γ ($\sim$ 1 MEV.)
1	3	20
2	10	400
5	300	3,000,000

e. Ground Shock and Craters

The air pressure resulting from nuclear bursts in the air (above the ground) creates some motion in the ground, but at almost all levels the air-induced ground motions are of less consequence than the direct air blast effects. Injuries can be sustained from sudden motions of the walls and floors of buried shelters at high overpressure levels, and such structures can be collapsed by the same pressures. But the danger from shock transmitted to occupants of surviving shelters is almost never severe in areas where the overpressure does not exceed 100 psi. For shelters intended to survive above 200 psi, some special consideration should be given to protecting occupants (with padding, with straps or bunks and hammocks) and to insuring that shelter appurtenances are secured or isolated so that

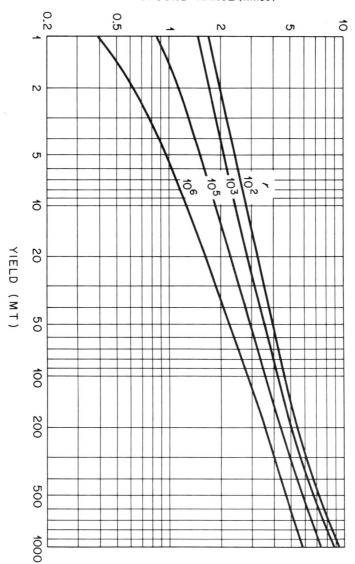

Fig. 5.7. Range of Prompt Radiation (Surface Bursts)

they do not become dangerous missiles within the shelter. Shelters in hard rock suffer less motions but higher accelerations, and are generally less likely to lead to ground shock casualties than shelters located in soil.

Even deeply buried shelters may suffer damage from bursts on or near enough to the earth's surface to create a crater. Such structures are relatively unaffected by air-burst weapons. They will be affected, however, by surface or underground explosions if these take place close by. The cratering action from nuclear explosions is well enough understood to predict with some confidence crater dimensions and also the extent of the damaging earth stresses as well as the magnitude and distribution of crater debris. Table 5.3 gives the approximate crater dimensions, i.e., the radii, depths, and volumes for large-yield surface bursts.

Table 5.3. Crater Dimensions—Surface Burst (Soil)

Yield (MT)	Radius (ft.)	Depth (ft.)	Volume of Crater (millions of cu. yds.)
1	410	120	0.9
10	780	200	5.4
100	1,500	330	33.

For special weapons able to penetrate deep into the soil before detonation, the crater and associated ground shock, debris, and local fallout are much greater. Table 5.4 presents estimates for a burst depth of 100 feet.

Table 5.4. Crater Dimensions—Explosion 100 Feet Underground

Yield (MT)	Radius (ft.)	Depth (ft.)	Volume of Crater (millions of cu. yds.)
1	1,050	290	14
10	1,900	430	69
100	3,300	630	305

Even though these craters are enormous, they clearly do not indicate that a target city could be "covered" in any sense by one or only a few craters. Debris is, however, distributed widely far beyond the crater edge, and such impressive masses of dirt earth ejecta can create heavy dust layers and serious showers of dirt clumps or rock projectiles far beyond the immediate crater lip.

Crushing stresses beneath a crater do not extend much more than one and one-third of the crater radii (five to seven times the depth), so that very deeply buried shelters should be immune to any but the largest imaginable weapons burst after considerable earth penetration, and even shallow buried structures may survive only a little beyond the crater's edge (a little more than half a mile from a surface-burst 100-MT explosion, and perhaps as close as 300 yards from a 1-MT burst).

6. *Exotic Nuclear Weapons*

There are several possible variations of the basic nuclear weapons just described. These variants would be of less importance in a large-scale attack because they are less efficient or less compact packages of destructive ability than the basic weapons.

So-called radiological weapons disseminate large amounts of radioactive materials. They can be nuclear bombs modified so that they produce special radioactive material in addition to the usual fission products (for example, cobalt bombs), or they can disseminate already radioactive materials in the form of a powder. The inclusion of such inert materials usually does not compensate for the consequent reduction in explosive yield. Furthermore, blast effects are so much more predictable than fallout effects that targeting calculations are usually based on the former.

If the neutron bomb (so called because it would maximize the number of neutrons resulting from its explosion) could be produced, it would prove to be an inefficient use of the available delivery capability, since the neutrons have very limited range.

Penetrating weapons offer the possibility of accentuating blast damage while suppressing thermal and nuclear radiation. The depth of penetration is generally limited to depths of, at most, around 100 feet in soil—and under most cities bedrock is much nearer the surface than this. For large yields, the cratering is increased without seriously degrading the blast or thermal effects, as compared with those of surface bursts. Fallout would be very much intensified very close by. The total explosive power of an earth-penetrating weapon would be smaller than that of a standard weapon of the same weight, but the difference in yield is not known.

7. *The Magnitude of the Threat*

The effects of a single nuclear explosion are reasonably well understood; the assessment of the damage from an attack is made uncertain, however, by lack of knowledge of the number of weapons, the yields employed, and the intended targets of the weapons delivered. These, of course, are factors which change with time.

Unclassified estimates of enemy weapons stores suggest that the Soviet Union has about 1,000 intercontinental missiles, about 150 long-range bombers, about the same number of medium-range bombers, and could launch about 130 missiles from submarines. They have sufficient nuclear weapons for explosions totaling 4,000 to 6,000 megatons.

Another way to arrive at the magnitude of the potential threat is to consider the targets presented by the United States and the magnitude of the attack necessary for an enemy to accomplish its objects. In this way, Martin and Latham in *Strategy for Survival* have outlined a possible attack of some 5,000 to 9,000 megatons distributed among 303 target cities. In many cases the actual targets are missile sites near the cities rather than the cities themselves. However, if an enemy's attack force is considerably lower—insufficient to knock out a significant fraction of our hardened retaliatory missiles—then it appears likely that key American cities and SAC bases would be the primary targets.

References

Glasstone, Samuel, ed. *The Effects of Nuclear Weapons*. Washington, D.C.: U.S. Atomic Energy Commission, 1962.

Martin, Thomas L., Jr., and Donald C. Latham. *Strategy for Survival*. Tucson: Univ. of Arizona Press, 1963.

Rothschild, J. H. *Tomorrow's Weapon—Chemical and Biological*. New York: McGraw-Hill, 1964.

The nuclear capability of the USSR was estimated in the Feburary 6, 1967, issue of *Aviation Week and Space Technology* (p. 28). According to all reports it has greatly increased since.

6

Medical
and Ecological Effects
of Nuclear Weapons

STANLEY I. AUERBACH
and SHIELDS WARREN

¶ The preceding chapter described the effects of nuclear explosions in terms of physical quantities, such as overpressure, radiation intensity, potential for igniting fires. This chapter tells us what the effect of a certain overpressure, of a certain amount of radioactivity, is on man, animals, and plants; what the effect of large fires would be on our fields and forests. It considers effects in the near future and also long-range effects. ¶ Although the present chapter does not describe in detail the methods for mitigating the effects of nuclear explosions on man and animals, it does contain a number of useful hints in that direction. In particular, it describes the medical problems in the absence of an extensive shelter system, and also the alleviation of these problems by the availability of different types of shelters.—E.P.W.

Shields Warren, M.D.
Scientific Director, Cancer Research Institute,
New England Deaconess Hospital;
Professor Emeritus of Pathology

¶ Shields Warren was born in Cambridge, Mass., in 1898. He studied at Boston University and received his M.D. from Harvard Medical School in 1923. He joined New England Deaconess Hospital in 1927 as pathologist and has been associated with that institution ever since. He also was professor of pathology at Harvard Medical

126

School from 1948 to his retirement as emeritus professor in 1965. ¶ Dr. Warren has led a most active life, both as a physician and as administrator and counsellor to a variety of institutions. He was consultant pathologist at eight hospitals, in addition to his leadership of reseach at Deaconess Hospital. He participated in the work of many national committees, including several organized by the National Academy of Sciences and the National Research Council. He is a member of forty scientific and honorary societies, including the Royal Society of Medicine, the Indian Association of Pathologists, the Pan American Medical Association, the Peruvian Academy of Surgery, and the Tokyo Pathological Society. Over the years he has received sixteen awards and medals and is considered to be an authority in many areas of medicine, in addition to his special field of pathology. His interest in the effects of nuclear radiaton on man and his environment stems from his long association in this area, including his assignment as Senior Medical Officer to the Atomic Casualty Investigation in Japan in 1947.

Stanley I. Auerbach
Staff Member, Oak Ridge National Laboratory

¶ Stanley Auerbach was born in 1921, received his B.S. and M.S. degrees in zoology from the University of Illinois, Urbana, in 1946 and 1947 respectively. In 1949 he received his Ph.D. from Northwestern University. He has taught biology at Roosevelt University and is a member of the Health Physics Division at Oak Ridge National Laboratory, where he is in charge of the radiation ecology research. Major areas of his work are in ecology, both animal and plant, and in biophysics, particularly radiation ecology. He is also interested in ionizing radiation in general, isotopes research, and environmental monitoring in health physics. He has published extensively in the unclassified literature, in particular on the ecology of invertebrates and on the behavior of radionuclides in various environments.

I *Introduction*

In spite of the awesome character of nuclear war, it is well to remember that man, plants, and animals have demonstrated again and again the persistence of species under highly adverse circumstances. Man survives in the Arctic and in the Sahara. Relentless war has been waged on rats since man first stored food, yet today the rat population is greater than it has ever been. Vegetables were growing well in the ashes of Hiroshima less than two months after the explosion. Therefore, we must give weight to the ability of man and his domestic plants and animals to survive a nuclear war, particularly when aided by an intelligently planned civil defense system and appropriate postattack strategy. Available knowledge clearly demonstrates that a shelter program can be effective in protecting man and that he will emerge from shelters into a damaged world, but not one barren and hopeless for the survival of the individual and of the human race. However, tremendous economic and sociologic adaptation may be required.

Man and his supporting environment are so interdependent that his mere absence for two or more weeks may be as disastrous as effects from limited numbers of nuclear weapons. He is the dominant factor in the ecosystems that serve him, whether it be food plants with need for cultivation, irrigation, weed and pest control or domestic animals with problems of feed, protection, control of disease.

A considerable body of basic information exists on the quantity of radiation necessary to cause mortality in plants and animals and man. A full review of these facts is beyond the scope of this chapter. Some salient aspects, the consequences of which will be discussed later, are the following: The fatal radiation doses, absorbed in hours or less, range from a few hundred rads (or roentgens) for man to over 100,000 rads for some insects or plants. However, living tissues have the capacity to a limited extent to repair damage resulting from radiation. Because of this, sublethal amounts of radiation delivered over weeks usually cause less biological damage than would result from a single dose of the same size delivered promptly.

What are some of the prompt doses required to kill various types of plants or animals? Trees such as oak, maple, ash, and other deciduous species appear to require a dose of about 10,000 roentgens before their top structures are killed. Little information is available about what dose is required to cause total death. For cereal plants such as oats, wheat, and barley about 4,000 r is fatal. Natural grasses and other species of plants usually found in meadows and grasslands appear to be more radioresistant, requiring doses in the neighborhood of 20,000 r to cause heavy mortality.

In the animal kingdom most of our information on the effects of ionizing radiation is based on mammals (including man) and insects. In general, radiation exposures of 1,000 r can be expected to kill most species of mammals. Adult insects are far more resistant. Doses of over 100,000 r have been reported as being necessary to kill adult insects, but there is so much variation between different species, it is difficult to generalize about them. Sterility of insects can result from doses one tenth those required to cause death. Earlier life stages of insects such as eggs, larvae, or nymphs are much more sensitive than adult stages.

For other plants and animals than these, the sensitivity to ionizing radiation ranges from hundreds of roentgens, the lethal dose for reptiles, to the hundreds of thousands or millions of roentgens necessary to kill bacteria and viruses.

Nature of Attack

Preparation against atomic warfare will provide adequate protection against other weapons, with only slight adaptation for protection against special weapons whether high explosive, incendiary, chemical, or biological. The probability of any given type of attack cannot be predicted and consequently preparation should be made to face the worst—the nuclear attack with attending fallout.

The nature of the attack itself is a decisive factor governing the extent and quantity of radioactive fallout. Bombs which are exploded high in the air to maximize blast and thermal effects will result in negligible fallout whereas those which burst on or in the ground will yield the greatest quantities of fallout. Between these general extremes there are many variable factors that will govern the extent and amount of fallout. Among these variables are the size and makeup of the weapon, target localities, time of year, and climate. Generally speaking, after a nuclear attack there would be two kinds of fallout. Local fallout is composed of radioactive debris. It is usually accompanied by a fair amount of radioactive gaseous or volatile fission products among which the isotopes of iodine are most important from the radiobiologic standpoint because of their selective absorption by the thyroid gland and the vulnerability of the thyroid to radiation injury. These gases may condense on particles or in water drops which in turn fall to the surface of the earth within weeks after the event. The local fallout would provide most of the radioactivity and likewise contribute the major part of the residual local contamination. The second type, worldwide fallout, results from the material injected into the troposphere, stratosphere, or upper atmosphere. This material returns to the earth at various times, in the course of months or years, depending upon latitude and climate. It is spread out over most of the Northern or the Southern Hemisphere, depending on the location of the explosion.

Most civil defense plans have thus far envisioned a single attack on a given target. However, the relative geographic locations and proximities of our cities are such that fallout from simultaneous attacks on cities upwind is likely to give the effect of repeated attacks. In general, the problem of sequential attacks or repeated fallout may be met in part by appropriate prolongation of the shelter period.

Uncertainty must always exist concerning the enemy's choice of target and type of attack. It may be assumed that targets and attacks would be chosen (a) to eliminate sites from which retaliatory attacks may be made, (b) to break morale with a minimum of physical damage, (c) to apply the most effective weapons for his purpose—namely, atomic bombs, with or without conventional weapons.

Assumption (a) indicates that civilian populations adjacent to strategic military bases or important missile sites would be in grave danger not so much from direct attack as from peripheral effects of attacks on the bases.

Assumption (b) suggests that centers of prime importance to government, to the economy, to distribution would be preferential targets.

Assumption (c) indicates that nuclear weapons would be used initially and that preference might well be given to "dirty" weapons (i.e., weapons which cause a great deal of radioactive fallout). Conventional weapons would be impractical in a direct attack on the United States. The relative ineffectiveness of chemical and bacteriological weapons and their delivery problems as well as their dependence on optimal weather conditions for effectiveness suggest that their utilization, if any, would be secondary and for harassment rather than for primary attack. Procedures effective against blast and fallout could be modified to provide considerable protection against biological and chemical attack. The United States has stated that its retaliatory response against a Soviet attack will be nuclear.

While the size of any attack is unpredictable, it may be assumed that no nuclear attack of magnitude less than 1,000 megatons would give an enemy hope of victory; one larger than 10,000 megatons would greatly strain the economy of an aggressor and, if effectively delivered, would leave little in booty or population to be taken over by the victor.

In spite of the inherent uncertainties, it is best to plan to mitigate conditions under the worst assumptions, since a more-than-adequate protection under less rigorous attack conditions will do no harm other than to add somewhat to the cost.

Depending on the length of warning, the response of the population to warning, and the adequacy of shelters, the effects of a nuclear attack will vary greatly. Assuming adequate warning and adequate shelter, there would be few initial casualties other than in regions under direct attack. The period of shelter occupancy would depend on the fallout pattern. Assuming inadequate warning and inadequate shelter, a great number of diverse effects would be encountered varying with such factors as type and magnitude of explosion, distance, height of burst, and climatic conditions.

Although a nuclear attack releases three different types of energy —kinetic (blast), thermal, and radioactive (both immediate and delayed) certain relationships hold so far as protection is concerned. Protection against kinetic or blast injury, whether primary or secondary, automatically includes protection against thermal injury and also, to a very considerable degree, against radiation injury.

Effects

Uncertainty concerning the effects of a nuclear attack on the environment, its subsequent recovery, and on man's ability to survive is related (a) to the inability to formulate a realistic estimate of the dimensions of a nuclear attack and (b) to the lack of a general body of information on the ecological consequences of radiation insult delivered to the environment on a large scale. Whenever there is uncertainty and a lack of information, a tendency exists to view a problem pessimistically. One might recall the dire predictions which preceded the introduction of the railroad and the automobile. Learned statements appeared to the effect that humans could not survive at the speeds which these devices would attain, and that the side effects of their noise or smoke would have dire consequences on plants and animals.

Blast and immediate radiation effects are but little altered by meteorological conditions at the target, but thermal effects are materially reduced by clouds, fog, or precipitation. Precipitation would increase the intensity of radioactivity of local fallout, including I^{131}, a radioactive isotope of iodine, but correspondingly would decrease the area of the local fallout. It would also increase local fallout from distance explosions.

Blast Effects

Injury from blast may be direct, which would be relatively unlikely at pressures under 10 psi; secondary from objects, such as the broken glass of windows set in motion by the blast wave; or tertiary from being hurled against solid objects by the blast. Fractures, contusions (including rupture of viscera), and lacerations would be produced by flying or falling beams, masonry, and glass and other debris or by impact of a translated body against them. If the velocity of secondary missiles or translated persons is less than 10 feet per second (produced by about 1.5 psi ovepressure), little harm will result. While no practical shelter system could be completely protective against a direct hit, shelters of 100- or even 50-psi resistance with antiblast doors would provide significant protection.

Thermal Effects

Thermal injuries may be direct from the flash itself or indirect from flames of ignited fires. Flash burns would occur primarily in those areas of skin directly exposed to the luminescence of the fireball and would be restricted or minimal in those areas covered by clothing. Persons within structures and away from windows or in shelters would be completely protected. A 1-megaton explosion will produce second degree burns at about 6 calories per square centimeter, or at a distance of 10 miles. Retinal damage or blindness from direct viewing of the fireball might be a hazard, even at distances of many miles, especially at night.

Effects of Fire

Secondary flame effects would depend on the character of build-ings and the extent of fires. Carbon monoxide poisoning is always a hazard in close proximity to fires. A word should be said here with reference to the possible exhaustion of oxygen by firestorms. This is relatively unlikely and could be a major factor only under highly specialized conditions.

The need for protection against fire has led to a kind of thinking, sometimes referred to as the "Smoky the Bear" complex which im-plies that all fire is bad. Certain areas because of topography, soil structure, draining, and related factors are more susceptible to ero-sion after fire. But in terms of the total continental land mass, these areas are limited.

Fire is an environmental factor which played an important and generally beneficial role in the development and maintenance of certain major ecological communities on this continent before the advent of colonization. The concept that fire inevitabily leads to desolation of the environment stems primarily from the projection of the destruction of renewable resources, such as timber or wheat fields, which are of immediate usefulness to man.

A considerable part of the United States is covered with vegeta-tion types which, if burned, would result in little or no long-term harm. The areas to which we are referring are the Great Plains region and the areas adjacent to it, originally comprising the prairies that extended from Indiana to the foothills of the Rockies and from the Canadian border to the Gulf of Mexico. Historical analyses and recent experiments have led ecologists to the conclusion that por-tions of the prairies were maintained and rejuvenated by periodic burnings. These fires had two major effects. They destroyed en-croaching tree and shrub growth and they served to make nutrients bound up in plant materials readily available for new growth, which in turn was more luxuriant than the previous growth. During the last several years experimental areas of original type tall prairie grass have been reestablished and subjected to periodic burning. The areas protected from burning tend to deteriorate into scrubby preforest type vegetation whereas the burned areas maintained their prairie aspect. At present there are approximately 75 million acres (about 115,000 square miles) in the Southwest covered with mesquite brush and chapparal resulting from the suppression of fire and overgrazing. Experimental burnings have resulted in the return of grasses. Large scale fires in the mesquite region likely would result in its reversion to useful grassland. It is also a well known ecological fact that young ecosystems are more productive in terms of energy content than older more stable areas. As an ecosystem develops toward a steady state (climax), more and more material is tied up in cellulose. Herein also lies the reason for the great productivity of the original prairies and their capacity to support millions of bison.

The foregoing is not meant to imply that fire is always beneficial, but rather that in considering the postattack fire problem in relation to civil defense feasibility, a balanced viewpoint is essential. Certainly there are areas, especially forested areas of the United States, which if burned would result in a loss of valuable, but ultimately renewable resources. It is also difficult to reconcile the dire predictions of fire spread with the wide possibilities of kinds of attack and with the varying susceptibilty of different parts of the country to fire. Maximum fire danger would result from weapons detonated in air, an attack which would result in minimum fallout. Consequently the time required to remain in shelters because of radiation would be much less than in a ground burst attack and more resources (people) would be available for countermeasures. At any given season all of the United States is not necessarily equally susceptible to fire ignition. In the summer of 1965 the northeastern part of the country was suffering from drought and probably was fire susceptible. In contrast the Southeast and the Great Plains had more than ample rainfall—a condition not conducive to ignition and fire spread.

Effects of Ionizing Radiation

Exposure to ionizing radiation will produce in those persons not sheltered or inadequately sheltered a variety of effects ranging from immediate, or slightly delayed, to late. We will consider problems chiefly encountered in the acute radiation syndrome as these would be the ones of primary concern during the shelter period. Under attack and shelter conditions accurate dosimetry will be difficult, and since the neutron component of the dose may be uncertain, symptoms may well serve as the best guide. Those who have received very heavy doses of whole-body radiation—5,000 r or over—will be disoriented promptly or in coma. Less heavily irradiated patients would show nausea, vomiting, and diarrhea. Most patients who have received doses of ionizing radiation over 300 r will show serious hemorrhagic manifestations (bleeding) within the first three days after exposure. The lethal dose for half the exposed population is about 450 r. The chance of survival of anyone who has received over 750 r is very slight. Some epilation usually occurs within the first week in patients who have received over 300 r. Weakness and fatigue is prominent in those who have received over 200 r. A period of rest is imperative for irradiated persons. There is no specific treatment. Remission of symptoms after a few days may be followed by relapse. In general, those who survive six weeks will recover. Any shelter adequate against blast of 30 psi or more will give effective protection against fallout radiation. One yard of earth cover reduces the intensity of fallout radiation by a factor of well over 100.*

Late Effects in Man

Late effects as well as immediate ones must be considered together with their burden on the postattack society. Among the many types of somatic injuries to be considered would be those involving

---

* Editor's Note—For the protection afforded by an earth cover against the prompt radiation from the explosion, see the discussion of the preceding chapter.

loss of limbs, of special senses, disabilities related to scars, muscular distortions, and badly healed fractures. These might well be on the order of five percent of the survivors, assuming no adequate civil defense. The risk of carcinogenesis and leukemogenesis is real but would be delayed for years or even decades and probably would not exceed five percent. Damage to protective mechanisms of the body such as immunity might be produced but this has been impossible to detect among the survivors at Hiroshima and Nagasaki. Among heavily irradiated survivors there might well be risk of sterility or of the procreation of individuals with hereditary defects, but on the basis of available data, as from Hiroshima and Nagasaki, such effects would be slight.

Emergency Medical Care

Depending on the degree of preparation made, and the availability of skill within any given shelter group, varying degrees of medical care might be available, ranging from that comparable with the service of a major hospital to the barest provision of non-sterile protective bandages and crude splints. It would be highly desirable to have knowledge of first aid so widely disseminated in the population that practically every group in shelters might have at least one person competent in the simpler forms of first aid. On the basis of a two-week shelter period most persons with minor trauma or first- or second-degree burns would be recovered by its end. Persons with third-degree or infected burns or severe trauma would require care over a period of months.

No fractures would be healed within the assumed shelter period. The time of healing ranges from a minimum of six weeks for simple fractures of nonweight-bearing bones in children to many months for compound or complicated fractures of weight-bearings bones in adults.

If the people enter the shelters before the attack arrives, the need for extensive first aid medical care will be relatively slight. However, first aid and medical services for casualties will have enormous demands placed upon them unless ample warning has been provided. The existence of an organized service during the shelter period will be impossible unless some form of grid shelter system* or other means of intercommunication is utilized, as many shelters would be entirely without medical personnel. In addition to the types of casualties that might be expected from an atomic, high explosive, or incendiary attack, everyday events such as birth and minor illnesses assume major medical importance under the conditions of shelter life. Provision of primitive sanitary facilities should not be difficult within most shelters, but rigid sanitary discipline would be required.

The key to prolonged shelter occupancy is organization and adequate leadership to maintain morale. Particularly important is the reassembly of families and the gradual reestablishment of contact with and control over the environment.

Variations in Populations to be Sheltered

Consideration of the probable types of people in shelters is of major importance from the medical standpoint. Because any attack to be effective must be simultaneous throughout the country, the difference in time zones would suggest that targets in different areas of the country would experience considerable variation as to population density and composition at time of attack. For example, able-bodied workers would predominate in nonresidential urban and industrial areas. Whenever possible, family groups should be maintained. While it is neither desirable nor feasible to segregate persons on the basis of age, some groups pose problems of special care.

In residential sections and areas near large medical or mental institutions there are many incapacitated persons who must be provided for. Ten percent of our population is under five years of age and 1.25 percent is over eighty. At any given time in the United

---

* Editor's Note—This will be described in Chapter 9.

States there are approximately 3,200,000 women in some stage of pregnancy. The number of patients in hospital beds throughout the country is probably on the order of 1,285,000. A small portion of these might be self-sufficient, but most will need special care. At any given time a portion of the population at home is also ill (1+ percent). Therefore, one must provide medical care and medical supplies for several million, particularly for the chronically ill who need continuing medication, as diabetics in need of insulin.

Between half a million and a million mentally ill people would require care. In 1966 there were about 550,000 patients resident in mental hospitals, as estimated by the national Institute of Mental Health. If current Massachusetts figures were projected for the country as a whole, 1 million mentally ill persons is a reasonable estimate. While some patients with certain types of mental disease may improve somewhat under stress, most mentally ill patients would have a disrupting effect on the maintenance of order and tend to frustrate joint efforts. In addition, approximately 160,000 prisoners would require some type of custodial care and segregation.

Radioactive Fallout and Residual Contamination

The residual contamination resulting from radioactive fallout is a facet of the postnuclear attack situation that least lends itself to tractable analysis. The complications are manifold.

The radionuclides comprising fallout can be lumped into two categories: (a) those which are short-lived and would be a problem for periods up to a year and (b) long-lived isotopes which would retain their radioactivity for many years.

Several of the short-lived isotopes such as radioiodine are readily accumulated by certain tissues and organs. Consequently, during the weeks and months after an attack precautions must be taken with regard to intake of food, water, and dairy products. In the case of food, including milk, commodities in storage and hence protected from fallout are an extremely important asset. Many short-lived radionuclides would be bound to the fallout particles from which they would not be readily released so that they would remain harmless. This is especially important with regard to water. Many of the fallout particles would settle in rivers and lakes. As a result many of the short-lived radioisotopes would lose much of their activity before being leached from the particles.

The two long-lived radioisotopes of greatest concern are strontium 90 and cesium 137, both of which have half-lives of about thirty years. They are metabolizable to a certain extent and hence are of major concern to man. Their concentrations in the soil may have little effect on plants and uncertainty exists regarding their long term effects on animals. The degree to which the continuous or discontinuous ingestion of these isotopes constitutes a health hazard has been the subject of considerable controversy.

The controversy is concerned with the minimum level of radiation exposure necessary to induce bone cancer, leukemia, anemia, genetic damage, and premature aging. Essentially, the argument centers about whether radiation damage, in terms of leukemia, for example, is a direct or linear function of the radiation dose or whether there is a threshold level of cumulative radiation exposure. This issue cannot be resolved with evidence presently available.

In regions of heavy local fallout, particles containing both Sr^{90} and Cs^{137} and other radioactive fission products will be entrapped by vegetation as well as by the surface of the soil. During the early weeks or even months following an attack, these areas of heavy contamination, be they crop-producing, forest, or grassland regions, pose no hazard for radioisotope intake simply because these areas probably will be too radioactive to be utilized in any fashion. This distinction is all too frequently beclouded in discussions of the feasibility of civil defense. References are frequently made to the fact that all crops will be so "poisoned" by heavy contamination that they will be unfit to eat. Ergo, we will be unable to grow food and consequently will face starvation or slow death induced by radioactive intake. Depending upon the time of year, crops may or may not be heavily contaminated. If an attack were made in October, most of the crops would have been harvested. If the attack took place in early summer, crops or other vegetation in heavily contaminated areas would be damaged by the radiation, precluding their use as food, even if it were possible to harvest them. Obviously this situation places a premium on maintaining at least a one-year supply of foodstuffs, a not unreasonable criterion for planning even apart from considerations of civil defense.* From the second year after an attack the problem will then be concerned with chronic input of Sr^{90} and Cs^{137} into the diet. Let us examine some aspects of this problem.

In the years following an attack Sr^{90} and Cs^{137} would enter the food plants via two routes—uptake by plant roots from the soil and by the contamination of leafy surfaces by radioisotopes coming down later as part of worldwide fallout. By far the greater quantity of radionuclides would be in the soil since they would have been derived from local fallout. Present thinking, therefore, leans toward the soil uptake route as being the more important pathway for entry of Sr^{90} and Cs^{137} into the diet and hence into human bodies. However, it is important to recognize that only a small portion of the radionuclides would be available for uptake at any time and, furthermore, that biological discrimination factors would generally be operative to reduce further the amounts entering the body.

Because most of the Sr^{90} and Cs^{137} would be in the soil where portions may be fixed in the soil or remain part of poorly soluble fallout particles, there would be time to institute many kinds of suitable countermeasures to reduce their intake by people. These countermeasures would include various kinds or combinations of plowing and planting to reduce the availability of the radioactive materials to plants, monitoring procedures to separate contaminated from uncontaminated food, feeding the former to animals thereby

* The food supply of the United States, much depleted by foreign aid, was sufficient for nutrition for about nineteen months even at the seasonal minimum, just before the 1967 crop became available. However, its composition was unfavorable; in particular, too much of it was corn.

taking advantage of a biological decontamination technique, and separation of Sr^{90} from milk by methods now available.

The other important pathway for entry into the diet is through drinking water. Here the problem would be most serious in the immediate months or first few years after a heavy fallout, although runoff from the land surfaces would represent a long-term problem. Unfortunately, we know little about the dissolution times of fallout particles and the rates of runoff from watersheds of varying ecological nature. On the other hand there are techniques for removing radioisotopes effectively from water. Increasing economic and technological recovery after an attack could provide the specialized means for decreasing the entry of long-lived radionuclides into the diet by this route.

Decontamination

Decontamination stations should be established in association with major shelters through which, after the strike, contaminated survivors could be transferred to clean areas. Mobile stations with adequate equipment to come from without the target zone would be of great importance. An important role that community, state, and federal hospitals might perform outside strike areas and where additional strikes might be expected would be the decontamination of survivors before their entry into the shelter system.

As egress from shelter first becomes possible, the protection of returning teams of shelter inhabitants who might have been contaminated during exploratory trips to the outside and the entrance of survivors potentially contaminated by fallout demands monitoring and in some instances decontamination. Assuming a grid type structure of shelters, communication is effectively maintained and the problems of distribution of medical, surgical, first aid, and sanitary skills can be better handled. Among the first priorities on emergence would be the preparation of decontaminated pathways to other shelters, to sources of water, and to stores of food and supply.

Effects on Animals

The uncertainties regarding the dimensions of an attack make detailed predictions on the effects upon animals and plants uncertain. Experimental data provide considerable insight on the effects of ionizing radiation. Domestic animals such as cattle, sheep, and swine would be killed by acute doses of 500 r. Death would not be instantaneous. Consequently, they could be used as food, since the edibility of their flesh would not be affected by the radiation. Animals protected by shelters would be in danger of internal contamination from their food. It is unlikely that this contamination would cause fatalities to significant numbers, so that there should be no difficulty in starting new herds.

Birds generally are more resistant to ionizing radiation than are mammals. Adult birds can survive a dose of 1,000 rads. Many species, such as our game birds, might be relatively unaffected by an attack either because they may be in a part of the country less affected by fallout, or (in the case of ducks) on water where local fallout would sink and otherwise be dispersed, thereby reducing the radiation dose.

Doses 10 to 100 times greater than those necessary to kill birds would be required to produce total lethality in adult insects. Since it is well known that birds feed on insects and for many, but by no means the majority of insect species, birds provide a constraint on insect population size, it has been postulated that insect plagues would be one of the major consequences of a nuclear attack. Without denying the plausibility of this line of reasoning, one can introduce additional ecological facts and arrive at a different conclusion. Many species of insects are controlled or restrained by other species of insects which prey on or parasitize them. Still other are controlled more indirectly through competition for food; by the availability of food itself; or by climatic factors such as cold versus mild winters, precipitation, and seasonal temperature regimes. Large doses of ionizing radiation such as would be experienced in areas of heavy fallout might result in death to birds with little subsequent effect on insects the proliferation of which would still be restrained by their normal insect and environmental controls. Conversely, the radiation could result in destruction of a large spectrum of insect species, because the attack might occur in early spring when many of the species were immature, close to the ground, or otherwise more prone to both the gamma and the beta radiation that would be present in large quantities on ground surfaces. Under such circumstances a general reduction in insect populations might result rather than the buildup of plague numbers. Moreover, the buildup of insect populations and their subsequent maintenance is dependent upon the supply of food. It is mainly in simpler ecological systems, such as the pine or spruce forests, or in agricultural ecosystems producing a single crop that we are most vulnerable to insect attacks. In complex ecosystems such as grasslands or deciduous forests, the interacting factors of competition, predation, food supply, and climatic factors might well override the perturbing influence of ionizing radiation. We do not mean to imply that there is no danger whatever of an insect threat to agricultural production following a nuclear attack, but rather to suggest that this same threat to large scale agricultural production exists today and is held in check by the use of various controls including agronomic techniques, insecticides, and biological controls. Therefore, the insect problem after an attack may be no more a result of environmental disturbance or imbalance than it is at present. Consequently, this aspect of recovery and perhaps others as well, and the means whereby recovery can be facilitated, may be primarily an economic matter rather than an ecological one.

Effects on Plants

The landscape is covered by plant systems organized in two different fashions. One system represents the dynamic end product of nature acting continuously through long periods of time. The second system represents man's organized efforts to achieve maximum utilization of the landscape for the production of food or fiber. How the massive radiation which would result from certain kinds of nuclear attack might affect these systems has been the subject of some speculation and to a much lesser extent the subject of experimental study.

Doses such as those resulting from fallout after an attack can be expected to kill or otherwise affect many plants and plant systems. In the case of crop plant systems which would be affected by doses ranging from 2,000 to 35,000 r, it should be borne in mind that these are annual plant systems, which can be reproduced in soils easily as long as seeds are available. Consequently, if a crop is lost due to nuclear radiation, it could be regrown the following year if the agricultural means are available. Radiation itself would not be sufficiently intense after a year's decay of the fission products to interfere significantly with plant growth, except perhaps in localized sites where there was particularly heavy, close-in fallout. If the land can be plowed and if there are seeds and insect control measures available, the damage done to our crop systems by ionizing radiation should be repairable. For the residual, long-lived contamination to have a deleterious effect on subsequent growth, according to present evidence the dose would have to exceed 5 r per day. While attacks of dimensions necessary to produce such long term chronic doses over large areas of land can be postulated, it is doubtful that the delivery capacity exists to achieve them.

Three kinds of plant communities cover the landscape. These are deciduous forests, coniferous forests, and grasslands or prairies. Coniferous forests are most sensitive to ionizing radiation; prompt doses of 1,000 r kill conifers. Deciduous forests and grasslands are much less vulnerable: doses of 10,000 to 20,000 r are necessary to kill deciduous forests. Furthermore there is some evidence, discussed later, suggesting that although the aboveground parts of deciduous trees may be killed by doses in this range, the roots remain viable and able to initiate new growth. Exposures in excess of 20,000 r and perhaps as high as 40,000 r would be necessary to kill the plants which comprise the grasslands, i.e., grasses, legumes, sedges, and flowering annuals.

Ecological Recovery

Nature is characterized by resiliency. The capacity for self regulation, i.e., the return to ecosystems which are peculiar to particular climates and topographies is a very powerful one. In spite of the drastic operations man has performed on the United States portion of North America, such as cutting the original forest, plowing the prairies, restricting fire, overgrazing, and altering the rivers, wherever he has ceased such operations nature begins to recover the land. A recent striking example is the removal of large areas of marginal land from agricultural use under the soil conservation program. These areas are once again covered with forest, albeit young forest, and are providing habitats for a variety of wild animals and birds which in turn increase in numbers.

Would ionizing radiation delivered on the scale of a nuclear attack cause complete destruction of life? The experimental evidence that ecosystems will recover from massive perturbations induced by ionizing radiation is meager but favorable. An unshielded nuclear reactor in northeast Georgia operated for a limited period of time in 1959 and 1960 and delivered two acute exposures to the surrounding mixed pine-hardwood forest typical of that region. The radiation resulted in a band of killed trees and other vegetation radiating out in a generally pie-shaped segment for several hundred feet from the reactor wall. Recovery of the forest is now well underway, initiated by new trees developing as sprouts from the roots of trees whose aboveground structures were killed by radiation. However, the pines in this area did not recover. Sprouting took place only from deciduous trees, and not all the species responded similarly; therefore, the forest growth present 3 to 5 years later was qualitatively different from that which was there previously. Another example are the islands Bikini and Eniwetok, which were used for the testing of nuclear weapons 6 to 8 years ago and were heavily damaged by radiation. These have had the vegetation return to a normal appearing cover.

As Ayres (1965) has pointed out, the concept of an "ecological catastrophe" seems to be a difficult one to render plausible, in the light of the available knowledge. This conclusion is not meant to imply that the magnitude and suddenness of a nuclear attack would not result in serious short-term environmental problems; but only that the problems are amenable to amelioration with the aid of previous planning. The fact that we lack some information should not be construed to mean that the information is unobtainable nor is it a valid reason for assuming that survival after a nuclear war is impossible and therefore civil defense is ineffectual.

References

Some of the basis for the data used in this chapter is contained in *The Effects of Nuclear Weapons* (Washington, D.C.: U.S. Atomic Energy Commission, 1962); most of it, however, is scattered in the literature on ecology. Robert Ayres' study *Environmental Effects of Nuclear Weapons* was published as a Hudson Institute Report (HI 518–RR) in 1965.

7   Civil Defense Abroad in Review

CURTIS E. HARVEY

¶ The future cannot be planned successfully without a knowledge of the present. The chapter which follows acquaints us with the basic facts about civil defense preparations in other countries. It shows that the neutral countries have done most toward protecting their people, the communist countries apparently less, and the NATO countries are far behind these. The reasons for the stagnation of the civil defense efforts of other NATO countries are probably similar to those of the United States.—E.P.W.

Curtis E. Harvey

Professor of Economics
University of Kentucky

¶ Curtis E. Harvey was born in 1930 in Romania. He spent ten years in that country and, subsequently, five years in German-occupied Czechoslovakia. He came to the United States in 1946. He studied economics at the University of California at Los Angeles, worked for a few years for that state's Compensation Fund, then became lecturer at the University of Southern California and took his Ph.D. there in 1963. ¶ Dr. Harvey's principal interest is in international trade and economic development. However, he also has an abiding interest in the problems of civil defense and has published on this subject. ¶ Dr. Harvey has traveled extensively in later years—in 1961–62 he was a Fulbright Scholar in Austria. Much of the material for the present study was collected on a recent trip to Europe. At present, he is professor of Economics at the University of Kentucky in Lexington, Kentucky.

A **Introduction**

t the end of World War II the United States was the only belligerent to emerge from the conflict unscathed. Virtually every other participant in that war was made acutely aware of one of the central elements of modern strategic doctrine: the distinction between the home and the fighting front had disappeared. In World War I army fought against army, leaving the major share of the homeland relatively untouched. In World War II selected homeland regions were attacked and devastated, but, basically, the outcome of the war continued to hinge on the effectiveness of the opposing armies, and on the amount of political, economic, and moral support they were able to command at home. Nevertheless, a new element to warfare was added: with the advent of air power the success of field armies could be affected by attacks on the home front. For the first time, civil protection, although of a primitive help-your-neighbor character, became necessary.

Since the end of World War II the realization that the homefront is vulnerable has been reinforced by the emergence of long range jet aircraft, intercontinental ballistic missiles, strategically placed bases, and sea launching missile capabilities. Today, because more sophisticated protection is possible, civil defense is considered an essential part of strategic doctrine throughout the world. But since most people instinctively refuse to think of the practical implications of nuclear war and since civil defense, in requiring public support, has become in many countries a matter of public discussion and debate rather than implemented policy, civil protective measures have generally not been deployed extensively or enthusiastically. Thus, even though civil defense, along with strategic offensive, strategic defensive, and general tactical forces, represents one of the four basic elements that make up a nation's military strength, it has generally been relegated to a position of secondary importance in the hierarchy of military priorities.

This chapter addresses itself to a review of civil defense in the context of its role as an integral part of foreign strategic thinking. Consequently, the individual countries reviewed are grouped in accordance with the strategic doctrine that each pursues—the nuclear powers, the neutral nations, the nonnuclear NATO countries, and the nonnuclear Warsaw Pact nations. While a more comprehensive effort might have included the nations of Africa, Asia, and Latin America, the focus of this chapter is directed principally on the developed nations of West and East Europe, Canada, and China.

The Nuclear Powers

A nuclear policy is an offensive policy in the sense that nuclear weapons are necessarily offensive weapons for deployment abroad. Only in recent years has technology advanced to a point where nuclear weapons are now being thought of as also capable of providing domestic protection.

But nuclear weapons, particularly missiles, still rank as strategic deterrents in the military arsenals of world powers, and not as shields. Military strategists and scientists, therefore, continue to devote most of their talents to the development and perfection of offensive weapons. This, of course, is consistent with the principle of "retaliatory response," but succeeds at the expense of a defensive protective posture. That this is true in varying degrees only is quite clear, but to date, no nuclear power has elevated civil defense to a position of equality, or anything resembling it, with offensive weapons development. The fundamental premise on which this revealed preference is based is quite clear—strategic planners and decision makers consider a dollar spent on offensive weapons to yield more additional protection than a dollar spent on defensive weapons.

That is to say, they argue that the nuclear age has made destructive power cheap, much cheaper than protective power deployed at home. While this argument may be relevant in partial application, it cannot effectively be applied on a global basis in a nonhomogenous world. Another chapter in this book treats this topic more fully.

United Kingdom

British strategic thinking, like that of most NATO countries, considers civil defense an integral and necessary part of the total defense system of the country. In conjunction with offensive weapons, civil defense plays a deterrent role in lessening the likelihood of conflict. Because natural disasters in England are sufficiently infrequent and mild, civil defense cannot be justified in these terms. It therefore becomes a defensive military system only.

The urgency of civil defense activities is usually dictated by the perceived likelihood of the threat of a nuclear exchange. The British government considers this possibility remote, but nonetheless desires to maintain a viable civil defense organization against the contingency of a change in the world situation. In view of the nation's current economic woes, civil defense expenditures for 1967–68 were reduced by 25 percent from 1964–65, viz., from £24 million to £18 million. This was $50 million, or about $1 per person, at the rate of exchange then prevailing.*

The British civil defense organization benefits greatly from operational experiences gained during World War II. Its origin actually can be traced to the 1930's when, under the threat of impending air war, the Air Raid Precautions Service was established. Following the conclusion of the war, the Service was abolished. Worsening international relations during the later postwar years, however, gave impetus to a renewed concern with civilian protection which

---

* EDITOR's NOTE—U.S. civil defense budget is somewhat less than 50 cents per person.

culminated in the passage of the Civil Defense Act of 1948, the legal basis for the organization in existence today.

The operational character of the present civil defense system in England is based upon two fundamental assumptions: one, that protection against nuclear blast cannot reasonably be provided, and two, that slow crisis escalation with adequate warning time will permit the evacuation of a considerable segment of the population.

Main responsibility for civil protection in England rests with the various state ministries, the heads of which direct the activities of the local authorities. Local expenditures are either wholly or partially (at least 75 percent) financed by the national government. In general, each ministry is expected to perform its function in wartime as it would during normal conditions. For instance, the Ministry of Transportation is in charge of road and rail transport and the ports, the Ministry of Health for hospital and ambulance service, the Home Office for police and fire protection as well as for total civil defense planning and coordination.

Because under the British electoral system each minister represents a particular constituency, he is much more sensitive to the pressures of public opinion than he would be if he were an appointed official. And since a very vocal segment of the population is strongly opposed to any and all expenditures on national defense, progress made so far in establishing a comprehensive and effective civil defense system has been generally sporadic and unenthusiastic.

The latest five-year review of the British civil defense organization took place in 1965. Recommendations which flowed from this review divided the civil defense organization into four functions.

The objective of the first function, that of the control system, is to direct initial lifesaving operations and to establish a framework within which available resources can be allocated efficiently in order to assure continued survival. The jurisdiction of the control system is divided into 13 regions which comprise 170 subregions, counties and county boroughs. Many of these contain several sectors or control-post areas.

The second function, the civil defense corps, aids local authorities in the performance of their emergency control duties. In addition, it provides expert professional advice in the chemical, climatic, and medical fields. The total strength of this corps has recently been reduced from 120,000 to 80,000, most of whom are volunteers drawn from auxiliary organizations such as the Red Cross, the St. John Ambulance Brigade, the Women's Royal Volunteer Service, and from universities.

The third function, the casualty prevention, encompasses three principal objectives—warning and monitoring, shelter, and dispersal. The warning and monitoring system is designed to give the public a minimum of four minutes of warning, but its capability to measure radioactive fallout and to transmit findings from 1,500 underground posts to 24,000 warning points seems more important. Since protection from blast is considered impractical, the casualty prevention measures focus on fallout protection. It is assumed that in general such protection is attained best at home, and families are encouraged to take measures to improve this protection. In addition, a public shelter system is now under consideration for those away from home or those whose domicile is unsuitable for shelter.

The third principal casualty preventive measure is a plan which anticipates the evacuation and dispersal of approximately 10½ million people in priority classes (mothers with children under eighteen, expectant mothers, and the elderly and infirm) to reception centers within a fifty-mile radius.

The fire and police services represent the fourth functional element of Britain's civil defense system. The basis of these services is peacetime strength. In addition to local fire personnel, which would come under national control in the event of an emergency, 14,000 auxiliary volunteers are trained for service.

The strength of the British police force is 100,000 men. Temporary constables, trained by mobile training units, supplement this force, which is also supported by territorial and Army Volunteer Reserve units. The function of the police force is to patrol their home areas although the mobile and "specialist" vehicle units can play a national role as well.

In summary, the British civil defense organization concentrates its efforts on what it considers to be the most valuable activities of casualty prevention and total systems control. Life-saving operations, which to the British hold little promise, are relatively neglected. Flexibility for future contingencies, however, is maintained.

Public response to civil defense programs in England is quite negligible, and at times even hostile, particularly under the pressures of the current economic instability and the "moral" objections to overt defense policies. The British continue to regard nuclear war as unlikely and large expenditures on protective measures ill-advised. Public apathy is probably the single most effective obstacle in the way of creating a comprehensive and fully operative civil defense system.

USSR

Changes in Soviet strategic thinking, in recent years, have been affected by two events: the increasing sophistication of air defenses and the growing realization that civil defense is part and parcel of a total national security system. During the 1950's Soviet strategists spoke only of total warfare with the inevitable deployment of mass nuclear weaponry. Today, however, Soviet thinking suggests that while each local conflict may lead to a full-blown atomic war, such escalation is not inevitable. The Russians consider it quite possible, for instance, that following a conventional or nuclear tactical exchange, hostilities will end without the unleashing of the power of the full nuclear arsenal. Against such a limited conflict, an effective civil defense system would be valuable even if it would be less effective in the event of a massive nuclear exchange. The emergence of this realization, particularly since Khrushchev's deposition, has induced Soviet strategists to embark on a comprehensive and accelerated true defense program which includes passive (civil) defense and active protection in the form of antiballistic missile systems. But since little is known regarding the extent and sophistication of the latter, this section addresses itself only to the traditional passive defense measures.

Soviet civil defense has its true origin in the air protection service of 1915—the so-called WNOS. During World War II civil defense activities were directed against the threat posed by German air power and continued along this line until approximately 1953 when Russia's nuclear capability reached greater maturity. During the mid-1950's, greater emphasis on civil protection resulted in the secret extension and enlargement of subway facilities in Moscow, Kiev, Leningrad, Tiflis, and Sevastopol, all of which added considerably to the survival potential of the population.

Prior to 1960 Russia's civil defense agency was part of the Ministry of the Interior, but since then has become an agency of the Defense Ministry. The entire system is founded on two pillars: the local civilian air defense organization (MPWO) and the paramilitary support units (DOSAAF). The MPWO covers the entire country down to the smallest village and includes specialized units responsible for firefighting, decontamination, communications, security, medical aid, etc. Each factory, each apartment house, each collective contains functional groups which make up the whole of the local area organization.

The function of training the members of these units is undertaken by the DOSAAF, a quasi-military organization of between 20 and 30 million "volunteers," membership in which is considered a patriotic duty. The DOSAAF, the USSR civil defense organization, in conjunction with the Red Cross and the "Red Half-Moon" auxiliary organization—the latter two contain 53 million members—provide a very intensive and extensive training system indeed. Twenty million reservists and 21 million members of the national youth organization swell the total training and civil defense corps even further. But admitted organizational and logistical shortcomings in the harnessing of this manpower render total effectiveness less imposing than one would expect at first.

Little is known regarding the scope of Russia's shelter construction program. What is known, however, is that the Soviets distinguish between permanent and emergency shelters. The latter are private, single purpose shelters usually found in rural areas that are considered less endangered. The former, which make up the great majority of shelters, usually have a dual function, and are public. Little encouragement seems to be afforded private family shelter construction. All public shelters are designed to provide protection against heat, radiation, fallout, chemical and bacteriological agents, and against some degree of blast. The tunnel and subway facilities in all major cities represent very good public shelter with those in Moscow estimated as able to provide shelter for a minimum of 200,000 persons.

With a reported annual civil defense budget of more than a billion dollars—more than twenty times our own expenditure for a population that exceeds ours by 15 percent—and widely organized public participation, the civil defense effort in the USSR appears to be in a stage of energetic and continuing activity. The Soviet military maintains with spirit and eloquence that a comprehensive civil defense system is a necessary element of an effective total-security defense system. It is the duty of every Soviet citizen to participate in civil defense exercises and to support the civil defense effort.[*]

France

It seems that the more optimistically a country evaluates its chances of surviving a nuclear war, the less it concerns itself with civil protection. The French are quite optimistic. Their strategic thinking leads them to believe that any nuclear conflict will in-

[*] A more detailed description of the USSR civil defense, in particular of their plans to evacuate their cities in crises, was given recently by J. Levy in *Survive*, Vol. 2, No. 2 (1969).

evitably be preceded by a lengthy period of crisis escalation, during which there will be ample time to put protective measures into effect. This theory underlies the French evacuation plans. Moreover, the French believe that the development of a comprehensive civil defense system could severely detract from the credibility of its *force de frappe*. Such convictions naturally do little to encourage civil defense planning.

The outstanding feature of French civil defense planning is Plan ORSEC. This contingency plan goes into effect in the event of a widespread disaster or emergency, during peacetime and wartime alike. Its objective is to nationally coordinate fire, health, police, and engineering services for effective deployment. The plan has its basis in law and has proved successful in fulfilling its intended mission in many instances.

Civil defense in France is under the jurisdiction of the Ministry of the Interior which coordinates civil defense requests and allocations from the various ministries, such as Health, Industry, Economic Affairs, the armed forces, etc. In the event of war, it is estimated that 1½ million technicians will be needed for duty. This manpower can be recruited from the fire services (There are 236,000 volunteers in France.), from special military forces, from public service personnel, from volunteers, and from conscripts. A law permitting conscription for civil defense purposes, if needed, was passed in 1964, and includes all eighteen- to twenty-year-olds and those in the forty-eight to sixty age group.

France does not possess a good warning system. In 1964 a total of 2,600 sirens existed, but most people were out of range of these. The underlying doctrine of the authorities is that ample warning time will be available, since a sudden outbreak of hostilities is considered unlikely.

As noted earlier, the cornerstone of French civil defense planning is the concept of evacuation. Considerable experience was gained during World War II when 3¼ million Frenchmen were evacuated from occupied zones. The basic organization which was in existence then is still in use today, although it has been modified to reflect new weaponry. Evacuation areas have been designated as A, B, and C categories, depending upon probability of threat, with A including all areas most likely to be hit by atomic weapons. Zone H was later added to reflect the danger of being hit by thermonuclear weapons. The residents to be evacuated include children first, and then all others considered inactive or engaged in nonessential endeavors. Essential personnel would remain in the danger areas, but could be removed to shelters in nearby "dormitory zones" for given periods of time. Whether evacuation will be voluntary or mandatory is, as yet, uncertain.

Aside from developing evacuation plans, little else has been implemented in France for civil protection. There is some emphasis upon postattack sanitation, food distribution, and selected industrial protection, but no shelter construction has been undertaken, even though the subways in Paris and other subterranean facilities elsewhere could easily be modified for such purposes. All in all, civil defense in France is not a very active topic of conversation or of policy formulation.

China

U.S. observers consider Chinese strategic thinking to be relatively primitive, at least in comparison with that of the other nuclear powers. The Chinese basically see in the nuclear arsenals of the United States and of the Soviet Union a continuance of the status of mutual deterrence. It is clear to them that the recent and future sources of international friction—Berlin, Cuba, South Vietnam, and now the Near East—are unlikely to lead to nuclear conflict and that they themselves hold the key to the eruption of a nuclear conflict in the future. But since, contrary to general public opinion, observers of China feel that this vast country does not intend and is ill-prepared to wage nuclear war, the lack of a comprehensive civil defense system is easily understandable. In addition, even if nuclear war were to break out, the loss of a portion of China's enormous population would certainly not represent a major impairment of China's political power. Thus, even though underground facilities for shelter protection are available in several of the large cities, little other effective civil protection does exist and more than the basic rudiments of self-protection are not actively supported by the government.

The Neutral Countries

Even a cursory review of the organization of civil defense in neutral countries reveals the fact that the neutrals have a keener interest and have made greater strides in homeland protection than most of their nonneutral neighbors. The fundamental explanation for this observation is quite simple—neutral nations are precluded by self-imposed edict from carrying armed conflict beyond their borders. The dictates of their security policy, therefore, lead to the development of a comprehensive defensive posture which necessarily features civil protection as a prominent element. After all, any armed conflict would be confined to the domestic front, thereby severely endangering the civilian population.

Sweden

This Scandinavian country, which has not engaged in warfare for over 150 years, pursues a policy of neutrality, but not of pacifism. It considers its armed forces a defense against invasion, its economic defense measures insurance against conditions of blockade, and its civil defense organization a safeguard against radioactive fallout and drifting war gas.

As in the case of the United Kingdom, Sweden relies heavily on evacuation as a protective measure. The spacious, underground, cave-type shelter facilities which are frequently featured in the popular literature—there are fourteen of these located in the nine largest cities—are intended to serve as the focal points for civil defense activities and are not expected to be used for mass occupancy.

Insofar as possible, the population will be evacuated and dispersed in an emergency. A low population density—43 persons per square mile—makes this a readily attainable goal. For the remaining population, shelters of varying degrees of protection are available (roughly 3.7 million spaces—the total population is about 7½ million). Approximately 2 million of these predate 1945 and therefore do not provide adequate nuclear protection, the remainder are of a newer vintage and give protection against fallout and against conventional bombardments. Since 1945 a law stipulates that each new structure is to contain a reinforced-concrete shelter equipped with an air-filtering system. Costs are borne by the owner, and in the case of multiunit buildings are passed on to the lessee, who is thus taxed indirectly for shelter construction. (Eighty-five percent of the urban Swedes live in apartments.)

The most ambitious protective effort in Sweden seems to have been reserved for economic resource protection. Employers in urban areas, realizing that shelter protection for their employees was not really very costly, began to store archives and other essential materials underground. In addition to these, in recent years, critical food industries, electric and water-filtering plants, generators, food stocks, essential defense industries, hospitals and schools have also begun to locate facilities underground. In order to ensure postattack survival, Sweden more so than any other country, has attempted to provide protection not only for its population but for economic resources as well.

The intent of Sweden's evacuation program is to evacuate approximately 90 percent of the urban population to distances up to 250 miles. Several very successful exercises have proved the feasibility of evacuations and dispersal. Well-designed and implemented plans stagger the departure time of the urban population (Priorities are built into the evacuation plan so as to guarantee the continuing functioning of the economy.), and temporary and final reception centers with protected supplies ensure adequate care.

The administrative responsibility for civil defense rests with each of the twenty-five provincial governors, but national coordination is ensured through the Office of the Director General of Civil Defense. A twenty-five-year-old law subjects each citizen between the ages of sixteen and sixty-five to draft for civil defense service. This establishes the pool from which the staff for manning the regional and local emergency centers is recruited. Training of this staff is both intensive and extensive, and recruitment is accepted by the population as a matter of fact.

In conclusion, public response to civil defense in Sweden nearly echoes official policy in an uncertain age—it is best to be prepared for the worst: for war. In order to implement such a preparedness policy, civil defense appropriations in Sweden will increase approximately 20 percent in the next three years.

Switzerland

By the mid-1950's Switzerland was in possession of a civil defense system capable of providing at least minimum population protection agains the effects from a nuclear war. Most households had food stocks for several weeks, and underground shelter facilities contained emergency hospitals and governmental and military stockpiles.

According to the 1962 Federal Civil Protection Law, all able-bodied males between the ages of twenty-one and sixty become eligible for service in an emergency, and women may serve on a voluntary basis. During normal times, service in civil defense is a substitute for military duty, and the entire organizational system of rank, promotion, and pay is patterned after that of the armed forces. In fact, even though civil defense is under civilian control, special army units are assigned to it for contingency support.

Although the overall implementation of civil protection in Switzerland is directed by the federal government, a considerable amount of responsibility rests with the individual cantons, communes, institutions, and individuals. The structure of responsibility is specifically defined under the law for each jurisdiction, as are the cost-sharing arrangements. Each commune is assigned its organizational structure, tactical units, manpower, and equipment, and it in turn assigns these down the organizational structure to the smallest unit—the Household Defense unit—which contains sixty to eighty persons.

Under existing law, businesses and institutions with more than 100 employees are required to establish tactical units comprising up to 20 percent of the work force. These units, which are an integral part of the local defense systems, are manned and equipped to take care of their own establishments and to render aid to the entire community when necessary.

The shelter construction program in Switzerland is quite extensive and is actively supported by federal and canton subsidies. All new structures—private and public alike—must contain shelters which can give protection not only against all nuclear weapons effects, but against chemical and biological agents as well. As of now, approximately one-half of the population can be thus protected. An acceleration in the current shelter construction program is expected to result in its completion by 1980, at which time protection for all 5.4 million Swiss will be available. About three-fourths of the construction costs of the program are borne by the federal and canton governments, the remainder is assumed by private owners.

Unlike Sweden, the Swiss do not have an evacuation program. The Swiss public is also more reluctant to accept the need for vigorous defense planning and organization than the Swedish public. Therefore, although supported by law, an intense campaign of public persuasion remains necessary in order to keep the population attuned to its responsibilities for protecting itself.

Austria

Austria, the most recent addition to the club of European neutrals—a status of neutrality was declared by its Parliament in 1955 and is written into the State Peace Treaty—is also the member with the least well-defined or implemented civil defense program.

Basically, this is so because the country does not yet have a clear idea of what its entire national security strategy can or should be.

As the Austrians see it, the continuance of neutrality in an armed conflict is directly dependent on adequate defensive preparations in four areas—military, civilian, psychological, and economic. Austrian officials consider psychological preparation the most important, but also the most difficult.

In the area of civil defense organization and implementation, Austria has just begun to grapple with the problem. To date, only 1 of the 9 states—covering but 5 percent of the total population—has enacted legislation which directs builders to include shelters in their structures that are capable of withstanding 5 psi overpressure. Another state is currently considering such a law. Since 1963 most federal buildings with a military function have been provided with shelters, but those who serve the civilian population have not. One of the biggest hurdles to program implementation to date has been an unenthusiastic and infrequent enforcement of this legislation. In fact, comprehensive legislation that would deal with a total civil defense system for the entire nation—as in Switzerland and Sweden—is still missing in Austria.

Some progress, however, has been made in informing the public of the hazards of nuclear and nonnuclear warfare and in training civil defense officials in the principles of emergency deployment, the need for and care of necessary equipment, structural reinforcement of living and working accommodations, proper organizational responsibilities, and others.

In case of a national emergency, three types of organizations can be deployed. First, the professional and voluntary fire services (The latter are rather large in rural areas.) can be called up, and the Red Cross, a broadly supported and popular organization in Austria, can be used to render first aid. Firefighting units have been given training in handling radioactive fallout. Second, a technical service, organized five years ago, is intended to be instrumental in approaching an emergency in a systematic and organized manner.

Finally, the third type of emergency "organization" is a collection of national self-protection units, composed mainly of local residents. The organization is not highly structured nor nationally directed because its members are expected to help only themselves or their immediate neighbors.

By and large, the main task of civil defense planners in Austria is to recruit public opinion for the support of a comprehensive civil protection program. To date they have been successful only in rural areas, while the urban population remains largely apathetic.

Nonnuclear NATO Countries

Military planning among the fifteen NATO-member nations is well coordinated and in a relatively high state of readiness. Civil defense planning, on the other hand, is poorly coordinated. This is somewhat surprising for one would have expected the nonnuclear members of NATO, in accordance with their oft stated fear that future conflicts would probably be fought on their territories, to have assumed the responsibility of protecting their human and economic resources. But this is not so, and sporadic attempts to internationalize civil defense activities of planning, financing, and implementation have generally failed, and civil protection remains the responsibility of each individual country. The reason for this failure is simple—people of each country have been able to generate enough opposition to civil defense to obstruct the development and implementation of a comprehensive program. This, of course, is true in varying degrees only. British legislators, subject to vocal anti-bomb and anti–civil defense demonstrations, have been extremely sensitive to public pressure. Some smaller countries, Norway and Denmark, for example, have experienced less public opposition. Thus, even though NATO does contain several committees charged with the responsibility of general civil emergency planning and with the solution of technical problems in transportation, communications, health, industry, and logistics, their role is essentially that of an advisor and storer of information. They are not in a position to insist on the carrying out of recommended policies, particularly when heavy national expenditures are involved. Consequently, it is not surprising to find great differences in the philosophy, organization, and effectiveness of civil protection among the nonnuclear NATO countries. The most essential characteristics of the civil defense systems of these countries are described below.

Germany

German officials believe that their strategic geographic position exposes them to the likelihood of becoming a principal battlefield in future wars. They fully appreciate the fact that 600 to 800 Soviet intermediate-range ballistic missiles are trained at their country and that each is capable of carrying a nuclear warhead. Their civil protection program, therefore, includes measures designed to counteract the potential effects from limited or tactical nuclear warfare and from a thermonuclear war.

Notwithstanding a very apathetic public and weary drawn-out debate, the Bundestag passed, shortly before its adjournment in late 1965, seven of the eleven proposed laws dealing with the establishment of a comprehensive civil defense organization. Prior to that date, little legislation governing civilian protection existed, and whatever protective measures had been taken originated from individual initiative.

Whereas the new legislation gives the federal government the right to take certain preventive and remedial actions, implementation of the programs has been slow, essentially a victim of government austerity. The new legislation stipulates the following government actions: to establish a compulsory civil defense corps; to permit emergency control over the acquisition of capital and money in circulation; to safeguard transportation resources; to secure and control food, agricultural, forestry, and wood supplies; to safeguard the water supply; to make compulsory the construction of shelters in all new public and private buildings; and to ensure that every

German citizen between sixteen and sixty-five is exposed to a minimum of ten hours of civil defense training. To date the accomplishments of eight years of civil defense planning in Germany are not very great. A warning system comprising 10 communications systems and 45,000 sirens is in operation, some public shelters located mainly near transportation centers have been constructed, 71,000 men have been trained in the civil protection service, and 300,000 persons are members of the local self-protection units. Finally, any resident is able to obtain free civil defense training if he so desires. For a nation with a population of 57 million, however, these achievements do not represent a very comprehensive or effective civil protection program.

German officials basically expect self-help and individual initiative to provide initial aid and protection during an emergency, a concept that has its origin in World War II. Even though the implementation of this concept was very successful then, its continued use as a foundation for modern civil defense planning in a nuclear age is open to question.

Although it is too early to assess the effects of the recently enacted legislation, and that of newly pending broad emergency powers for the federal government, it can be said that a greater amount of civil protection consciousness is emerging in West Germany. Economic and political conditions permitting, this could ultimately result in the development and implementation of an effective civil defense program. With a high population density (about 550 persons per square mile) and high urban concentration, Germany's civilian population continues to be vulnerable and relatively exposed to nuclear or conventional attack.

Canada

Canada's strategic planners recognize that the threat of nuclear attack is real, but also that it is not immediate. This recognition has given rise to two policy objectives regarding civil defense: one, to maintain a state of readiness for a potential emergency, and two, to harness as much public support for civil defense as possible without creating undue anxieties.

To date a substantial portion of the Canadian plan to establish a comprehensive civil emergency organization has been implemented. In addition to the national center in Ottawa, 6 Regional Emergency Government Headquarters, 24 Zone Headquarters (9 of which have been completed so far), and 350 municipal Emergency Government Headquarters (of which 160 are complete), have been established. In addition to this organizational framework, Canada has put into operation a 24-hour warning system capable of disseminating emergency warning through a network of sirens. The system is activated on the basis of information received from NORAD in Colorado. An emergency broadcasting system which can transmit instructions and information to the public supplements the federal warning system.

Canada does not, as yet, have a shelter policy, but intends to establish one soon. Toward that end it is presently conducting a shelter survey in order to establish the available and required shelter space in public buildings.

Since 1962 Canada has been engaged in a stockpiling program that has as its objective the prepositioning of medical and other supplies essential for coping with mass casualties. The first phase of this program resulted in a stockpile worth $20 million, and it is closely coordinated with Red Cross requirements. In the event of an emergency, the normal public services, such as fire, police, and first aid protection, will be supplemented with approximately 150,000 volunteers dispersed throughout Canada. These include auxiliary policemen, auxiliary firemen, radiological defense workers, wardens, medical workers, welfare workers, and others, all of whom have received some training in the application of protective measures, or have attended the Canadian Emergency Measures College at Arnprior.

Canadian planners fear that national security conditions and threat estimates have changed so much since the last reorganization of emergency planning in 1959 that the existing civil defense system may have become obsolete. As a consequence, they are currently engaged in a reevaluation of the existing program of Emergency Measures Planning in order to identify those elements and changes that must be made in order to bring the program up to date.

Denmark

The Danish civil defense organization has its origin in legislation passed as early as 1935. Subsequent amendments have updated the early organization so that today civil defense consists of three elements—warning, evacuation, and shelter.

The civil defense office in Denmark is part of the Ministry of the Interior. During an emergency, all activities designed to protect and save the population will be directed from dispersed reinforced civil defense command posts, all of which are heat- and blastproof.

The warning service includes 700 sirens and is integrated into the Air Force warning system. In case of emergency, evacuation of all cities with more than 10,000 residents is planned. Thereafter, first aid and other immediate help will be given by the self-protection services, the local protection units, and the National Civil Defense Corps. Main emphasis in civil defense planning remains on local self-help units which depend on volunteers for maintenance of strength. The number of volunteers, however, has fallen far short of the number needed in an emergency. However, emergency manpower is available from the National Civil Defense Corps, service in which may be substituted for regular military duty. Approximately 1,200 Danes yearly elect to do this.

Denmark also has a relatively well-developed shelter system. By mid-1965, 766,000 shelter spaces with fallout and limited blast protection had been built, and 75 large dual-purpose public shelters could provide protection for an additional 300,000 persons.

In conclusion, even though some well-organized opposition to the concept of civil defense does exist in Denmark, the national program continues to be implemented at a respectable pace.

Norway

The Norwegian civil defense system bears a great resemblance to the Swedish and Danish organizations. Jurisdiction over it, however, rests not with the Department of the Interior, but with the Justice and Police Department. Service in civil defense is compulsory for men and women between the ages of eighteen and sixty-five, unless, of course, they are serving in the military services. In order to establish comprehensive coverage, civil defense manpower is allocated to various functional services: protective units, industrial protection, evacuation units, railroad protection units, block protection, household protection, and, national reserve commandos. According to the 1960 civil protection plan, approximately 16 percent of the civil defense forces are assigned to staff and communication services, 29 percent to communal firefighting, 13 percent to recovery and clearing, 4 percent to local firefighting, and 8 percent to atomic, bacteriological, and chemical protection. The remaining 30 percent were assigned to individual localities for general duties associated with fire combat.

In the event of war the Norwegians expect to evacuate approximately 15 percent of the population, while the rest will find protection in shelters.

By 1964 the shelter protection system in Norway had proceeded to a point where 540,000 private and 122,400 industrial shelter spaces were available. An additional 146,700 people could find protection in public shelters.

Thus, Norway, as a whole, has been quite successful in the implementation of its civil defense program; 1966 per capita expenditures on civil defense were a comparatively high $1.92, nearly four times that of the United States.

Netherlands

Plagued by vocal and sustained pacifist opposition to civil defense, and by topographical characteristics that are devoid of mountains and feature a high water table, shelter construction in Holland has proceeded slowly. By 1965 total public shelter capacity was estimated at only 70,000, which included three sections of the Rotterdam subway system. A 1955 law requires multifamily buildings to contain a substructure for potential shelter use, but progress in enforcement has been slow. The focus of 1967 civil defense expenditures, therefore, is on a nationwide fallout shelter survey which is to determine the exact status of the shelter program and future requirements. Additional efforts are centered on training and expanding firefighting, police, and first aid reserve units and on readying these forces for use during natural disasters.

Iceland

This island, with a population of 186,000, is just beginning to concern itself with civil defense. A 1962 law serves as the foundation for a comprehensive civil defense program. It established a Bureau of Civil Defense in the Ministry of Justice with responsibility for first aid, self-help, evacuation, and the construction of private and public shelters. In addition, the law authorizes the drafting and training of men between the ages of eighteen and sixty by the Department of Justice. In brief, Icelandic civil defense still appears to be in an embryonic stage. An official awareness of the need for an effective civil protective system, however, seems to assure the continued development and implementation of the program despite some public opposition.

Italy

In Italy civil defense measures are the subject of much public debate. So far, the main task of civil protection has been assumed by the firefighting units and by the Red Cross. In recent years, however, reservists, deferred male residents, and specialists (doctors, technicians) have been recruited and combined into the so-called "Colonne mobile" for regional civil protection deployment. In an emergency these units are intended to supplement the mobile

"Colonne" of the Carabinieri, which are police units trained and equipped for regional use.

Belgium

In Belgium civil protection is the responsibility of the "Corps de Protection Civile," a civilian organization composed of officials from local, regional, and national sources. Only in the event of warfare will members of public service units, uncalled draft eligibles, and specialists—civil engineers, doctors, technicians—be called into the corps.

Luxembourg

In 1960 this small grand duchy organized a "Brigade grand-ducale des volontaires de la Protection Civile" (civil protection brigade), which today has 4,000 fully trained and equipped members capable of rendering aid against radiation and contamination. The Brigade is also motorized with ambulances and other vehicles for deployment anywhere within the country. Twenty-five corps centers are dispersed throughout the region and the "Centre de Messages" collects and evaluates information concerning the severity and location of damage and casualties. For such a small country, the civil protection service appears well planned and well organized.

Portugal

The Portuguese civil defense organization is part of the Department of Defense. Portuguese officials consider civil defense part of total military strategy and, as a result, have insisted on receptive public opinion and public participation in civil defense activities. Thus, in an emergency governmental agencies can be integrated for effective coordination, civil defense units composed of workers in all essential industries can be deployed, and trained local volunteer corps in towns and small cities have been set up to assist in measures leading to greater self-protection.

No shelter construction program is in existence in Portugal, although the subway system in Lisbon and other subterranean facilities can serve as potential shelter in an emergency. In order to test the functioning of the system, periodic exercises are held, and, as a whole, they have been considered successful by Portuguese authorities.

Turkey and Greece

These two southernmost members of NATO have not been particularly active in the development of protective measures for the home front. Potential efforts have largely been frustrated by limited resources and by vocal opposition.

In Greece the Directorate of Civil Defense falls under the jurisdiction of the Ministry of Public Order and is headed by a Gendarmerie General. In fact all civil defense officials are members of either the police or the gendarmerie (rural police). The Directorate includes three divisions which concern themselves with civil defense organization, plans and training, and technical matters. A training center for civil defense is located near Athens, and regional units, each under the command of a colonel, are dispersed throughout the country for use in disasters. Local competence for civil defense is the responsibility of police, and each station has a siren to warn the population of impending emergencies.

Greece has no shelter construction program; shelter protection consists of what remains from World War II days. But these old shelters, although initially reinforced, have not been maintained and are incapable of providing protection against nuclear weapons.

In summation, Greece has regarded civil defense the responsibility of the military and the police—it is not considered a civilian function.

Turkish civil defense efforts are of relatively recent vintage. A 1959 law set up procedures and regulations for civil defense planning in cities and towns and, more specifically, for public buildings and institutions. In addition, rules governing evacuation, dispersal, and intergovernmental relations in an emergency were also established. A second law, passed in 1960, assigned responsibility for civil defense matters to the Ministry of Interior and established a staff college for civil protection training. But despite this legislation, implementation has been slow and resources scarce. Civil defense as a system is only in its infancy in Turkey.

The Warsaw Pact Nations

The East European members of the Warsaw Pact (Romania excepted), unlike their counterparts in NATO, pursue a strategic policy that is essentially imposed upon them by the Soviet Union. Thus, they consider the protection of human and economic resources an essential element of total national security and have attempted, in the past ten years, to fill the gap between a well-defined military establishment and a lagging civil defense organization. As a whole they have been moderately successful. While their foreign policy berated Western civil protection developments and branded them as "aggressive war mongering," they quietly went ahead with their own plans to establish a civil defense organization. However, an effective implementation of a comprehensive program is not in evidence.

Just as France's defection has significantly blunted NATO's strength, Czechoslovakia's and Romania's national reassertions have effectively weakened the Warsaw Pact Organization. One can no longer speak of one, wholly integrated Communist military establishment. Romania's Ceausescu plays the role of DeGaulle in Eastern Europe and Czechoslovakia's adherence to the Pact remains a forced one.

Because of the exposure and accessibility of the Soviet Union through the northern tier countries—Poland, Czechoslovakia, and East Germany—Soviet strategists have traditionally been most concerned about safeguarding this vital buffer. Hence, their defense measures carry a distinct northeast European flavor. Romania, Hungary, and Bulgaria concern them less. Twenty-four of Russia's twenty-six divisions stationed in Europe are based in Poland and East Germany, and Czechoslovakia's and Poland's military establishments are the largest and best of the Soviet's allies.

Along with military aid, Russia has repeatedly encouraged its allies to develop and expand their civil defense establishments. Detailed and specific information regarding the civil defense activities of its allies, however, is largely unavailable. Whatever information has been made public reveals a rather mixed picture. A brief survey of the status and development of civil protection in several East European countries follows.

In the German Democratic Republic (East Germany), civil defense legislation began to emerge in 1956 and since then has been amplified to include nearly all protective activities commonly associated with homeland protection. Civil defense activity is organized under the jurisdiction of the Ministry of the Interior, is called the "Kommando des Luftschutzes," and fulfills the following needs: communication, warning, fire protection, care of the population, medical assistance, recovery, and retrieval. Assigned to the "Kommando" are 10 armed battalions with a total strength of 10,000 men, stationed in various regions and intended to secure and police affected areas.

Like the quasi-military DOSAAF in the Soviet Union, the GDR has an organization—"Gesellschaft fuer Sport und Technik"—which since 1952 has served as a premilitary training reservoir. Its 500,000 members are actually included in a count of the total armed forces personnel of the GDR.

Since 1962 a self-protection service has been in the process of development, which, although not compulsory, nonetheless suggests in its recruitment circulars that evasion of one's responsibility severely weakens the country's defenses. For each 80 to 100 residents, a self-protection unit has been organized to provide first aid, fight fires, and report damages and hazards.

Shelter construction in the GDR is largely absent. World War II shelters are maintained, but new construction suffers from a scarcity of building materials. In late 1965 reports indicated that a large World War II underground V2-weapons plant, as well as various tunnel systems near Nordhausen, were being used for the stockpiling of potatoes, fruit, vegetables, etc.

Information on civil defense activities in Poland is rather sparse. A recent interview with the Polish director of civil defense reveals that an estimated half million Poles have been trained in the rudiments of protection against nuclear war and that a sizable number of bunkers have been constructed in Warsaw.

The other East European nations have not progressed very far in the direction of establishing a comprehensive and effective civil defense system. Although they all possess legislation that establishes a civil defense organization and participation therein, public response and support has been unenthusiastic. This is particularly true of the less developed countries of the southern tier—Romania, Bulgaria, and Hungary. Periodically, therefore, officials attempt to kindle general interest in civil protection, but the elicited response is rarely significant. One such instance occurred in June 1967, when Bulgarian Deputy Premier and Civil Defense Director Mihailov urged the citizens of his country to take a more active part in civil defense matters. From his remarks emerged the fact that a 1962 law makes service in the Bulgarian civil defense corps compulsory for residents aged sixteen to sixty (women only to fifty-five) if they have not participated in the military services. Training in the use of protective measures against nuclear, chemical, and bacteriological warfare is compulsory for the entire population in Bulgaria. In addition to the above, Mihailov called for shelter construction and population dispersal plans, all of which indicates that a comprehensive civil defense system is currently not in effective operation in Bulgaria.

Conclusion

While a spirit of detente has, in the past few years, invaded the international relations of nations that belong to what Mao Tse-tung called the "City World," many countries of the bellicose "Village World"—Asia, Africa, and Latin America—continue to encourage and actively support so-called "Wars of National Liberation." The world is far from tranquil and friction abounds. And even though the thrust of China's militant policies seems to have been blunted temporarily by internal strife, the destruction of the "City World" continues to be a central feature of its international aspirations and goals.

Against the Chinese threat and that of other potential nuclear powers, the developed European nations of the northern hemisphere offer a destructive deterrent capable of annihilating a large portion of humanity. This deterrent is almost entirely founded on offensive weaponry, for in the thinking of strategic planners technological development to date has made offensive nuclear deterrents less costly and more readily deployable than passive protection at home. The perpetuation of such offensive deterrents, however, at the expense of even limited defensive measures, creates an imbalance in the structure of military capacity that may be difficult to modify in the face of a sudden change in an enemy's threat posture. Thus, most Western strategic thinking is couched in static terms, for it fails to consider that modern technology with its swift breakthrough potential could propel a hostile nation into relative offensive superiority very quickly, thereby leaving an opponent vulnerable to partial or mass destruction. In addition, Western planners assume only rational enemy strategy, which disregards the possibility of irrational behavior on the part of a potential aggressor or acts which may in fact be entirely rational to him, but completely nonsensical from a Western point of view. Therein lies the case for civil defense—a need to be prepared in order to reduce a country's vulnerability to unforeseen and sudden technological breakthroughs in foreign offensive and defensive military capabilities and a need to protect the nation against unanticipated or irrational aggressive threats and nuclear blackmail. Many of us are particularly afraid of this. But the case for civil defense has been made successfully only in the Scandinavian countries and in Switzerland, and to a lesser degree, in the Soviet Union. The remaining nations, including the United States, have failed to balance their military capacity between offensive strength and domestic survival and therefore continue to leave the home front, despite retaliatory capabilities, exposed to the debilitating effects of limited or even broad nuclear attack—and to the threat of such an attack.

8 Active and Passive Defense

ALBERT L. LATTER
and E. A. MARTINELLI*

¶ The physical principles underlying civil defense are simple: they can be understood by physicist and nonphysicist alike. However, civil or passive defense is not the only true defensive defense: it is possible to aim at the destruction of the nuclear bombs of the attacker before they have a chance to explode sufficiently near to cause destruction. This is called active defense; its methods are almost infinitely more demanding, technically, than those of civil defense. They require the finding of an object of a few feet in diameter at distances of hundreds of thousands of feet and of shooting it down as it approaches twenty times faster than the speed of sound. However, in principle, the problems of active defense are amenable to solution and the recent installation of such defense by the USSR, implementing their solutions of these problems, has caused a great deal of anxiety in our military circles. The present chapter compares active and passive (civil) defenses; it tries to determine the conditions under which one or the other, or a combination of the two, is most advantageous. Much of the contents of this chapter has not appeared in the literature before.—E.P.W.

* This chapter does not represent an official position of any agency of the United States Government.

Albert L. Latter
Division Head, the RAND Corporation

¶ Dr. Albert L. Latter was born in Indiana in 1920 and received his Ph.D. in theoretical nuclear physics from the University of California at Los Angeles in 1951. He is presently head of the Physics Department of the RAND Corporation in Santa Monica, California. Dr. Latter's research has been primarily concerned with nuclear weapons and their effects. He has written numerous papers—several of them classified—on a variety of subjects including nuclear physics, equation of state, seismic signals from nuclear explosions, neutron transport, nuclear weapon design, etc. His principal interests are in strategic weapon systems—ballistic missiles and ballistic missile defense. Because of his familiarity with these subjects, he was asked to contribute to this volume. Dr. Latter is chairman of the Nuclear Panel of the Air Force Scientific Advisory Board and a member of the Air Force Ballistic Systems Division Advisory Group. He is co-author (with Edward Teller) of *Our Nuclear Future* and was a recipient of the E. O. Lawrence Award in 1964.

E. A. Martinelli
Associate Division Head, the RAND Corporation

¶ E. A. Martinelli was born at Lucca, Italy, in 1919. He received his Ph.D. in Nuclear Physics from the University of California at Berkeley in 1950. He was one of the original members of the University of California Radiation Laboratory at Livermore and acquired his knowledge of the design of nuclear weapons there. He joined the RAND Corporation after leaving Livermore Laboratory and is now the associate head of the RAND Physics Department. His research at RAND has been primarily concerned with nuclear weapons and their effects. ¶ Dr. Martinelli's interest in problems of ballistic missile defense dates from 1954. He has served on several ballistic missile defense advisory panels. He has written several papers in the field of nuclear physics and more recently some papers relevant to the detection of underground nuclear explosions.

T his book deals primarily with shelters, a passive form of defense. However, passive defense cannot be discussed meaningfully without understanding the relationship to active defense, i.e., intercepting and destroying the attacking bombers and ballistic missiles. Both active and passive defense have the same purpose—to save lives and the tools necessary for recovery. This chapter will describe the technical aspects of active defense, particularly ballistic missile defense, then discuss the difficult question: which is more effective, active or passive defense—or some combination of the two?

Bomber Defense and Ballistic Missile Defense

Ten years ago active defense referred to defense against high-altitude bombers. Then the intercontinental ballistic missile (ICBM) was developed and the defense picture changed drastically. Our bomber defense had no capability to intercept ballistic missiles. Moreover ballistic missiles could destroy vital elements of the bomber defense, which meant that the bomber defense became ineffective even against bombers. This situation led to a period of intense effort to develop a defense against ballistic missiles, with relative indifference toward possible improvements of the defense against bombers.

During the past ten years considerable progress has been made on ballistic missile defense, but just as bomber defense without ballistic missile defense is of little value, so also is the opposite true. Cities need not be attacked in the first minutes of the war; hence bombers can be used for this purpose just as well as missiles. Indeed there is a good reason for an aggressor to concentrate his initial attack on military targets. These targets, particularly aircraft and missiles, must be struck quickly—by missiles—in order to keep retaliation to a minimum.

The remainder of this chapter will be concerned only with the problem of ballistic missile defense. But the reader should keep in mind that effective bomber defense is itself a difficult problem, which would not be solved automatically if the ballistic missile defense problem were solved. The heart of the difficulty is this: within or near enemy territory modern bombers can fly at low altitude—a few hundred feet above the ground—so that detection by ground-based radar is possible only at short range. As a result, a number of bombers can concentrate their attack in a narrow corridor—avoiding most of the defenses and saturating the rest. The problem is further complicated if the bombers are equipped with many small, nuclear-armed missiles which are fired outside the range of the bomber defense radar, and fly at such a low altitude that they cannot be intercepted by the ballistic missile defense. With such missiles even a single bomber might saturate the short-range defenses.

Approaches to the bomber-defense problem using air-based missile and radar platforms to achieve area coverage, as well as invulnerability to missile attack, look promising but still have major technical difficulties.

Technical Aspects of Ballistic Missile Defense

To understand the ballistic missile defense problem it is necessary to know some of the characteristics of an ICBM. For this purpose it is convenient to distinguish three fairly distinct parts of the ICBM trajectory.

The first is the launch phase when the rocket motors are firing, and the ICBM rises with increasing speed. Thousands of delicate components must operate in a precise manner during this phase, and the missile is in its most vulnerable state. Small perturbations can grossly affect its overall performance. This part of the trajectory lasts a few minutes and terminates when the final-stage rocket motor is turned off, well outside the atmosphere.

The next phase, beginning when the nose cone, containing the nuclear warhead, is separated from the rocket and lasting until the nose cone returns to the atmosphere (an altitude of a few hundred thousand feet) is called the midcourse phase. This phase is by far the longest part of the flight; it takes the missile from a point essentially over its home base to a point above its target in enemy territory. The nose cone, with the warhead inside, flies freely during this phase, similar to a cannon ball, except that the trajectory is outside the atmosphere. For the nominal ICBM range (5,500 nautical, that is 6,300 ordinary, miles), this part of the trajectory lasts approximately 20 minutes and reaches a height above the horizon. The nose cone does not slow down appreciably until it is quite close to the ground (50,000 feet or less depending upon detailed design) so that most of the terminal phase of the trajectory is traversed at the speed of 4 miles per second. The duration of this phase, considered to begin at an altitude of a few hundred thousand feet, is less than one minute.

Difficulties with Launch Phase and Midcourse Ballistic Missile Defense

The description given above suggests that it would be advantageous to attack the ICBM during the launch phase. The missile is over enemy territory, it is moving relatively slowly, and it is most vulnerable. Even nonnuclear weapons could be effective in destroying the missile, and nuclear weapons would have large kill radii. Launch-phase defense has the additional advantage of area coverage, i.e., providing protection for the whole country. Systems using this approach have been studied. The most studied system, BAMBI (Ballistic Missile Boost Intercept), consists of satellites that detect ICBM launches by infrared emission from the rocket motor. On detection the satellite releases an infrared homing missile with an intercept range of a few hundred miles.

The difficulty with this concept is that, to handle a concerted attack of ICBM's a large number of satellites must be on station.

A large number on station implies a much larger number in orbit—perhaps thousands. Studies of the BAMBI system, making reasonable estimates of reliability and kill probability, lead to astronomical costs for such a defense. To make matters worse, it may be feasible for the offense to employ cheap infrared decoys that could drain the satellite interceptors and allow the real missiles to go unscathed.

Midcourse ballistic missile defense, like launch-phase defense, has the advantage of operating far from friendly territory and providing area coverage. In addition it has the advantage of requiring only a small number of ground-based installations. The latter fact makes this type of defense especially attractive from the point of view of cost. Unfortunately, midcourse ballistic missile defense faces a great difficulty.

Because the midcourse phase is beyond the atmosphere, there are no drag forces operating during this phase. Therefore any objects, no matter how lightweight, if dispersed with the nose cone, will follow along in essentially the same trajectory. This property of the midcourse phase permits the offense to employ lightweight decoys to fool radar, which is the only practical method of detection during this phase. For example, metallized balloons shaped like the nose cone can provide indistinguishable radar echoes, or light metal wires of appropriate length to backscatter radar waves efficiently can be dispersed around the nose cone in a huge cloud to produce so much clutter in the radar receiver that the nose cone signal is effectively lost. To be sure of destroying the warhead, the defense would be forced to attack each balloon decoy or the entire cloud of wire, thereby expending a prohibitively large number of interceptors.

Despite this difficulty, a midcourse defense could be useful against limited missile attacks or primitive attacks that do not employ sophisticated decoys. Such attacks should be considered in evaluating the worth of a defense since nuclear technology is bound to spread to less-developed countries. For this purpose midcourse defense might provide a substantial degree of protection for the whole country for only a few billion dollars. Midcourse defense can also be useful as an adjunct to an expensive terminal system designed to cope with large, more sophisticated attacks. Such a system is discussed in the next section.

Nike-Zeus

The problem for midcourse defense is decoys. But effective decoys are heavier and harder to make if they have to penetrate the atmosphere. This fact has led the United States to spend most of its effort on defenses that intercept during the terminal phase of the trajectory.

To perform the standard functions of defense (i.e. to detect and track incoming objects, to discriminate warheads from lightweight decoys, and then to launch and direct interceptors to the target), a terminal ballistic missile defense system has the following major components: an acquisition radar, target-track radars, a computer for data processing, nuclear-armed interceptors, and radars to track them. The acquisition radar detects and identifies the incoming objects, gives this information to the tracking radar, which follows the objects on their courses and causes the intercepting missiles to be committed. The main point for the reader to appreciate about these components is that they are big, complex, and expensive.

To see why, remember that the terminal phase lasts less than a minute. Much of this time may be spent in discriminating decoys from the warhead before an interceptor is actually launched. To insure that an intercept takes place at a high altitude—where ground effects from the enemy explosion, as well as the defense explosion, are negligible—the interceptor must be fast. To carry a warhead, guidance and control equipment, and rocket motors to maneuver at high altitude, the interceptor must be big. The interceptor used in the Nike-Zeus system—the first U.S. system of this kind—weighs more than 20,000 pounds, is almost 50 feet long, and travels at an average speed of a little more than 1 mile per second.

The acquisition radar must also be big. The typical nose cone is much smaller than an airplane, and because of its more regular shape, it can be designed so that it does not reflect much of the radar wave back to the receiver. To see such a target at the necessary range of a few hundred miles requires a powerful radar with a big antenna. Because of the threat of the submarine-launched missile and the round-the-world missile, as well as the ICBM's, the narrow-pencil radar beam must be scanned over a large fraction of the sky, and the scanning must be rapid because the time the missiles are in view is so short. In the Nike-Zeus acquisition radar, the scanning is done mechanically by large-scale precision machinery.

Another major complication is caused by the need to carry out many intercepts simultaneously. To accomplish this task Nike-Zeus provides a separate target-track radar for each object, and while it is smaller than the acquisition radar, the target-track radar is still a large and complex device by usual standards, and therefore very expensive.

Finally, the short time scale of the ballistic missile defense problem forces the defense to rely on automatic processing of target data. To cope with many simultaneous objects and to perform calculations necessary for discrimination and tracking, a large digital computer is an essential component of a terminal defense system.

Nike-X

Nike-Zeus was a successful program; all the components worked. Prototype tests have been carried out in Kwajalein in the Pacific against targets launched from Vandenberg Air Force Base in California. But, in the last analysis, many experts felt that the decoy problem had not really been solved.

The Zeus interceptor, to achieve an acceptable intercept altitude, has to be committed very early in the terminal phase, at a time when there has been only a small amount of atmospheric interaction with the incoming objects, which, it was feared, was not adequate for discrimination of lightweight decoys. Also U.S. high-altitude nuclear tests revealed that at the altitude at which the Nike-Zeus system has to operate, the acquisition radar can be blacked out by high-altitude nuclear explosions deliberately set off by the enemy outside the reach of the defense.

To cope with both these problems, it was proposed that the Nike philosophy of permitting only negligible damage to the ground be altered so that the commitment and intercept altitudes could be lowered. Out of this concept has come a new system, currently under development, called Nike-X.

The essential component of the Nike-X system is a new interceptor, the Sprint, which can attain its maximum speed in a very short time. This interceptor allows the defense to wait as long as possible for discrimination and still achieve an acceptable intercept altitude. Also included in the system are some Zeus interceptors in order to preserve the capability of intercepting at high altitude when feasible. The combined system has the capability to intercept at both high and low altitudes and is much more difficult to overcome than either singly. In addition, the Nike-X system has a new acquisition radar, which employs electronic rather than mechanical scanning of the beam and allows many more objects to be tracked simultaneously.

If the development program goes as expected, the Nike-X system should be effective in intercepting enemy warheads that are aimed directly at the defended cities. Unfortunately, for a terminal defense like Nike-X, the warheads can be made to impact on the ground outside the reach of the defense, allowing the winds to carry radioactive fallout over the cities. Such fallout is without effect on houses and other structures but its radiation is dangerous to man. For this reason the Nike-X system cannot stand by itself. Fallout shelters to protect people from the radiation are a necessary adjunct.

Actually, the Nike-X becomes more effective if the population has some protection from blast and heat as well as fallout. That way the intercept altitude can be made very low without excessive damage to the population if the enemy warhead is detonated before the intercept occurs. The lower the intercept altitude, the more certain it is that decoys can be distinguished from the warhead.

So far we have been concerned with the technical feasibility of terminal defense. But we must ask: if the system is feasible, what is its value? Frequently, it is assumed that feasibility implies great value, but the answer is not so simple. The defense interceptors are very expensive. To insure that none of the warheads "leaks" through the defense because of unreliability of the system components, more than one defense interceptor may have to be fired at each threatening object. The cost of these interceptors plus the cost of radars, computers, etc., though perhaps not as high as that of the ICBM they destroy, is measured in millions of dollars per object shot down. Such a defense may be valueless if for the same cost the offense is able to overwhelm the defense with warheads and decoys.

Which side has the advantage in this game depends sensitively on the minimum weight for an effective decoy and on a myriad of other details. For the Nike-X system, the answer is not known, and the estimates are secret. In his statement before the Armed Services Committee of the U.S. House of Representatives in February 1965, Secretary of Defense McNamara stated that analyses indicate that the advantage probably lies with the offense by a factor of about two or more. However he also pointed out that the United States has great economic superiority over other nations and hence may be able to afford this kind of disadvantage. Moreover, while we must consider the possibility that the Soviets would try to offset our defense by increasing their offensive forces, we naturally hope that they would not react that way at all. Although this is not the official point of view, we believe that it might better serve the ends of both countries if the Soviets were to choose instead to strengthen their own defenses.

Comparison of Active and Passive Defense

We must now turn to the question we asked at the beginning of this chapter: which is more effective, active or passive defense—or some combination of the two? In the last section we pointed out that the Nike-X ballistic missile defense may be overcome by additional offensive forces with the cost-advantage (probably) on the side of the offense. The obvious question at this point is: Can the effect of blast shelters be offset in the same way?

A simple argument gives the answer. Assume that warning time is too short for evacuation, and people must be sheltered close to where they live or work. The cost for shelters is so much per person depending upon the hardness level, i.e., how much blast pressure can be tolerated. Hence, the cost to defend a given area to a given hardness is proportional to the population density. On the other hand, the cost to the offense to destroy the area depends only on the area and is independent of the population density. It follows that the exchange ratio—the defense cost relative to the offense cost to offset the defense—is favorable to the defense in all those places where the population density is sufficiently low.

The critical population density depends upon several factors: the offense cost to deliver a nuclear warhead, the defense cost of a shelter space, and the shelter hardness. The reason that the hardness plays a role is that the cost of a shelter space happens to be almost independent of hardness, at least up to a blast pressure of about 100 pounds per square inch (psi), while the offense cost per person killed increases rapidly with increased hardness. If 100-psi shelters cost $300 per space and the offense cost to deliver a 10-megaton warhead is $35 million, the critical population density is about 15,000 per square mile. A range of 10,000 to 25,000 probably covers the uncertainties in the cost figures.

More than 90 percent of the people in the United States live in places where the population density is less than 15,000 per square mile. All these people could be protected by 100-psi blast shelters that cost less than the missiles required to destroy the shelters. It follows that for this major portion of the population, if a choice were made between purely active terminal or purely passive defense, passive defense would be preferred.

We are left with the question: What kind of defense should be provided for the remaining population—less than 10 percent—that live in the densely populated areas? For these areas, with the assumptions that we have made about cost and effectiveness of pure passive or pure active defense, neither approach is satisfactory. Both can be offset for less cost by the offense.

Of course, there is the possibility that some new ballistic missile defense, as yet uninvented, could be less expensive than the Nike system, or that people could be evacuated from the densely populated regions, for instance, by a system of tunnels as described elsewhere in this book. Another possibility is that a combination of active and passive defense might be more effective than either by itself.

That such a cooperative interaction between the two types of defense should exist, can be seen this way: if there are only blast shelters, no active defense, the offense need not use decoys or multiple warheads and can devote his entire missile payload to the most efficiently packaged nuclear weapons. Against ballistic missile defense only, the offense can afford to employ a large fraction of his payload for penetration aids such as decoys or multiple warheads since even a small warhead on target is adequate against an unsheltered populace. When both types of defense are present, however, the offense is forced to compromise.

A simplified analysis of this complex offense-defense game shows that a cooperative effect does exist and specifically, if M_a is the price in missiles that the defense can exact for each life destroyed using active defense only, M_p is the price using passive defense only, then, by proper allocation of resources between the two, the price can be raised to something like the sum, $M_a + M_p$. For the low-population regions, as might be expected from our previous argument, M_p turns out to be much larger than M_a, which means that passive defense dominates, and the cooperative effect is negligible. For the high-population density regions, however, M_a may become comparable to M_p—depending on detailed cost assumptions—and the cooperative effect can be as much as a factor of two. A factor of two seems significant when one remembers that tens of billions of dollars are involved and that much of this money would be spent in these high-population density regions in order to make them no more attractive as targets than the rest of the country (in terms of population destroyed per missile). In fact, a factor of two would go a long way toward overcoming the disadvantage of the defense in the high-population density areas. For these areas, therefore, an optimum defense probably would consist of a combination of active and passive types. Of course, the analysis permits a precise determination of the optimum distribution of active and passive defense. We can actually calculate, for a fixed total defense budget, how much should be spent on each type in each part of the country. Unfortunately, the results of such an analysis cannot be taken too literally, since they are terribly sensitive to technical inputs, many of which are unknown. The best one can do with these technical inputs is to make plausible assumptions of the sort underlying Secretary McNamara's statements (in 1965) to Congress on Nike-X, and then quote the results in no more detail than they deserve. In this spirit, for defense budgets up to, say, $50 billion, the situation can be represented fairly well by three categories.

First, there are the rural areas and small towns, where, because of low-population densities, direct attack is unprofitable. This category, comprising roughly half the population, would receive fallout protection but no special protection from blast and no terminal ballistic missile defense.

The second category is the suburban areas. To make this category no more attractive as a target than the first category, blast protection, as well as protection against fallout must be provided, but still no terminal ballistic missile defense. The level of blast protection might range from 10 to 100 psi depending upon the total defense budget, the population density, and the increase in cost with increasing hardness of the shelters. If the cost increase is as low as indicated in the next chapter, the hardness may well be 100 psi almost everywhere. This second category comprises roughly 40 percent of the population.

The third category is the large central cities, which are prime targets for attack. For this category all types of defense are provided—fallout, blast, and ballistic missile defense. The fraction of the budget devoted to active defense increases with the population density and reaches a maximum in the New York metropolitan area of 25 to 50 percent, depending on cost assumptions.

We have already emphasized that quantitative results of this type of analysis cannot be trusted because of technical uncertainties. Actually, the most important of these uncertainties have to do with active defense. Vital parameters such as decoy weight and warhead characteristics may differ appreciably from what is assumed, since our knowledge of present enemy technology is limited, and there is always the possibility of future invention. Furthermore, the performance of active defense under wartime conditions is unpredictable because realistic testing is impossible.

On the other hand, blast shelters that work—at least up to 100 psi or so—involve only straightforward engineering well within the present state of the art. For these reasons passive defense, at least for population, seems to be a more *assured* damage-limiting measure than ballistic missile defense, and hence the preferable form of defense. Moreover, in the analysis it has been tacitly assumed that a shelter hardness greater than 100 psi is not practical. If this assumption proves false and much harder shelters can be built for a modest cost increase, the analysis would tend to favor passive defense even more heavily. If for example, 500 psi is achievable at a cost of $500 per person, even for a large defense budget—$50 billion—the allocation for active defense would be negligible everywhere, even in New York City. These considerations suggest that all defense money should be spent on passive measures. However, there are some factors that work in the opposite direction.

We have been assuming that the only purpose of defense is to maximize the number of lives saved against a well-planned attack on U.S. cities—the sort of attack the Soviets might be capable of launching against us if they were to strike first. We have also assumed that there is adequate warning of the attack from long-range radars or other intelligence sources, so that people have time to get into the shelters.

The picture is somewhat modified and favors greater emphasis on ballistic missile defense if the protection of houses, structures, and other material assets is taken into consideration as well. It is difficult to be quantitative because a detailed evaluation would involve a comparison between the values of such disparate entities as human lives and factories.

The picture is further modified if the missile attack comes with little or no warning. With passive defense only, people would not have a chance to get into the shelters, and such an attack would be devastating. But active defense, being continuously alert, can counter the early-arriving missiles and provide additional time for occupying the shelters.

Finally, consideration should be given to attacks that are limited in the number and sophistication of arriving warheads, for instance attacks by lesser powers. In this case, ballistic missile defense—even an area defense—might be able to destroy all the incoming warheads and provide complete protection for lives and property. With passive defense only, there would necessarily be some lives lost and appreciable damage to property.

For these reasons, it seems clear that a portion of the defense budget should be allocated to ballistic missile defense. There is, of course, no exact way to determine what this portion should be, and some judgment must enter into the final decision. For a budget of $50 billion, we would suggest spending most of the defense money, $35 billion for fallout and blast shelters; about half the remainder for a midcourse (area) ballistic missile defense designed to provide some protection for the whole country, including our strategic missiles, strategic bombers, and bomber defenses; and the rest for a terminal ballistic missile defense to protect the most populous urban areas.

9

Improved Shelters
and Accessories

J. C. BRESEE
and D. L. NARVER, JR.

¶ This is one of the key chapters of this book. It describes the ways shelters can reduce the danger to human life (discussed in Chapter 6) from the phenomena resulting from nuclear explosion (described in Chapter 5). It distinguishes between two types of shelters: the fallout shelters, which protect from fallout's delayed radiation but provide little protection against the blast accompanying the explosion, and blast shelters, which provide protection against all direct effects of an explosion. The latter are either isolated shelters (each of which accommodates a limited number of people) or interconnected (in which case the whole shelter system under a city is accessible to everyone who has reached it anywhere). The authors strongly favor the interconnected system. The blast-shelter system discussed here is the tunnel-grid system, toward the development of which the writers have contributed decisively. This system can be built for the single purpose of protection; alternately, it can serve a peacetime need (such as underground communication, automobile parking, housing of utility ducts), but it must be built strong enough to afford protection if the need should arise. ¶ It is assumed in most of the chapters, and in particular also in the present one, that civil defense is the only means available for protection, and the degree of protection afforded by blast shelters, in particular, is discussed under this assumption because active defense has so many unknown elements that its effectiveness is very difficult to avaluate. However, as the preceding chapter demonstrates, it can contribute significantly to the reduction of casualties, even if the extent of this contribution is difficult to assess.

The chapter ends with a discussion of the warning system and its functions.—E.P.W.

James C. Bresee
Project Director, Civil Defense Research Project,
Oak Ridge National Laboratory

¶ James C. Bresee was born in New York in 1925. He received his Sc.D. degree from the Massachusetts Institute of Technology in 1953. In 1951 he joined the MIT faculty and was in charge of practice schools at Parlin Station, New Jersey, and Oak Ridge, Tennessee. He joined the staff of the Chemical Technology Division of Oak Ridge National Laboratory in 1954 and, prior to his present assignment, conducted and guided research in radiochemical separations, mass transfer, chemical kinetics, and in the field of radiation hazards and unit operations. He was a member of the Harbor Project; his interest in civil defense grew out of this study. He became director of the Oak Ridge National Laboratory Civil Defense Research Project in 1965.

David L. Narver, Jr.
Vice-President, Holmes & Narver, Inc.

¶ David L. Narver, Jr., is vice-president, Advanced Technology Group, for Holmes & Narver, Inc. A civil-structural engineer with registration to practice engineering in many states, he has been involved in nuclear weapon test programs since 1949. He was co-head of the group that instrumented the many structures tested during Operation Greenhouse and was chief project engineer for all structures constructed for the first two series of thermonuclear testing. He was the first chairman of the American Society of Civil Engineers' Committee on Nuclear Structures and Materials and has published articles on the properties of structural materials and problems of nuclear blast designs.

General Description of Protective System

Shelters and a warning system are the most important elements of civil defense. The purpose of the shelter is to reduce the weapons effects described in Chapter 5 to the level of human tolerance described in Chapter 6. For nuclear weapons, these effects can be divided into two categories, immediate and delayed. We shall call those effects "immediate" which manifest themselves within the first minute of a nuclear explosion; all other effects, "delayed."

This definition leads to some difficulty. Blast effects severe enough to cause structural damage extend down to the region of 1 psi, (pound per square inch) particularly for megaton weapons. (Sonic booms of less than one-third psi have broken windows.) The time of arrival of the blast wave from a 15-megaton explosion, at the point where its pressure has been attenuated to 1 psi is about 6 minutes. Yet, blast effects will be treated in all cases as immediate effects. On the other hand, the radiation is conveniently divided by the 1-minute line into two parts: the prompt radiation resulting from fission and fusion, and the delayed radiation resulting from fission products.

Shelter and Accessories for Delayed Effects

The most common shelter for protection from the delayed effects of nuclear weapons is the fallout shelter. The hazardous effect is penetrating radiation from particles vaporized or entrained from the surface of the earth which have collected fission products from the weapon. These settle in areas adjacent to the explosion as fallout particles. Protection from the radiation of the fission products attached to this dust or fallout is provided by massive shielding (heavy materials such as earth or concrete) between the fallout and the shelter inhabitants. The thickness of the shielding needed depends, of course, on the intensity of radiation emitted by the fallout, i.e., the amount and age of the fission products attached to the fallout particles and, of course, on the proximity of these particles.

Important shelter accessories include ventilating equipment, food, water, sanitary supplies, radiation monitoring, and facilities for communication with other shelters. Other elements of principal importance in a later rebuilding period will be discussed in later chapters.

Protection from Initial Weapons Effects

The initial weapon effect against which it is most difficult to provide protection is blast. While for small tactical nuclear weapons, the lethal effects of prompt radiation can extend beyond those of blast waves, the weight of such weapons for a given yield is so high that they are unlikely to be employed against civilian populations. Large nuclear warheads are the most probable threats to people. Hence, protection against blast from large weapons will be, in general, the most important factor in the design and cost of the shelters which are expected to protect people against the immediate effects of explosions.

Blast shelters must have great structural strength to resist the blast wave. They must be equipped also with blast doors in the passageways and blast valves in the ventilation ducts and in all pipes that have an access to the outside.

General Requirements for Shelters

In evaluating shelter concepts, the following features are important:

1. *Availability.* Is there space for everyone?
2. *Accessibility.* Can people reach shelter in time?

3. *Liveability.* Can the occupants survive once they are in the shelter? To assure this, the shelter must protect against radiation and blast; it must also provide food, water, fresh air, sanitation, etc.

4. *Mobility.* How difficult is it to reunite family groups?

5. *Community needs.* Can medical and governmental authorities (e.g., policemen and firemen) assist everyone?

6. *Egress.* Is it possible to leave the shelter safely in the presence of local hazards? Can rubble, radioactivity, or fire block the exits?

7. *Population density.* Can the number of people per square mile be reduced either quickly or at least within a few hours after taking shelter?

Shelter design basically consists of determining the least expensive system which protects the occupants against possible damage from nuclear weapons, with the features listed above serving as a design checklist.

Radiation is not sensed by any of the human sense organs—one cannot see, smell, or hear it; hence, another very important consideration, particularly for small shelters, is the information and judgment required to decide how long it is necessary to remain in the shelter. It must be assumed that many small shelters, particularly those created at the last minute, will not have radiation detection devices. Fortunately, a great many persons now possess battery-operated transistor radios so that central authorities can provide some guidance to isolated shelters concerning the necessary sheltering period. Nevertheless, the temptation to leave a shelter prematurely will be great.

Fallout Shelters

As was mentioned earlier, fallout shelters are effective in lessening the effects of delayed radiation. Such shelters' protection from blast is generally low. Hence, a fallout shelter will be useful principally in areas beyond the blast damage region.

Three types of thermonuclear attacks can result in hazards for which a fallout shelter, even in urban areas, provides adequate protection. First, ballistic missile attacks against U.S. military targets, such as our Minuteman silos, which are located mainly in remote western areas, could produce dangerous fallout in many areas not subject to the initial effects of these weapons. This is a particularly important hazard since destruction of hardened missile silos probably requires ground bursts, which cause a great deal of local fallout. Second, attacks against certain urban areas (perhaps containing important industrial targets) can result in dangerous fallout in nearby cities. On the other hand, blast effects and damage to a soft target can be maximized by air bursts which cause little local fallout. Finally, a city protected against the immediate effects of ballistic missiles may be enveloped with radioactive fallout by an upwind ground burst. Fallout shelters can render such an attack ineffectual.

Let us now look at the hazards to urban areas caused by a direct attack. The following calculation illustrates the magnitude of the damage which could be inflicted by a nation with advanced nuclear capability.

In the older 48 of the 50 United States, some 70 percent of the population is located in approximately 1 percent of the area: according to a forecast for 1975, 140 million people will reside within 40,000 square miles. If large thermonuclear weapons were detonated in the air over the most densely populated areas, a few hundred such weapons could cover these 40,000 square miles with substantial blast effects. For example, about 250 10-megaton weapons could produce 10-psi or larger blast waves over approximately 1 percent of the area of the United States. A 10-psi blast wave and the accompanying 300-mph wind from a 10-megaton weapon would severely damage most aboveground structures. In addition, in clear weather fires could be started over a wide area.

The total area covered by at least 10 psi is cut in half when a nuclear weapon is detonated on the earth's surface and the danger of large fires would also be greatly diminished. On the other hand, the threat would be increased by intense radiation from local fallout. Consequently, it is not obvious whether a blast-fire or blast-nuclear radiation attack would be preferred by the enemy if the urban populations were his target. In either case a serious effort to reduce urban damage and casualties would require the next step beyond full fallout protection: blast shelter, ballistic missile defense, or both.

People in urban areas, even outside areas subjected to blast, can expect fallout in a short period of time (within about a half hour) after an attack. Hence, urban shelters should be essentially complete, so that the time before the arrival of fallout is available for moving people into the shelters.

The impossibility of foreseeing the time at which an attack may be launched makes planning for the number of shelter occupants difficult. For example, a home shelter may have to function without one or both parents or may have to include several guests who are unable to get to their own shelters. Large buildings in metropolitan areas have population fluctuations from many thousands to essentially no occupants, all in the matter of a few hours. Consequently, the full fallout shelter plan of the federal government has assumed that at least 20 percent more space will be needed than there are people to be sheltered.

Adequate ventilation of fallout shelters, of course, is very important. A great deal of information has been made available on ventilation systems not requiring electricity, operated by either bicycle drives or hand cranks. An example of one such system is shown in Fig. 9.1. There is, in addition, new information on a very simple, inexpensive, easy-to-construct, manually operated air pump which may be very useful in shelters in the warm and humid regions of the country.[1] A drawing of the pump is shown in Fig. 9.2.

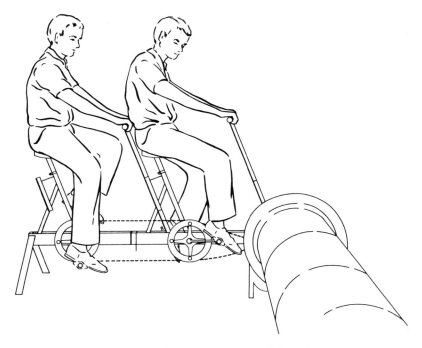

Fig. 9.1. Fallout Shelter Ventilation Unit in Operation

The unit contained in the package ventilation kit can be operated manually or electrically. (Source: *Annual Report of the Office of Civil Defense for Fiscal Year 1965.*)

A final word of caution would be appropriate concerning blast protection afforded by fallout shelters. Assuming that the shelter is underground in a reinforced concrete structure, the basic structural elements may survive rather intense blast waves. Many such buildings in Hiroshima "suffered remarkably little damage externally"[2] as close as 1,950 feet from the explosion. The shelter entrance may be baffled to prevent thermal radiation from shining directly in. However, intense and dangerous shock waves from large thermo-

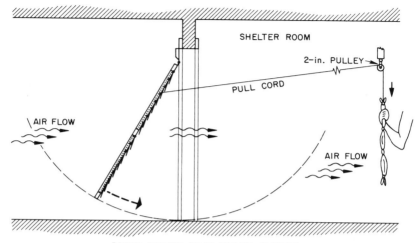

POWER STROKE (FLAP VALVES CLOSED)

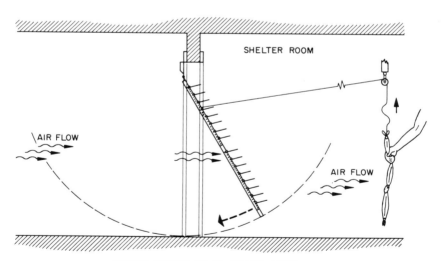

RETURN STROKE (FLAP VALVES OPEN)

Fig. 9.2. Punkah-Pump; Vertical Sections through Doorway

nuclear weapons, carrying high pressure air, persist for several seconds, and this "reservoir" of compressed air can penetrate through openings and around corners with only moderate loss of intensity. Unless the shelter remains reasonably airtight, it will provide only moderate protection because the entering blast and heated air will injure those inside.

Shelters from Initial Effects (Blast Shelters)

Blast shelters differ from fallout shelters primarily in that the complete facility can withstand the force of the air and ground shock waves, the initial nuclear radiation, and the sudden intense heat flash from the explosion as well as the large amount of heat resulting from possible fires started by the initial flash. As was suggested earlier, an important protective element is a strong door at all entrances. It is also necessary to provide for suitable atmospheric environment—reasonable air temperature, humidity, and oxygen and carbon dioxide content while the shelter is closed up to resist blast and fires.

Let us first examine the entrance design problem. Unless people can enter and then be protected as soon as they are in a shelter, the shelter is not very effective. Ideally, the entrance should allow a continual, high flow rate of people into the shelter while preventing the entry of any damaging weapon effect. Blast resistant doors suitable for very large pressures have been built and subjected to tests. Hardened military installations are equipped with such doors, but these do not permit the passage of a large number of people during the possibly short period available before an explosion. The design problem is further aggravated by the high emotional stress that could prevail after the nuclear attack warning—particularly if the explosion is conceived as imminent.

Several designs for the entrance way have been proposed which offer partial solutions to the problems listed above. The entrance may be simply a revolving door which must be, of course, strong enough to resist the expected blast pressures. This provides constant protection of the inside against the blast, but, because one cannot see through it, it might cause psychological difficulties at times of stress. This difficulty could be decreased by holding "open house" demonstrations of a public blast shelter equipped with revolving doors.

The "anticipatory" door is another design that has been proposed. It is a sliding door, and its closing is actuated by an aboveground trigger which is sensitive to one of the immediate weapon effects. This trigger would have to be properly maintained. If the trigger is actuated by the blast, it would have to be located far enough away to allow the door to close before the arrival of the shock wave. A third design envisages the closing of the door to be actuated by the shock wave arriving at the door itself. If this design is used, some of the shock wave will enter the shelter but with diminishing intensity. A door of this type would also have to be very rugged to be able to withstand the effect of being slammed shut by a force which may amount to several tons per square foot of door area. There are also designs intermediate between the second and last of those described. All these doors are weapon-actuated and have the advantage of keeping the passageway open until the attack actually occurs.

A last design, the "air lock" scheme, is illustrated in Figure 9.3. It is similar to systems used in cold climates to keep the cold air out of the house whenever someone enters or leaves. An almost continual movement can be maintained through two, or better three parallel airlock doors, and the filling operation can be almost completely independent of attack time. Such a system avoids the need to deny access to later arrivals in order to protect those inside when some stragglers may yet be coming in. The inside is always protected, yet accessible to stragglers. However, the shelter must have enough entrances so that all who need to enter can do so within the warning time. This should prevent a premature rush to the shelters. Even more important, in our opinion, is the requirement that if people should start moving to the shelters before the enemy

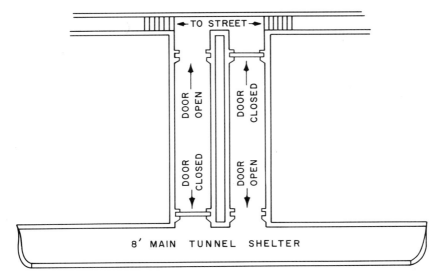

Fig. 9.3. Airlock Type Entrance

In the situation illustrated, people coming from the street would enter the corridor on the left. Those already in the corridor on the right would leave for the shelter proper. In the next stage, all open doors would close, and all closed doors would open. People who are in the corridor on the left would leave for the shelter proper, those coming from the outside would enter the corridor on the right. When this has happened, the doors would again assume the position shown above and the process would repeat itself.

attack has started, such movement shall not induce the enemy to precipitate action lest his strategic position deteriorate. It does not deteriorate if people could move to the shelters in time even when his attack is underway. Hence, delaying his attack and continuing negotiations would not make his attack less effective if it should have to be undertaken anyway.

In addition to keeping the nuclear weapon effects inside the shelter within human tolerance levels, the air in the shelter must be maintained in suitable condition, even if conditions outside, for instance heavy fires, require a temporary closing of the ventilation system. The human body consumes oxygen and gives off carbon dioxide, moisture, and heat. If the amount of any one of these items deviates too far from normal, sickness and even death can result. As an example, normal air contains 0.04 percent carbon dioxide, though 2 to 3 percent is tolerable. At 4 percent there is considerable discomfort, at 11 percent unconsciousness can occur, and exposure at 25 to 30 percent for a few hours can result in death. If a person were in a sealed room where the average volume per person is 50 cubic feet, in a little more than 2 hours the carbon dioxide content would increase to 4 percent, and in about 6 hours to 11 percent. From the standpoint of heat, an air temperature of 92° F with 90 percent relative humidity results in a dangerous rise in breathing and pulse rates and a sense of panic. Let us suppose, for example, a 50-cubic-foot space allotment per person and an initial temperature of 70° F with a relative humidity of 50 percent. Someone entering in a state of exertion and tension could give off as much as 1,000 Btu per hour (about 2 to 3 times the normal rate). Under this condition, unless some cooling were provided, it would take only about 4 minutes for the air to reach 92° F and 76 percent relative humidity. Cooling by the shelter's walls ameliorates this situation only moderately. All this calls for an effective control of the atmosphere.

Let us return briefly to the seven desirable features listed at the beginning of this chapter and note some of the difficulties encountered when trying to provide these in isolated (that is, unconnected) blast shelters.

1. *Availability*. The location of people in urban areas varies a great deal with the time of the day and the day of the week. If overcrowding of isolated shelters is to be avoided, these must have, in every region, sufficient capacity to accommodate the largest number of people who can be expected to be in the area at any time of the day or week. This requires a considerably greater

number of shelter spaces than the number of inhabitants in the city. No such excess of shelter spaces is necessary if the shelters are interconnected because local overcrowding in some parts of the city can be relieved by movement through the tunnels to areas where there are vacant places.

2. *Accessibility.* Isolated shelters do not present particular problems in this regard.
3. *Liveability.* The remark under 2 applies here also.
4. *Rejoining of family.* If there is no passageway between shelters, members of a family may become widely separated. If there is not much radiation from fallout outside, they may try to rejoin each other when no more explosions are expected, but this will remain dangerous and may lead to confusion.
5. *Community needs.* In the same way that families may be separated, so medical and government authorities will be unavailable to many shelterees in isolated shelters.
6. *Egress.* Since isolated shelters have few doors to the outside, these may be blocked by rubble. In addition, the radioactivity resulting from fallout may render it dangerous to leave the shelter long enough for moving outside the area of bomb damage.
7. *Population density.* Since people will not be able to move far before seeking shelter, there is much less opportunity for substantial concentrations of people to be reduced before their positions are essentially fixed for the period of heavy radiation outside.

The difficulties enumerated can be reduced by connecting shelters with tunnels, but the cost of tunnels would be quite substantial.

A solution which overcomes the disadvantages just discussed is that of using a series of long (many miles) parallel tunnels as shelters and having these tunnels connected by another series of long parallel tunnels which are perpendicular to the first series. With such a system, one could enter any place in the city and

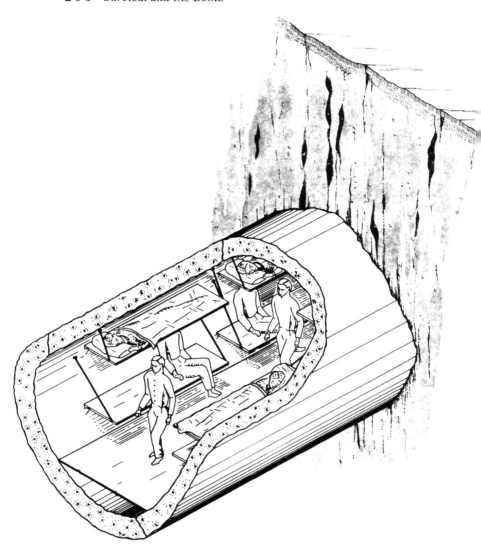

Fig. 9.4. Section of Tunnel-Grid Shelter

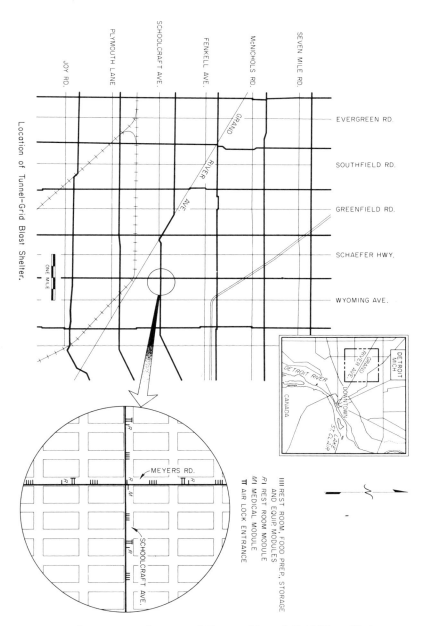

Fig. 9.5. Location of Proposed Detroit Tunnel-Grid Blast Shelter

within a relatively short period of time (a few hours) walk to any other portion of the city, thus making possible the reuniting of families, distributing of doctors and governmental authorities, minimizing duplication of spaces, and providing for redistribution of population while in a sheltered condition. Such a system was first documented by Howard Harrenstien of the University of Arizona.[3] It has also been studied by members of the Civil Defense Research Project at the Oak Ridge National Laboratory where it is called a tunnel-grid blast shelter. A general study of the tunnel-grid blast shelter concept was followed by a special adaptation thereof to a twenty-five-square-mile section of Detroit, Michigan.[4] Figure 9.4 shows a typical cross section of the main tunnels. This arrangement could shelter some 5,000 persons per mile. The entrance illustrated in Figure 9.3 permits the passage of 1,800 people in about 10 minutes. There is always a closed door between the blast shock and the shelter so that it never becomes necessary to close doors suddenly. The main tunnels are located as shown in Fig. 9.5; this also shows the relative locations of the various primary components which service the shelter, namely restrooms, storage and food-preparation units, air-handling modules, and power generation plants. With the tunnels roughly a mile from each other, the shelter system could accommodate a population density of 10,000 persons per square mile for a month at a 1965 construction cost ranging from $400 to $500 per person, depending on the excavation method used. It should be stressed that underground blast shelter costs (and even feasibility) in areas of high water table are not well established and require further work.*

Conversion of Other Installations to Shelters

The discussion so far has related to the creation of fallout and blast shelters for shelter use only. We will now consider the possi-

---

* EDITOR'S NOTE—A recent suggestion, made by J. M. Reynolds and Roger W. Richardson of Louisiana State University to build the shelters inside the levees which guard against floods, may be helpful.

bility of upgrading or modifying proposed or existing urban facilities to provide, in addition to their normal function, protection from
varying amounts of the initial and delayed effects of nuclear weapons. This concept has been successfully applied by the Office of
Civil Defense to provide protection in public buildings against delayed effects and has been called slanting. While examining urban
facilities, we will stress those which have elements of interconnec-
tion so that the general requirements described in items 4, 5, 6, and
7 of the design checklist can be at least partially satisfied.

Facilities with peacetime use which can protect against blast
and radiation are almost always located below grade. Examples
of such facilities which either are or can be easily interconnected
include modern subways, underground garages and highways,
underground pedestrian walkways, utility tunnels, and even large
storm drains.

In none of these facilities would there be adequate blast protection without modification of the normal structure. The two most
important modifications are the provision of blast doors and of
blast valves in ventilation ducts. These two modifications would be
responsible for most of the additional expense of the installation,
and they could be delayed. At the time of construction, only blast
resistance of the main structure would have to be assured. Hence,
one can identify three levels of cost: the cost of the facility for peace-
ful use only, the cost of the facility fully equipped for normal and
emergency use, and the cost of the facility in a form which would
allow inexpensive conversion to an emergency facility at a later
date. As a facility is built, extra thickness to concrete ceilings can
be inexpensively added, but after completion the same addition
might not only be much more expensive but might also seriously
degrade the peacetime utility of the facility. On the other hand,
the installation cost of emergency electric generators or blast doors
would be relatively independent of time (except for possible inflation), provided that space for their installation had been designed
into the original facility.

Underground Garages and Highways

As the cost of space in crowded urban areas increases and as an increasing value is attached to retaining the land surface for recreation and beauty, more and more underground parking facilities are being constructed. George Hoffman while at the RAND Corporation[5] suggested that tunnels could be used for highways in cities and for automobile parking, and, if tunnels continue to become less expensive, the country may enter an era within the next decade when surface and subsurface roads are about equally expensive to construct and maintain.

Although Hirschfeld[6] has disagreed with some of Hoffman's cost data, he also expressed optimism that increased use of tunneling machines should reduce future tunnel costs. This optimism is being borne out by experiments being conducted by several organizations on new methods of rock breaking, especially the high pressure water jet method.[7] There is reasonable hope that a significant reduction in cost of tunneling can be achieved.

To evaluate the present-day feasibility of the construction of highways and parking facilities in tunnels and to establish the cost of dual-use blast shelters in very crowded urban areas, a conceptual design study was carried out by Holmes & Narver, an engineering company in Los Angeles. The study concerned the planned six lanes of underground highway in midtown Manhattan, connecting Lincoln and Queens-Midtown Tunnels, with adjoining parking facilities for 30,000 automobiles.[8] Holmes & Narver was assisted by members of the System Development Corporation, Santa Monica, and by Hoffman. The plan of the complete system is shown in Fig. 9.6.

The plan envisages a network of parking tunnels under virtually all cross-town streets between 63rd and 13th Streets, with connections to the cross-town highways provided by tunnels under the north-south avenues. The tunnels would be in bedrock, more than one hundred feet below the surface, so that there would be no inter-

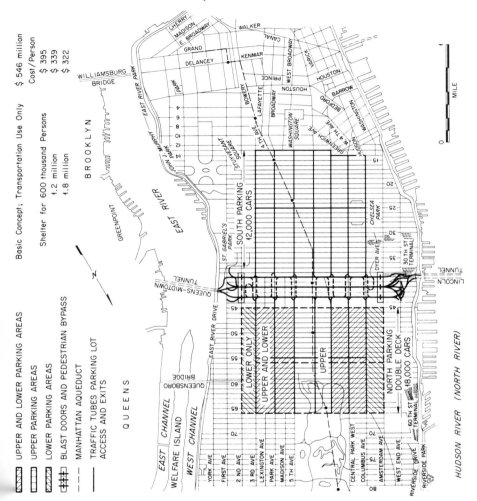

Fig. 9.6. Proposed Dual-Use Shelters for Manhattan

Interconnecting traffic tubes and underground parking areas. (From "Engineering Study of Underground Highway and Parking Garage and Blast Shelter for Manhattan Island." ORNL–TM–1381.)

ference with the foundation of buildings, city utilities, and subways. If further studies indicate that an underwater nuclear explosion in the Hudson or the East River might fracture the rock and allow water to enter the tunnels, these would have to be subdivided with waterproof bulkheads. Access to the transportation system would be through escalators.

If no consideration is given to later use as a shelter, the facility would cost $546 million. If it is built so that it also provides shelter of the same quality as the single purpose Detroit shelter, the cost would be increased $300 to $400 per space, depending on the number of spaces. The possibility of providing 100-psi protection for the residents of one of the most densely populated areas in the world at costs below single-use costs by taking advantage of the cost-sharing advantages of dual-use shelters indicates the importance of pursuing the concept further.

Modern Subways

A distinction needs to be made between old and new subways, largely for present purposes, on the basis of ventilation methods. Older systems do not have air-conditioned cars and are ventilated by using the trains as pistons which pull air in and push it out through large ventilation openings to the surface. Only little additional ventilation is provided for smoke removal in the event of a fire. The ventilation openings are so large and so numerous that the cost of hardening a system like the present one in New York is probably quite high. Modern subways with the much larger heat loads from air-conditioning equipment in cars are equipped with complete forced ventilation through exhaust ducts. These can be rather easily equipped with blast valves.

Subway tubes have greater strength than stations. Hence, one might first imagine using the space between stations for mass shelters. A cross section of a 16-foot-square tube prepared suitable for emergency shelter use is shown in Fig. 9.7, indicating how as many as four or even five people per foot of tunnel might be housed. On

Fig. 9.7. Subway Tunnel Equipped for Emergency Habitation

the other hand, because of ground-water problems, the new Rotterdam subways uses only the stations as blast shelters.[9]

Another approach to interconnected blast-shelter design is that of Stockholm in which subways can be used as passageways to reach underground parking garages, which become 150-psi blast shelters in an emergency.

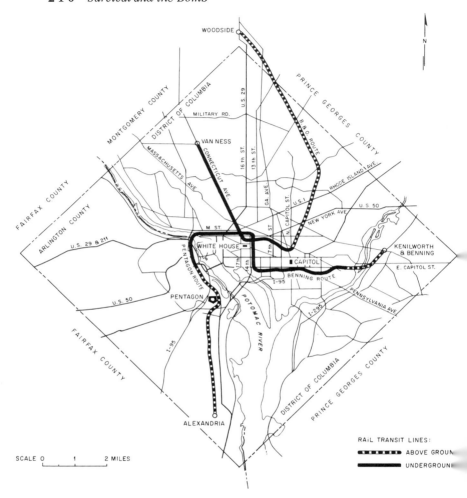

Fig. 9.8. Plan of New Washington Rapid Transit System

An example of a modern subway, the design of which might be
modified to provide a substantial amount of blast-shelter space, is

the new Washington, D.C., subway. The plans are still in flux but the potential shelter capacity is likely to exceed 370,000 people.

Utility Tunnels

Utility tunnels (some called "Utilidors") have been widely used in cold climates to prevent damage to water and sewer lines by permafrost and to permit repairs under all weather conditions. Relocating electrical utilities underground has also aesthetic motivation; this partially explains the extensive use of utility tunnels on university campuses. In some cities underground pipes are city owned and space is leased principally by utility companies.

Ease of maintenance of utilities and increased beauty are two important goals as our cities are gradually rebuilt through urban development and similar programs. Over a period of time, networks of larger utility tunnels (more extensive, perhaps, than the Detroit tunnel grid) might be installed under most regions with a high density of urban population. A schematic representation of a nine-foot utility tunnel and a possible revision for shelter use are shown in Fig. 9.9. Such tunnels would provide a great deal of protection in case of an emergency.

Protective Capability of 100-PSI Shelters

A sample calculation of the life-saving potential of blast shelters may render the preceding discussion more concrete. We choose, as an example, an enemy strike with 10-megaton weapons aimed so as to produce the maximum number of casualties. We assume that the urban population is protected at residential locations with 100-psi blast shelters, and that the shelters provide complete protection up to a blast pressure of 100 psi but no protection above 100 psi. Table 9.1 compares the number of 10-megaton weapons with the percentage of the U.S. population who live outside the lethal radius of the weapons.

One feature of interconnected blast shelters has not been con-

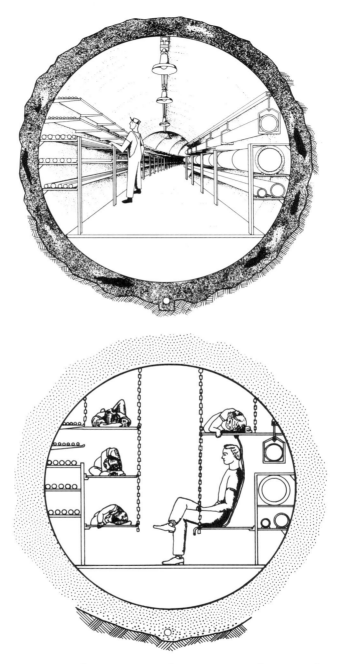

Fig. 9.9. The Conversion of a Nine-Foot Utility Tunnel
for Shelter Use

Table 9.1. Population Protection by 100-PSI Shelters*

Number of 10-Megaton Weapons (Targeted for maximum casualties)	Percent of 1970 U.S. Residential Population Outside Lethal Area	Population Densities in Target Areas (people/sq. mile)
25	97	24,800
50	95	20,000
100	92	14,200
200	88	11,000
300	84	9,100
450	80	7,400
600	76	6,250
750	73	5,500
900	71	4,750

* R. A. Uher, "The Effectiveness of Blast Protection Against an Anti-Population Attack," ORNL–TM–1725 (Oak Ridge, Tenn.: Oak Ridge National Laboratory, 1968).

sidered in the calculations leading to Table 9.1, the potential ability to provide blast protection near a person's work or residential location and then to reduce high population densities by movement of people through the shelter grid while they are protected. If the population density values listed in the table can be reduced by movement through a shelter system, then the residential population within the lethal area would be further reduced. The number of fatalities would be reduced also by the installation of active defense, as has been discussed before.

Improved Warning Systems

In the present national civil defense warning system, information that an attack against the United States is underway may come from several sources, but in case of an intercontinental ballistic missile attack, principally from the Ballistic Missile Early Warning System (BMEWS) of the North American Air Defense Command (NORAD). The system detects ballistic missiles which may strike the United States by means of the three large radar installations, one each in Alaska, Greenland, and England. When the NORAD commander in Colorado Springs concludes that the nation is being attacked, he informs a civil defense representative at the command

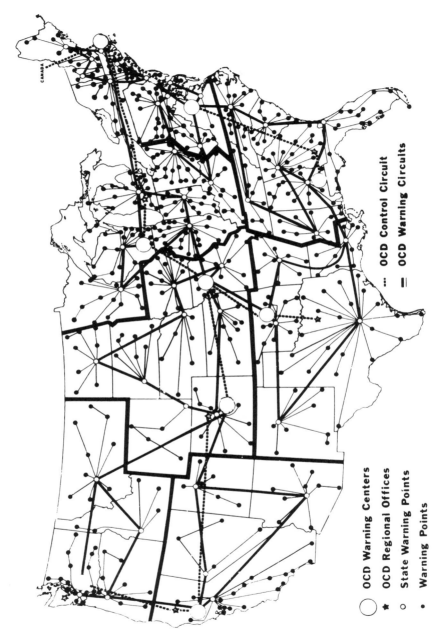

OCD Control Circuit

OCD Warning Circuits

OCD Warning Centers

OCD Regional Offices

State Warning Points

Warning Points

Fig. 9.10. National Warning System (NAWAS)
(Source: *Annual Report of the Office of Civil Defense for Fiscal Year 1964.*)

center, who transmits the warning to the country through the National Warning System (NAWAS) (see Fig. 9.10).

This network extends through regional and state warning centers to municipal offices which are continuously occupied. They are, as a rule, in police and fire stations. Upon receipt of the attack warning appropriate local officials sound the local alarms, mostly outdoor sirens, to indicate that protective actions should be taken immediately by going to shelter.

At the same time that NAWAS is sending out the attack warning, through a different network the Emergency Broadcast System is activated to supply verbal confirmation of the siren warning. Typically, an announcer might state: "The country is being attacked. Go immediately to the nearest civil defense shelter." Thus, someone hearing the siren could verify that the emergency was real. However, many people inside buildings in urban areas might not hear the outdoor warning system.

An effective indoor warning system is under development by the Office of Civil Defense. A radio signal would turn on receivers over which emergency information and instructions would be broadcast. These receivers could be located in any room of a house, office, or factory, and would allow national or local leaders to communicate with most citizens rapidly, when their protection required it.

Would an expanded civil defense program have different warning requirements? Would a shift in emphasis from fallout shelter, protecting from delayed effects, to blast shelters against all immediate effects, significantly change the warning problem?

We will now assume that all the country is protected by an "area" ballistic missile defense, that is, by interception outside the atmosphere of large unsophisticated enemy warheads. In addition, certain critically important military installations and several dozen large metropolitan areas have backup protection by Nike-Sprint missiles, which attack threatening objects which penetrate into the atmosphere. We will further assume that early in the 1970's an abortive coup d'état somewhere results in a small number of sophisticated missiles launched toward a mixture of military and population-industry targets in the United States.

News of political troubles might provide a considerable amount of warning during the days or even weeks preceding the attack. We shall assume, nevertheless, that the only attack warning comes from BMEWS (or possibly a forward-scattering radar installation which detects the actual missile launchings). A take-shelter warning is delivered by siren and radio-repeater to essentially all the U.S. population fifteen to twenty minutes before the first impact or airburst is expected.

Community shelters in cities may range from the basement fallout type (in lower population density areas which are twenty or more miles from important military or industrial targets) to blast shelters in interconnected transportation tunnels or single-use tunnel grids (in densely populated areas or areas near military targets). Rural shelters are all assumed to be individual family fallout shelters.

Assuming the warning was heard, understood, and believed, significant movement toward shelter would begin within approximately five minutes and would continue until all were under cover. The total movement time might be as long as one hour (high-rise building evacuation might require twenty to thirty minutes) in large and congested cities. Within ten to fifteen minutes after the bulk of the people began to move to shelter (mostly on foot through the city streets), missile-ABM engagements would begin in space and in the stratosphere over the United States, or in considerably shorter time in the case of a submarine attack on a coastal city. In the vicinity of these engagements, it would probably be safer for those who have not yet reached shelter to seek immediate if temporary cover (in parked automobiles or basements) rather than to continue toward better shelter. Information on the proximity of the enemy missiles will be available from the computers which will control the launching, guidance, and detonation of the nuclear-tipped Spartan and Sprint missiles.

With the advent of ballistic missile defense, we suggest that an improvement to the single signal system ("Go to shelter, regardless of your present location.") would involve the use of the old aircraft warning system—a go-to-shelter signal which means that an attack is underway against the country and a take-immediate-shelter signal which means "interrupt your movement to your assigned shelter location and protect yourself as best you can."

For an attack of a limited duration or for one that occurs in waves, there would be time for movement to shelter to be resumed. If an upwind groundburst has occurred, at least fallout protection will be required. Thus, successful intercept of all dangerous objects during an attack on an area defended by both Spartan and Sprint missiles does not eliminate the need for improved shelter and the need to abandon the unventilated basement or unshielded automobile.

Summarizing the suggested shelter warning doctrine, a single go-to-shelter signal should go to the entire population until the local threat can be identified from the ballistic missile defense radar and computer. The take-cover signals should be issued. At the end of the local engagement, movement to shelter should be resumed.

Notes

1 Cresson H. Kearney, *Mechanized Durability Tests of a Six-Foot Punkah-Pump*, TM–1155 (Oak Ridge, Tenn.: Oak Ridge National Laboratory, 1965).

2 Samuel Glasstone, ed., *The Effects of Nuclear Weapons* (Washington, D.C.: U.S. Atomic Energy Commission, 1962).

3 *Local Civil Defense Systems* (Tucson: Engineering Research Laboratory, Univ. of Arizona, 1964).

4 Donald T. Robbins and David L. Narver, Jr. (Holmes & Narver, Los Angeles), *Engineering Study for Tunnel Grid Blast Shelter Concept for a Portion of City of Detroit, Michigan*, TM–1223 (Oak Ridge, Tenn.: Oak Ridge National Laboratory, 1965).

5 G. A. Hoffman, *Urban Underground Highways and Parking Facilities*, RM–3680–RC (Santa Monica, Calif.: RAND Corp., 1963).

6 R. C. Hirschfeld, *Report on Hard-Rock Tunneling Investigation,* prepared for the U.S. Department of Commerce (Cambridge: Massachusetts Institute of Technology, 1965).

7 John L. Kennedy, "Erosion Drill Shows Astonishing Speed," *Oil and Gas Journal,* Jan. 27, 1969, 92, 93.

8 H. F. Perla and H. F. Haller, *Engineering Study of Underground Highway and Parking Garage and Blast Shelter for Manhatten Island,* TM–1381 (Oak Ridge, Tenn.: Oak Ridge National Laboratory, 1966).

9 *Proceedings of the Symposium on Protective Structures for Civilian Populations,* April 19–23, 1965 (Washington, D.C.: Subcommittee on Civil Defense, National Research Council, National Academy of Sciences, 1965), p. 252.

10   Decontamination

FREDERICK P. COWAN
and CHARLES B. MEINHOLD

¶ Decontamination could be very useful in areas not significantly affected by blast but visited by heavy fallout. It could greatly abbreviate the period which has to be spent in the shelter, making the outside and its installations accessible much sooner than they would be otherwise. If this permits the resumption of production, it would contribute to a speedier recovery.—E.P.W.

Frederick P. Cowan

Head, Health Physics Division,
Brookhaven National Laboratory

¶ Dr. Cowan was born in Bar Harbor, Maine, in 1906; he received his A.B. degree from Bowdoin College in 1928 and his Ph.D. from Harvard in 1935. He then served as instructor and assistant professor of physics at Rensselaer Polytechnic Institute from 1935 to 1942. From 1943 to 1945 he was a research associate in the Radio Research Laboratory at Harvard, after which he joined the Engineering Division of the Chrysler Corporation. He became a member of the Brookhaven National Laboratory staff in 1947 and is presently in charge of the Health Physics Division. ¶ Dr. Cowan served as a consultant to the Federal Civil Defense Agency from 1951 to 1955 and was president of the Health Physics Society in 1957–58. He was a member of the American Board of Health Physics from 1962 to 1966, having served as chairman from 1963 to 1964 and as chairman of the Board's Examination Panel from 1959 to 1961. He is a member of the Subcommittee on Heavy Particles of the National Council on Radiation Protection, chairman of the Task Group on Neutron Instrumentation of the International Commission on Radiation Units and Measurements, and a member of the AEC Advisory Panel on Accelerator Radiation Safety. In 1965 Dr. Cowan was elected to membership on the International Commission on Radiation Units and Measurements, and in 1967 to membership on the National Council on Radiation Protection.

Charles B. Meinhold

Associate Health Physicist, Health Physics Division, Brookhaven National Laboratory

¶ Mr. Meinhold was born in Boston, Massachusetts, in 1934 and received his B.S. degree in Physics from Providence College in 1956. He did graduate work at the University of Rochester under an AEC Fellowship in Radiological Physics. He joined the Health Physics Division at Brookhaven National Laboratory in 1957 where he now has an appointment as an associate health physicist. At Brookhaven he is responsible for the training activities of the Health Physics Division and assists in the supervision of the operational health physics program. ¶ Mr. Meinhold is a member of the Health Physics Society, having served on various committees, and is active in its New York Chapter, having served in all offices. He is certified by the American Board of Health Physics. He has been active in the radiological aspects of civil defense on both the local and state levels since 1957. He is presently serving on a Task Group of the International Commission on Radiation Protection for the revision of its Publications 3 and 4.

Introduction

One of the major hazards to individuals surviving the immediate effects of an atomic attack is exposure to gamma radiation from highly active fallout of fission-product-bearing debris. As explained in earlier chapters, provision of adequate shelters is the primary method of reducing such exposures. An important secondary method, especially during the recovery phase, is decontamination.

Except in areas where fallout is mild or has not occurred at all, people, after an attack, will be in shelters from which they can emerge for increasingly long periods only after the radiation has decayed to acceptable values. Not only is it important that their stay in shelters be made as short as possible, but operation or restoration of vital facilities such as power plants, water works, food distribution and processing systems, medical installations, communication centers, and transportation systems should be undertaken promptly. Achievement of both of these objectives can be considerably furthered by decontamination of selected areas and installations. For instance, for an urban environment, one study[1] demonstrated that:

1. In most cases the time during which access to important facilities must be denied can be reduced by a factor of 10 (e.g., from two months to less than a week) using practical methods of decontamination.

2. Radiation levels inside of selected structures can be reduced by a factor of 5.

3. Radiation levels outdoors in selected areas can be reduced by a factor of 20.

4. These results can be achieved without excessive exposure to individuals carrying out the decontamination.

The very substantial reduction of the sheltering period that can result from decontamination may be illustrated as follows. Let us consider a situation in which outside levels at t = 1 hour are 1,000 r/hr., and the shelter reduces the radiation intensity by a factor of 100. If we use typical decay data, we find that the dose received during a two-week stay in the shelter will be 30 r if radioactive decay is the only additional factor reducing the dose rate. If the occupants emerge from the shelter after this two-week period, the total future dose without decontamination will be 700 r, which is objectionable. If the outside levels are reduced to 1/10 by decontamination, the total dose will be 30 + 70 r or a total of 100 r. Without decontamination, the period in the shelter would have to be extended to 40 weeks to obtain the same total dose value of 100 r. Although long sheltering periods may in some cases be reduced by the effect of rainfall or by transfer of people to less-contaminated areas, it is clear that decontamination is a very important technique for hastening the process of recovery.

Although the gamma radiation from fallout is the major concern, the effects of beta radiation should not be overlooked. Fallout material left on the skin for an extended period of time can cause serious burns, and if inhaled or ingested in sufficient quantities, it can result in internal damage. Grossly contaminated clothing may contribute to such skin exposures or indirectly to the ingestion of radioactive material. Thus it may be necessary to resort to decontamination of body surfaces, clothing, food, or water.

The basic method of decontamination is to transfer the radioactive material from one location to another that will lead to less exposure of personnel or interference with necessary activities. Alternatively, the material may be left in the same place and the radiation at a selected location reduced by shielding. A very substantial improvement in the postattack situation can be achieved in this way, but since decontamination requires the investment of manpower, fuel, and some exposure to those doing it, only a limited amount can be accomplished. In this connection, it is appropriate to list a few basic principles before proceeding to a discussion of specific methods:

1. The planning of decontamination should be an important part of the preattack civil defense activity.
2. Areas or facilities chosen for decontamination should be those most needed during the postattack period.
3. Methods and plans should be adjusted to obtain the maximum

possible benefit from a given investment of manpower and personnel exposure.

Although these principles are merely an application of sound common sense, efficient use of them calls for a fairly complex evaluation of many factors. The rest of this chapter will be devoted to a general discussion of these factors and to an evaluation of the usefulness and limitations of decontamination as a radiation countermeasure.

Methods of Decontamination

The radioactive fallout following an atomic bomb explosion consists of tons of finely divided sand or cindered dirt particles which were produced in the mushroom cloud through the processes of vaporization and condensation, or were sucked up by the high winds associated with the cloud's rapid rise to high altitudes. The highly radioactive fission products and other activated atoms are trapped in or on the particles which, except for those falling close to the point of explosion, are quite small. Thus, beyond the area of gross physical damage caused by blast and fire, fallout particles will range in size from 20 to 200 microns (0.0008 to 0.008 inches). Such particles settle very slowly in air and are carried along primarily by air currents. Furthermore, the particles which are carried to greater distances from the point of origin are only the smaller ones. Particles of sand grain size predominate in the vicinity of the explosion while fine dust is the major constituent farther away. In areas of heavy fallout, the deposit may amount to as much as a pound per square foot. The following are some important considerations relative to the problem of decontamination:

1. The mass of the radioactive material itself is a tiny fraction of the mass of the inert fallout material with which it is associated. Thus, in discussing the mechanics of removal, fallout may be considered as a type of dirt.
2. In general, the amount of radioactive material removed is proportional to the total amount of fallout material removed.

3. Although the solubility of fallout particles depends on the composition of the ground where the detonation took place, it is fair
   to say that detonations over land will produce essentially in-
   soluble particles while detonations over water will produce
   much less but fairly soluble fallout material. This soluble material will have a much greater tendency to adsorb to surfaces.
4. Under most circumstances one is dealing with small particle
   sizes.

The methods applicable to radiological decontamination are
those available to dirt removal in general. Some common examples
are sweeping, brushing, vacuuming, flushing with water, scrubbing,
surface removal, and filtration. In addition, the radioactive material
can be shielded by plowing, spading, covering with clean dirt or by
construction of protective dikes. Such methods may utilize power
equipment or depend upon manual labor. Their effectiveness will
vary widely, depending upon the method of application, the type
of surface, the conditions of deposition, etc., and there will be
similar variations in the exposures received by those doing the
decontamination.

Although the efficiency for removal of the fallout material by
brushing or sweeping is rather low, since the fine particles tend to
adhere to all but the smoothest of surfaces, these methods will find
wide application because of the availability of equipment and the
speed of such operations. An additional problem inherent in sweeping operations is the recontamination of areas previously cleaned
unless great care is taken to confine the collected material. A vac-
uum cleaner overcomes this problem and is quite effective, especially if combined with a brushing action to dislodge the particles.

Flushing with water can be very effective, particularly if the
water is under pressure, the surface is smooth and proper drainage
is available. Under certain conditions, the use of water flushing
during the deposition period can be of great value. The water will
tend to fill the surface irregularities and prevent entrapment of

particles. Soluble materials will be kept in solution, thereby reducing the chance of surface adsorption.

Removal of the contaminated surface when feasible will normally provide the greatest reduction in fallout levels. The resultant large quantities of material to be disposed of, coupled with the long work times required, reduce its overall effectiveness somewhat. In the winter, however, when fallout is deposited on snow, removal may be relatively easy.

Since gamma radiation is quite penetrating, only a limited reduction in radiation levels can be achieved by plowing. However, as the example early in this chapter indicates, a reduction of the activity by a factor of 5 may be of decisive significance. Likewise, large quantities of clean dirt are required to achieve significant reductions by covering the contaminated areas. On the other hand, the surface material removed by a scraper can be quite useful at the periphery of the cleared area where it can be used to form a protective dike or to cover contamination in a buffer zone. The use of such material for a protective dike may seem surprising since it is contaminated. However, in the process of removal by a scraper, the radioactive surface layer is mixed with the underlying clean dirt so that much of the dike's radioactivity is buried and ineffective.

Both experimental and theoretical studies of decontamination as a civil defense countermeasure have been supported by the Department of Defense and by the Atomic Energy Commission. Much of the work has been carried out in connection with weapons tests or at military installations. There is an extensive literature on the subject and a selection of important papers is listed at the end of this chapter.[2] Although these documents and others constitute a reservoir of source material, they are, in general, too detailed and compendious for wide application. However, the Office of Civil Defense has produced excellent summaries in Part E, Chapter 7 of the *Federal Civil Defense Guide.*

The effectiveness of a number of decontamination methods is shown in Table 10.1 which contains a selection of typical data taken from this guide. Decontamination factor (DF) is the fraction of the radiation of the contaminant that is not eliminated. Larger and smaller values can be obtained in most cases depending on the effort expended. The fact that DF can vary all the way from 0.01 to 0.50 means that careful planning in regard to areas to be decontaminated and equipment to be used should be carried out in advance so that the maximum benefits may be derived from the manpower and fuel available for this work in the postattack period.

Table 10.1. Methods of Decontamination

Surface	Method	Man-Hours per 1,000 Sq. Ft.	Decontamination Factor
Pavement	Motorized sweeper	0.02	0.06
	Motorized flusher	0.01	0.02
	Firehosing	0.5	0.03
Tar and gravel roofs	Firehosing	0.3	0.07
	Firehosing plus scrubbing	2.0	0.02
Composition shingle roofs	Firehosing	0.2	0.05
	Firehosing plus scrubbing	2.0	0.02
	Hand sweeping	1.0	0.12
Unpaved land	Scraping	0.11	0.02
	Six-inch earth covering	0.25	0.15
	Plowing	0.4	0.20
	Grading	0.016	0.07
	Hand shoveling with wheelbarrow	2.25	0.12
Bare frozen ground	Motorized sweeper	0.027	0.1
	Firehosing	0.27	0.5
Packed snow	Motorized sweeper	0.017	0.02
	Firehosing at 15° F	0.45	0.12
Undisturbed snow	Blade plow	0.003	0.03
	Rotary plow	0.019	0.10

Decontamination of Urban Areas

A number of factors make large-scale decontamination useful in urban areas. Much of the area between buildings is paved and, thus, readily cleaned using motorized flushers and sweepers, which are usually available. If, in addition, the roofs are decontaminated by high-pressure hosing, it may be possible to make entire buildings habitable fairly soon, even if the fallout has been very heavy. The effectiveness of the decontamination of one roof may be reduced if nearby roofs are left contaminated. It should be added that rather narrow buffer strips (decontaminated areas) around urban buildings will suffice since much of the radiation that would be received from more distant points is automatically eliminated by the shielding provided by adjacent buildings.

The value of high-pressure water flushing in urban areas is further enhanced by the presence of storm drains and sewer systems which will effectively carry away the contamination. The availability of high-pressure water from fire hydrants is another important advantage but one which necessitates careful planning and coordination for maximum benefit. It is, naturally, possible only if the water supply is adequate. An important incentive for concentrating on the decontamination of urban areas is the large number of people benefiting from a given decontamination operation.

The best results will frequently be obtained by application of the so-called island concept. Central locations containing shelters, supplies, equipment, and other essential facilities are chosen as "islands" for decontamination. Such islands start as small staging areas for decontamination crews and expand outward to include the required area. An outer buffer zone, decontaminated but not yet usable, will also be required. Island areas can be linked to each other, and to isolated key facilities that have been decontaminated, by access routes; i.e., decontaminated streets with decontaminated buffer strips along their sides wide enough to make the routes usable. The possibility of using this island concept effectively depends in great measure on the wisdom of the preattack planning in properly locating facilities and supplies and in designating potential island areas. Thus it is desirable that equipment to be used for decontamination be protected from fallout and other hazards and that it be stored where it will be readily accessible to those who will operate it.

Two detailed studies of decontamination as applied to urban areas have been carried out for the Office of Civil Defense. One[3] dealt with the city of Paterson, New Jersey, and the other[4] considered selected locations in New York City. Although not directly applicable to other locations, the ideas and methods utilized will be of value elsewhere. It should be realized that great local variations in the levels and distribution of contamination will occur. Hence, preattack plans must be somewhat flexible and actual decontamination must be based on postattack measurements of radiation levels and adjusted to take advantage of the existing situation.

Decontamination of Suburban and Rural Areas

Decontamination activities organized on a community or group scale, while still useful, will have somewhat more limited application to suburban and rural areas as compared with the central urban areas just discussed. The buildings are smaller, lower, and of lighter construction so that they provide relatively little shielding to each other. Decontamination of roofs is still important but to achieve useful reductions in dose rate, the areas surrounding the buildings must be decontaminated, and these will often contain lawns, fields, bushes, and trees that are much more difficult to decontaminate than pavements.

Radiation levels in homes and apartment houses will originate from fallout on the roof, on the nearby ground outside, sticking to walls, or collecting on projecting surfaces, such as window ledges. Thus efforts should be concentrated on these areas. As in the city proper, large parking areas (such as those associated with shopping centers or theaters) or wide roads will be paved and, hence, easier to decontaminate. A number of large buildings will become habitable much sooner than the average small home and the decontamination plan may well be adjusted to facilitate transfer of people from shelters to such buildings.

Over 80 percent of the fallout on the roofs can be removed by either sweeping with a corn broom, or any stiff broom, or by flushing with a garden hose. This would reduce the radiation levels in the basements quite significantly by eliminating most of the radiation coming from the roof which would pass through the house. It would have much less effect above grade because much of the radiation there comes from the fallout on the ground around the house. The above grade situation can be further improved by a factor of about 4 if a 30-foot buffer zone around the building is decontaminated. This can be accomplished by sweeping or flushing paved areas and by digging up the grass areas and carting the material away. Even turning over the ground should be helpful.

The island concept discussed in the previous section can be applied as a community effort in suburban business areas, small towns, or selected facilities needed for various reasons. Decontamination of some streets may also be carried out by heavy public-owned equipment but clean-up activities for individual homes or farm buildings, for the most part, will be the responsibility of the occupants. Flushing, hand sweeping, and hand spading will be the major methods in such cases, although farmers will often have motorized equipment that can be put to good use. One procedure, potentially useful in rural areas, is to push the radioactive material into a ditch. This results in high radiation levels only above the material since the sides of the ditch provide lateral shielding.

Preattack Planning

There has been frequent reference in the preceding paragraphs to the importance of advance planning of various aspects of decontamination to be carried out when conditions make it possible for people to come out of shelters for limited periods of time. Since food supplies in shelters are limited and living conditions poor, it is important to get the occupants out of them and to get outside facilities operating as soon as possible.

One of the important decisions that must be made is when it will be advantageous to start decontamination. This decision depends on numerous factors including the following:

1. The outside radiation levels and their rate of decay.
2. The protection afforded by the shelter involved and the exposures accumulated while in the shelter.
3. The total exposure considered to be acceptable in a limited recovery period of time, such as two years.
4. The length of time during which people can reasonably be kept in shelters.
5. The number and nature of the areas that must be decontaminated.
6. The achievable decontamination factors and the individual exposures to achieve them using available equipment and methods.

Exposures of people involved in decontamination work consist of three components: that received in shelters, that received carrying out decontamination, and that accumulated during the rest of the recovery period. For a given total and local situation, an optimum plan and time should be worked out in advance because of the many technical and logistic factors involved, this advance planning should be done by specially trained civil defense personnel and should be coordinated with other aspects of civil defense planning.

If the operations described in previous sections are to be effective, extensive education, planning, and preparation must be undertaken during the preattack period. As with all civil defense activities, education of the general public is a basic requirement. First, to foster a spirit in which decontamination is recognized as an effective protective agent, and second to provide simple instructions which the individual can employ with maximum benefit.

Extensive training of decontamination specialists, for both the technical and operational aspects, should be accelerated. The technical specialist must be trained in the evaluation of methods (effectiveness, man-hours required, resources required), in the evaluation of radiation contributions (shielding, distance, fraction from specific areas), and in many aspects of radiological defense (permissible dose, radiation decay, recovery from radiation injury, types of radiation, etc.). The operational crew must have prior training in the methods to be employed. The difficult problem will be in keeping these crews active and ready. It has been recommended, for this reason, that the training of policemen, firemen, and even of army recruits, should acquaint them with the hazards of nuclear war and with the methods of civil defense.

Major aspects of the preplanning are the selection of the areas to be given the highest priority for postattack decontamination and the designation of the specific methods for each location. The decisions should be the responsibility of government officials but should be based, in a large measure, on the advice of decontamination and radiological specialists. Once these decisions are made, plans for locating personnel, equipment, and supplies should be formulated. The personnel to be involved must have excellent fallout protection prior to their work activities so that the major part of their allowable exposure may be utilized in the decontamination missions.

Decontamination of People, Clothing, Food, Water, and Equipment

Since fallout is basically dirt contaminated with radioactive substances, it can be largely removed from the skin by washing with soap and water. Grossly contaminated individuals should, if possible, be decontaminated before entering a shelter in order to protect themselves and the other occupants. The beta radiation given off by fallout is normally of little concern, but if the skin of an individual is contaminated, burns may result unless the material is removed. Not all the radioactivity will be removed by washing but that remaining will not be large enough to be harmful.

Loose contamination on clothing may contribute to the beta burns just referred to and may contribute to harmful internal dose if it gets into the air or into food. Thus grossly contaminated clothing should be cleaned or changed before an individual enters a shelter or its living area. Most of the contamination can be removed by shaking or brushing and this will suffice in most situations. More thorough decontamination may be accomplished by ordinary laundering procedures. Skin and clothing decontamination may also be necessary under some circumstances during the recovery period, especially for decontamination crews.

To be a problem in relation to food, fallout must get into the food actually eaten by people. Thus canned foods, foods in tight containers or wrappings, and foods inside of stores will not be affected. It is only necessary to avoid contaminating the food after opening the package. The same can be said for items that are peeled before eating, such as bananas or apples. Vegetables exposed to fallout in the garden will be grossly contaminated but may still be usable after washing if protected by an outer skin or husk or if penetration of fallout into the edible portions is not excessive. Since food supplies may be limited, conservation of existing sources will be important.

Most water supplies are such that contamination due to fallout should be minor.[5] Thus, water from wells or from closed systems using wells will be clean. Reservoirs will receive fallout, but much of it will settle to the bottom, be diluted by the huge volume of water, or be removed by the filtering and purifying systems. Cistern water may be very contaminated if contaminated rainwater or water from contaminated roofs has been collected. Milk from cattle who have fed on contaminated vegetation may contain large quantities of radioactive iodine for a period of a month or more. Decontamination is practical only with special equipment, but milk can be used for durable products such as powdered milk or cheese since the radioactive iodine decays with a half-life of eight days. Thus, after a month only 7 percent of the initial radioactivity remains.

After a fallout episode, much equipment will be contaminated and will require decontamination before it can be used. Examples would be motorized sweepers, bulldozers, snowplows, automobiles, and railway rolling stock. Initially at least, removal of the loose contamination will be the major necessity, and the methods already discussed, brushing, hosing, vacuuming, scrubbing, etc., will be applicable.

Summary

This very brief and qualitative discussion of decontamination has attempted to show that decontamination is an important adjunct to shelters as a civil defense countermeasure. Under some circumstances it can greatly reduce the length of stay in shelter or the total exposure, or both. Under other circumstances it is of more limited utility but should still be selectively utilized. To a large extent, effective decontamination is merely the application of sound common sense based on a knowledge of the nature and probable distribution of fallout. Advanced planning by knowledgeable individuals has been stressed as an essential ingredient for success. Probably the most important single point that we can make is that decontamination techniques are available and can greatly reduce the effects of fallout, hasten the emergence of individuals from shelters, and expedite the establishment of viable individual and community life.

Notes

1 J. T. Ryan and others, *Radiological Recovery Concepts, Requirements and Structures*, AD 450606 and AD 450598 (Durham, N.C.: Research Triangle Institute, 1964).
2 See "Selected Bibliography," which follows.
3 W. L. Owen and J. D. Sartor, *Radiological Recovery of Land Target Components*, USNRDL–TR–570 (San Francisco: U.S. Naval Radiological Defense Laboratory, 1962).
4 J. T. Ryan and others, note 1.
5 *A Prototype Manual on Civil Defense Aspects of Water Works Operation*, AD 445513, prepared for Office of Civil Defense, U.S. Department of Defense (Arcadia, Calif.: Engineering Science, 1964).

Selected Bibliography

1 J. C. Maloney and others. *Cold Weather Decontamination Study, McCoy, I, II,* and *IV.* NDL–TR–24, –32, and –58. Edgewood Arsenal, Md.: Nuclear Defense Laboratory, U.S. Army Chemical Corps, 1962, 1962, and 1964.

2 Carl F. Miller. *Fallout and Radiological Countermeasures.* Vol. I, AD 410522; Vol. II, AD 410521. Menlo Park, Calif.: Stanford Research Institute, 1963.

3 J. T. Ryan, J. D. Douglas, Jr., and H. E. Campbell. *Radiological Recovery Concepts, Requirements and Structures.* AD 450606 and AD 450598 Durham, N.C.: Research Triangle Institute, 1964.

4 W. L. Owen and J. D. Sartor. *Radiological Recovery of Land Target Components.* USNRDL–TR–750. San Francisco: U.S. Naval Radiological Defense Laboratory, 1962.

5 *A Prototype Manual on Civil Defense Aspects of Water Works Operation.* AD 445513. Prepared for the Office of Civil Defense, U.S. Department of Defense. Arcadia, Calif.: Engineering Science, 1964.

6 J. D. Sartor and others. *Cost and Effectiveness of Decontamination Procedures for Land Targets.* Camp Stoneman Tests. USNRDL–TR–196. San Francisco: U.S. Naval Radiological Defense Laboratory, 1957.

7 Second Camp Stoneman Tests—
W. B. Lane and J. D. Sartor. Vol. I. *The Production Dispersal and Measurement of Synthetic Fallout Material.* USNRDL–TR–334. 1960.
W. L. Owen. Vol. II. *Performance Characteristics of Wet Decontamination Procedures.* USNRDL–TR–335. 1960.
H. Lee, J. D. Sartor, and W. H. Van Horn. Vol. III. *Performance Characteristics of Dry Decontamination Procedures.* USNRDL–TR–336. 1959.
H. Lee. Vol. IV. *Performance Characteristics of Land Reclamation Methods.* USNRDL–TR–337. 1959.

8 J. C. Maloney and J. L. Meredith. *Simple Decontamination of Residential Areas, McCoy III.* NDL–TR–33. Edgewood Arsenal, Md.: Nuclear Defense Laboratory, U.S. Army Chemical Corps, 1962.

9 C. H. Wheeler and M. V. Cammarano. *Civil Defense Manual for Radiological Decontamination of Municipalities.* NP–13126. Caldwell, N.J.: Curtiss-Wright, 1963.

11

Economic Recovery*

JACK HIRSHLEIFER

¶ A nation with large parts of the population just emerging from underground shelters, subsisting on the fruits of past production, is not truly a nation. The hostilities of a nuclear war may be of short duration, but the war is not fully over until the nation is once again a functioning unit. For this, restoration of the economy is a precondition. ¶ The chapter considers the problem of recovery first in the historical setting. It then analyzes the physical conditions for an early resumption of economic production and the measures of preparedness which could enhance it. A similar analysis of the organizational problems follows with special emphasis again on foresighted preparations. The chapter ends with a review of the planning that has been carried out so far by the Office of Civil Defense and the Office of Emergency Planning. Throughout the chapter there is an undertone of the importance of maintaining motivation and morale—the subjects of the last chapter.—E.P.W.

Jack Hirshleifer

Professor of Economics,
University of California at Los Angeles

¶ Jack Hirshleifer received his Ph.D. in economics from Harvard University in 1950. He was employed by the RAND Corporation for a number of years and has taught at the University of Chicago; he is now a professor of economics at UCLA. His professional

---

* This chapter does not represent an official position of any agency of the United States Government.

work has been in the areas of resource economics (in particular, water supply), the economic theory of investment and decision under uncertainty, and managerial economics (with special reference to optimal behavior of decentralized enterprises). He was a member of the Project Harbor study group. He has written widely upon problems of post-attack recovery, including:

"War Damage Insurance," *Review of Economics and Statistics* (1953)

"Compensation for War Damage: An Economic View," *Columbia Law Review* (1955)

"Some Thoughts on the Social Structure After a Bombing Disaster," *World Politics* (1956)

Disaster and Recovery: A Historical Survey, RM–3079–PR (Santa Monica, Calif.: RAND Corp., 1963)

Disaster and Recovery: The Black Death in Western Europe, RM–4700–TAB (Santa Monica, Calif.: RAND Corp., 1966)

I. The Possibility of Economic Survival and Recovery

Our society has not, to this date, seriously attempted to adapt to an overwhelmingly significant change in the environment of human existence—the possibility of nuclear war. The reasons are various. First, we have been, understandably, far more urgently concerned with deterring potential attackers from deliberately initiating such a war, and also with reducing the possibility of its occurrence through accident or misunderstanding. Second, even granting the desirability of a damage-limiting posture, there is a widespread belief that physical protection of population from modern nuclear threats is hopeless. This belief is erroneous, as has been shown in earlier chapters. Finally, many who would concede the possibility of vastly increasing the number of those who will survive the direct physical effects such as blast and radiation, still cannot conceive that a functioning economic system could be reconstituted after such a shock. They picture the hapless survivors as doomed to ultimate starvation, or at best to a meager existence in a world bearing no resemblance to predisaster America. Hence the familiar refrain: "If the bomb comes, I want to be the one who goes first." This belief is, to a degree, self-fulfilling; the less the rational forethought and meaningful effort devoted to the problem, the more difficult and more costly will be the achievement of recovery in terms of otherwise avoidable sacrifices of human lives and values—and the poorer the prospect for ultimate success.

What are the prospects for recovery from nuclear war? There are certainly going to be great human losses due to privation and disease even after the cessation of the direct physical effects of bombing. Equally obviously, the society will be permanently scarred and modified in ways we can hardly imagine. Since history cannot be expunged, certain losses are indeed irrecoverable. But what we ordinarily have in mind by failure to recover would be a situation in which the survivors of the military blows could not reconstitute a viable socioeconomic system. This would be the case if the society degenerated to robber bands living by mutual pillage, or tribal clans grubbing for subsistence. Somewhat less drastically, we can imagine a surviving integrated community, but one unable to reverse an inexorable downward spiral as irreplaceable capital equipment and stocks inherited from predisaster times are gradually used up.

To get an overall view of the likelihood of this sort of development, we should first turn to history.[1] While no nation ever experienced a disaster quite like a large-scale nuclear war, the record of human existence includes some fearsomely destructive events. Historical disasters may be divided into two categories, according to whether they are of localized or generalized extent. A *localized* disaster is usually associated with a specific incident: earthquake, tornado, air-raid, siege, etc. Though geographically limited it may be exceptionally violent, as in the case of the destruction of the 30,000 inhabitants of St. Pierre in the 1902 eruption of Mt. Pelee on Martinique. (The lone survivor of that catastrophe happened to have an excellent shelter—he was in a solitary-confinement cell of the local prison.) The most severe of the more recent localized disasters have been air-raids, especially the nuclear attacks on Hiroshima and Nagasaki and the incendiary bombardments of Hamburg, Dresden, and Tokyo. *Generalized* disasters—catastrophes encompassing whole societies—are exemplified by destructive wars, famines, revolutions, and pestilences. In the past these have ordinarily taken months or years of time to develop their full effects. Nuclear war would probably combine the suddenness usually characteristic of localized disasters with the enormous scale attained in the great generalized catastrophes. So each of the two historical types of calamity is of some relevance.

Economic recovery from localized bombing attacks in general has been quite remarkable.[2] In Hiroshima, for example, power was generally restored to surviving areas on the day after the attack, and through railroad service recommenced on the following day.[3] By mid-1949 population was back to the preattack level, and 70 percent of the destroyed buildings had been reconstructed.[4] In general, populations of damaged areas have been highly motivated to stay on,[5] even in the presence of severe deprivation; once having fled, they have been anxious to return. The thesis has even been put forward that a community hit by disaster rebounds so as to attain higher levels of achievement than would otherwise have been possible.[6] While this cannot be proved from the historical record, there is clearly a strong tendency to return to previous levels and growth trends.[7] The evidence suggests that disaster in some way liberates springs of energy and unselfish activity not ordinarily called upon in periods of normalcy.

The historical record is not so clear for the larger-scale, slower-developing generalized catastrophes. Cases in recent history are few, and so particularized by special circumstances that it is difficult to draw firm conclusions. Over the broad sweep of history, however, the experience has been on the whole again surprisingly favorable. In the midnineteenth century John Stuart Mill commented on:

. . . what has so often excited wonder, the great rapidity with which countries recover from a state of devastation; the disappearance, in a short time, of all traces of the mischiefs caused by earthquakes, floods, hurricanes, and the ravages of war. An enemy lays waste a country by fire and sword, and destroys or carries away nearly all the moveable wealth existing in it: all the inhabitants are ruined, and yet in a few years after, everything is much as it was before.[8]

And in the twentieth century the industrial recoveries of Germany and Japan since World War II have continued to excite wonder, as has the impressive progress of Russia despite revolution and exceptionally destructive wars.

However, there are a number of seemingly less favorable recovery experiences. Among those sometimes mentioned are the alleged depression in western Europe following the Black Death of 1348– 50, and the century-long population decline of Ireland after the potato blight and famine of the 1840's.[9] Actually, in the decade after the Black Death, there was quite a rapid recovery from the original disaster.[10] What might be argued is that the rate of economic progress of western Europe in the following century was perhaps slower than might have been expected, though that is difficult to establish.[11] In any case, the major impediments to growth in that period appear to have been the losses associated with continuing onslaughts of plague and repeated destructive wars—rather than failure to recover from the original blow.[12] As for Ireland, a crucial point not to be overlooked is that the abolition of the English corn laws in 1846 permanently impaired the economic viability of Ireland's major export industry. And the potato blight, like the plague 500 years earlier, did not strike only a single blow but rather remained as a recurring source of economic loss.

A further remark of John Stuart Mill is of interest here:

The possibility of a rapid repair of their disasters, mainly depends on whether the country has been depopulated. If its effective population have not been extirpated at the time, and are not starved afterwards, then, with the same skill and knowledge which they had before, with their land and its permanent improvements undestroyed, and the more durable buildings probably unimpaired, or only partially damaged, they have nearly all the requisites for their former amount of production.[13]

Mill's remark, about the significance for recovery of the degree of depopulation, is consistent with the observation that destroyed cities recover only slowly, if at all, when the destruction takes the form of near-total depopulation (Carthage, Pompeii, St. Pierre, Jerusalem after the exile to Babylon, and again after the Jewish-Roman Wars are among the possible examples). It is also consistent with the viewpoint that a nation's wealth, and more particularly the source of its recovery capability, lie more importantly in its human rather than its material resources. Human knowledge, skill, energy, and industry count more than bricks, mortar, and machines—as the postwar recoveries of Germany and Japan, despite the ravaged state of their cities and industrial plants, proved once again in the twentieth century. In short, we all depend on one another much more than we depend on material objects.

The argument about the overriding importance of population survival does have its limits, as Mill suggests. If the ratio between population and resources gets too far out of line, very serious economic difficulties may be encountered. Population-protection policies against the direct bomb hazards can conceivably be pushed too far, achieving a degree of only-temporary survival not maintainable in terms of resources. Or perhaps the disruption consequent upon the attack may make impossible the utilization of resources that physically survive. These topics are taken up in the following sections which discuss, respectively, resource availabilities in comparison with the needs of the postattack society, and the possibilities for successfully marshalling the resources so as to meet those needs.

II. *Resource Availability Versus Needs*

Any attempt to assess the prospects for maintaining the survivors of nuclear attack, and for reorganizing the available human and material resources so as to achieve a meaningful recovery, is beset by crucial quantitative uncertainties. The first of these concerns the scale and pattern of attack. On the matter of scale, the difference between being attacked by Russia and being attacked by China (or Cuba!) comes immediately to mind. Or, consider the difference between a Russian "all-out" attack and a Russian "limited" attack designed to achieve some political or strategic purpose short of total nuclear holocaust. The pattern of the attack also may be critically important. The thrust could be directed primarily against American offensive military sites (especially missile and bomber bases) as a preemptive move, or alternatively against cities; as an economic catastrophe, the latter would be much more serious. Technical details may be of great importance: ground-burst bombs will spread lethal fallout while air-burst bombs will not, whereas fire hazards will be greater from the latter. And finally the state of our defenses must be considered: active defenses may destroy some incoming bombers and missiles, and passive defenses will further reduce the impact upon people and material property. It is impossible here to devote the space necessary to provide quantitative detail on the implications for survival and recovery of these many possibilities. Instead, the discussion will concentrate on the permanent underlying factors, favorable and unfavorable, and the generalizations about the vulnerability picture that remain applicable under a wide variety of circumstances.[14]

In the immediate aftermath of the attack the society will enter what may be called the emergency phase, defined essentially by the priority of direct life-saving tasks over all ordinary economic activity. This period may vary from days to months in different localities, depending upon the severity of destruction. Civil defense operations, with the assistance of military forces and surviving agencies of government, would be directed toward extricating and transporting survivors from damaged or contaminated areas, feeding and clothing refugees, and maintaining or restarting communications, power, water, sewage, and other vital utility services.

Activities here must meet urgent time-constraints, to make the impaired environment livable again or to move survivors to lesser-damaged areas before the limit of human ability to subsist without such help is reached. A major feature to appreciate is that different parts of the nation will suffer varying intensities and types of damage. Even in some areas of essentially complete property destruction, there will nevertheless still be considerable population survival if blast shelters have been provided. Other areas will have lesser degrees of blast and fire damage or fallout contamination, or combinations thereof; with good shelter, population survival in such less severely hit areas might approach 100 percent. And, finally, extensive regions may remain more or less untouched. During the immediate aftermath of the attack, communications will be disturbed in the damaged areas and transportation largely stopped except for the most critical movements; the survivors will have to subsist mainly on locally available stocks, often under conditions of great privation. After the end of the emergency phase, whether or not that has been efficiently managed, a degree of stability will have been attained. Those who have not perished in the emergency period will have been relocated, if necessary, and arrangements for regular food supplies will have been organized. At this point civil-defense operations in the ordinary sense terminate, and the problem shifts to economic reconstruction.

The reconstruction effort must also meet critical deadlines. The problem here is to reintegrate the surviving pieces of the economic mechanism into a functioning whole so that production in all essential lines can be started up in time to meet urgent needs as they come due. In the case of food, for example, reserves created to support the price of agricultural products and other stockpiles provide a year or more of leeway[15]—but by the end of this time there must be new production, or substitute arrangements through imports. Restoration of utilities to at least a minimal level of functioning will be quite urgent in point of time, while restoration of clothing production can be deferred for a long period. Again, failures here will be reflected in mortalities and intense suffering.[16]

The key industrial determinants of the prospects for successfully negotiating the reconstruction phase, so as to start on a course of meaningful recovery, are (a) the relative balance of supplies and survival requirements after attack and (b) the interactions of industries in the productive process. The first factor on the favorable side is that the peacetime economy has great aggregate resources relative to rigorous needs. About one-half of the current gross national product would suffice to provide the present population with per capita living standards at the prosperous level of 1929. And in the reconstruction period, of course, we will not need to devote effort (in any large degree) to amusement and entertainment, to production of automobiles, to missions into outer space, and perhaps not even to armaments. Furthermore, there are enormous productive reserves in our society that are not ordinarily used: factories could operate more than one shift, labor could work overtime, the unemployed could find work, and marginal workers such as the retired, students, and housewives could enter the labor force. Finally, the unavoidable fact of heavy mortalities will reduce some demands upon the economic mechanism.

On the other hand, the resources of the economy are physically vulnerable and concentrated in cities where they can be efficiently destroyed. Tables 11.1 and 11.2 are illustrative of this concentration. The first table indicates that, for example, the top 200 areas[17] (ranked by population) contain 47.5 percent of population and 58.9 percent of "survival industry";[18] ranking by survival industry in Table 11.2, the top 200 account for 41.2 percent of population and 70.6 percent of survival industry.

A major implication of these comparisons is that the industries necessary for survival could not be destroyed without substantially eliminating much of the population requiring support. The co-located population figures in the tables provide an indication of

Table 11.1. Concentration of Resources: Areas[17] Ranked by Population

Number of Areas	Population (Percent)	Recovery and Military Support Industry (Percent)	Survival Industry	Petroleum Refining	Electric Power	Ports
10	11.9	16.2	15.5	.6	7.2	31.7
20	17.9	26.6	25.1	2.5	10.2	42.4
30	22.0	30.3	30.2	3.3	11.7	51.2
40	25.4	34.8	34.1	8.2	14.0	54.8
50	28.2	39.7	37.4	15.8	16.4	70.7
60	30.6	44.2	40.4	22.2	18.3	74.5
70	32.5	47.4	42.2	25.5	19.5	76.8
80	34.3	49.5	43.6	26.9	20.8	76.8
90	36.0	53.2	46.2	27.8	22.0	77.6
100	37.4	56.4	47.9	30.8	23.4	79.0
120	40.0	58.9	50.0	31.7	24.7	80.8
140	42.2	62.4	52.5	42.4	26.0	81.2
150	43.2	63.5	53.5	45.1	26.9	82.6
160	44.2	65.2	54.5	45.2	27.8	83.4
180	45.9	66.9	56.3	45.5	29.4	85.3
200	47.5	69.7	58.9	47.4	31.2	88.2
250	51.0	73.6	61.5	55.9	33.7	90.7
300	54.0	77.3	64.3	70.5	36.4	93.2
350	56.6	80.1	66.6	72.3	38.9	93.6
400	58.9	82.4	69.2	76.0	41.3	94.5
450	60.9	84.5	70.4	77.5	42.4	94.9
500	62.8	86.1	72.3	77.6	43.7	100.0

Source: Sidney G. Winter, Jr., *Economic Viability After Thermonuclear War: The Limits of Feasible Production,* RM–3436–PR (Santa Monica, Calif.: RAND Corp, 1963), p. 211.

Table 11.2. Concentration of Resources: Areas[17] Ranked by Survival Industry

Number of Areas	Population (Percent)	Recovery and Military Support Industry (Percent)	Survival Industry	Petroleum Refining	Electric Power	Ports
10	10.8	20.5	19.9	1.8	7.1	27.4
20	15.3	27.5	29.2	2.4	9.9	37.5
30	17.7	30.5	35.4	10.7	12.9	49.1
40	19.9	34.8	40.1	14.6	14.7	52.1
50	21.2	36.8	44.0	22.2	16.8	55.8
60	23.3	41.4	47.6	22.8	17.7	56.8
70	25.1	44.5	50.6	25.3	19.7	57.9
80	27.9	46.8	53.2	25.4	20.4	57.9
90	28.8	48.5	55.4	25.4	21.3	57.9
100	30.2	50.8	57.4	25.5	21.7	65.0
150	35.7	57.8	65.4	39.5	26.6	66.0
200	41.1	64.9	70.6	43.0	29.8	73.6
250	44.6	67.4	74.0	47.4	32.9	83.3
300	48.0	70.6	76.7	51.9	34.7	83.6

Source: Sidney G. Winter, Jr., *Economic Viability After Thermonuclear War: The Limits of Feasible Production*, RM–3436–PR (Santa Monica, Calif.: RAND Corp., 1963), p. 209.

the fraction vulnerable to the direct effects of the weapons, while part of the remaining population would be vulnerable to long-range fallout. Of course, a very effective civil defense program, providing high-grade shelter (or evacuation where appropriate) would very substantially enhance population survival relative to industrial capacity. While this will make the ratios under study more adverse, a well-rounded civil defense program would at the same time provide a much better postattack capability for utilizing such resources as remain, and may even incorporate (through underground construction and related measures) protection for essential elements of industrial capacity.

The overall indications, therefore, are that the population-resource ratio would not be shifted beyond the more austere levels of recent historical experience—even without taking account of the enhanced utilization of resources that will be possible. Thus, so far as aggregate capacity is concerned, the ratio of resources-to-population does not seem likely to decline to a level that is really critical.

The vulnerability of the economic system, then, does not lie as much in its geographical concentration as initially appears. Rather, aside from the organizational or functional problem to be discussed later, the key source of vulnerability is *interdependence*. Interdependence derives from the division of labor that makes modern economies so productive, but this specialization means that destruction in one area or industrial sector may have far-ranging impact. Of course, it is possible to exaggerate these collateral effects. Before 1914, for example, it was seriously argued that the growing economic interdependence among nations would make a world war impossible. And during World War II our strategic bombing planners thought at one point that destruction of most of Germany's ball-bearing factories would bring her war machine to a halt. Nevertheless, for the much heavier levels of destruction we are contemplating here, interdependence will certainly entail critical disruptive effects. We cannot have production without transportation, nor transportation without fuel. Nor can we have any of these without the necessary skilled labor—which depends upon provision of food and shelter, relating back once again to the availability of electric power, transportation, etc.

The offsets to interdependence as a source of vulnerability should also be considered: inventories at every stage of the productive process provide buffers in the short run, and rationing can limit supplies to the most essential users. In the longer run, reallocation of effort and substitution—the shifting of resources from one employment to another—will break the bottlenecks. The problem of postattack resource management in the reconstruction phase is to regulate the sequential processes of rebuilding and repair in the light of these considerations, with an appreciation of the relative essentiality of each industrial sector and economic activity.

To give one concrete instance, it seems very likely that electric power will be uniquely significant throughout. Even in the emergency phase, power may be vital to permit continued shelter occupancy where the population is pinned down by fallout contamination.[19] Power is a necessary input to other utility systems, such as water, gas, and sewage (whose continued functioning or restoration is second in order of urgency). Arrangements will have to be made for emergency repairs, load-shifting, replenishment of coal inventories, etc. Power cannot be stored, of course, but the inventories of fuel and repair parts will be crucial. Supplies and skilled labor can be brought in from undamaged areas to accelerate restoration of service, and (as in the recent Alaska disaster) emergency generators can provide substitutes for network power for the most critical uses. With a power network restored, even on a severely rationed basis, attention can be directed to starting up less immediately urgent activities.

III. *Policy, Controls, and Incentives*

The problems of the emergency and reconstruction phases are not merely the mechanical or physical ones. Restoration of a functioning economic system must be achieved through an existent social organization, itself vulnerable in a variety of ways to the effects of bombing.

As mentioned earlier, the historical record does not justify predictions (appearing in the more lurid fictional treatments) of complete breakdown of law and order, with the collapse of all established authorities and norms of behavior. A somewhat less extreme possibility, worthy of some concern, would be a shift away from national loyalties and identifications to regional or local ones. Undamaged areas might refuse to share their resources or accept privations in order to assist the recuperation of damaged areas, to provide for refugees, etc. The vulnerable concentration of the federal bureaucracy in Washington raises the spectre of sheer incapacity of government at the national level. On the other hand, some elements of national authority will survive to reconstitute a legitimate government, and this government will possess what seem to be overwhelming sources of strength as against local separatism. Aside from moral authority, the national government will command a number of vital resources; a near monopoly of information as to the overall military, political, and economic prospects; access to overseas assets and sources of assistance or trade abroad; and, most important, surviving military forces.

We can presume, then, that there will be a national government engaged in some kind of overall regulation of the economic system designed to achieve the goals of postattack survival and reconstruction. Nevertheless, failures or mistakes of policy may lead to important losses in economic performance. For example, the attempt of the early Bolsheviks to run Russia without monetary exchange under the system of "war communism" led to economic catastrophe; ultimately, ideology had to give way to the New Economic Policy in the interests of survival.

In the emergency phase, and particularly in the more heavily damaged areas, the immediate economic task of sustenance— essentially the distribution of existing stocks simply to maintain life and health—will necessarily take priority over the longer-run task of production. For temporary sustenance, the dominant theme will be equity in rationing, in the interests of maximizing survival. In the reconstruction phase, the dominant theme will have to become *efficiency* in the utilization of resources, often at the expense of standards of equity applicable in normal times. For example, to assure that everyone capable of productive labor will be working, all personal income payments associated with property ownership may be blocked or placed under moratorium. Also, limited food supplies may be strictly reserved for productive workers, with some disregard of the disabled or unemployable.

To direct and regulate postattack emergency and reconstruction efforts, responsibilities have been assigned to a considerable number of government agencies. Oversimplifying somewhat in the interests of brevity, responsibility for postattack social functioning is now divided between the Office of Civil Defense (OCD) and the Office of Emergency Planning (OEP); the latter is a small advisory agency attached to the Executive Office of the President. OCD's sphere is primarily in the direct lifesaving aspects of postattack rescue, casualty treatment, decontamination, evacuation, etc. It also includes support of civil government. Thus OCD will have primacy in the more immediate postattack phase time-wise, and in the more damaged regions area-wise. Because of budget deficiencies, progress in ability to manage such large-scale postattack activity has been even slower than in the shelter program; all OCD can actually do now is to advise local government, and grant some token financial support for local planning. So on the one hand we have a need for strong action, on the other hand a failure to provide for it. Unless much more effective preparations are undertaken to support the functioning of civil government, it seems (to this observer) that martial rule in damaged areas will be inevitable.

OEP's main responsibilities are for preattack preparations to enhance the nation's mobilization base, i.e., the capability for producing the war materials needed, and for laying down the principles of postattack management of the surviving economy. Some progress has been made in assuring continuity of government, by legal provision for lines of succession and by physical preparation of dispersed (and, in a few cases, protected) alternative headquarters for government agencies. In the field of postattack economic management, OEP's thinking has been directed toward perfecting and updating the financial, industrial, and consumer controls developed during World War II. The key concepts and developments (at the time of writing) are as follows:

1. The postattack economy is to continue privately owned and operated, subject to governmental control and direction.
2. On the consumer level, there is to be detailed rationing of commodities and a general price freeze.
3. Producing firms will acquire allocations of resources on the basis of claimancy proceedings, in which an appropriate government agency will balance the relative urgency of the various claims against the supplies available. Unlike the practice in World War II, when at various times different agencies controlled such resources as manpower, rubber, steel, etc., the present concept envisages unified and centralized claimancy.
4. Vital information will be provided by the Program Analysis for Resource Management (PARM) System, an interindustry economic model associated with large-scale data-processing facilities. The PARM model is a mathematical simulation of the national economy, so designed as to take account of the interdependence of industries, locations and magnitudes of inventories, time-lags in construction, etc. This model will automatically incorporate damage-assessment information and will provide estimates of the feasibility of proposed recovery plans.
5. During the period when federal control may be incapacitated, the stabilization task (rationing, price controls) and the resource-management task are both to be delegated to local authorities.
6. A currency reserve has been stockpiled for government needs.

Whether this approach is workable in the postattack era seems very much open to doubt. The history of American economic mobilization in World War II has dominated current planning, which is understandable. But relevant historical experience is hardly provided by what happened in the unattacked United States, or even in Germany under continued but non-atomic bombing. A closer analogy may be the situations of Italy, Germany, and Japan in the confusion of war's aftermath. In each of these cases the problem was to put a shattered mechanism together again amidst damage and social disruption. The attempt to export familiar types of U.S. wartime economic controls failed conspicuously in these situations: the production recovery was disappointing for some time, while black or gray markets predominated in economic transactions. It seems evident, restrospectively, that much wiser policy would have dictated control of inflation by limiting the emission of purchasing power without attempting to freeze prices and economic relationships at unrealistic levels. Indeed, the real beginning of postwar recovery of each of these countries was associated with just such a shift of policy.

On the other hand, confusing the attempt to restore production on a private-enterprise basis will be the destruction of assets, titles, records, financial institutions, and corporate headquarters. Private business might be paralyzed, often rendered insolvent, even in undamaged areas. Can we have confidence that currency, not to mention bank checks, will receive acceptance in exchange for real goods? One is tempted to believe that it may be necessary to cut through the difficulties by what might be called disaster socialism, direction of all economic activity by fiat. Indeed, something like this seems unavoidable for damaged areas in the emergency phase; food and shelter will have to be diverted to immediate life-supporting needs regardless of ownership status. Furthermore, the persistence of physical dangers in some areas, particularly the problem of long-term contamination by fallout, seems to dictate the continuance of quasi-military control over some portions of civil life and productive activity. But on the other hand, the experience of Russian "war communism" confirms what we know already—that an army is not an efficient means of organizing production for the long pull.

To risk a prediction, quasi-military rule will prove to be unavoidable for the damaged areas in the emergency phase, and it will be gradually relaxed as physical hazards abate. In the undamaged areas and in private productive activity in general, new forms of government intervention will be found necessary: guaranteeing of private transactions with financial institutions, emergency credit provisions, sweeping moratoriums on various classes of property incomes, perhaps a currency reform, etc. The object here will be to find a way, despite unavoidable inequities, to liberate private productive energies from the dead weight of past claims and contractual arrangements. An ultimate equitable rearrangement and settling of accounts (deferred to the indefinite future) will be promised.

IV. *Implications for Preattack Preparation*

Nothing in the analysis above serves to disprove the contention that, by all accounts, the first priority is to save population. However, a well-rounded civil-defense program must recognize the life-saving implication of meeting emergency postattack needs: rescue and evacuation, feeding of survivors, etc. The first requirement here is organization, which must then be provided with stockpiles of food, clothing, and fuel; emergency communications; and transportation, etc.

To facilitate recovery, hardening of facilities and provision of surplus and buffer stocks of key equipment and inventories are indicated. In any case special attention should be paid to the functioning and rapid repair of the key utility networks: power, gas, water, and sewage. Even a limited budget can do a great deal in this area. There is also a very serious need for research in what may be called emergency technology (see Chapter 12), and in the analysis of economic and social systems under conditions of stress and its aftermath.

From the long point of view a postattack period of privation and impoverishment is definitely to be expected. But the historical record does not justify pessimism on the score of ultimate recovery—unless, indeed, the destruction level contemplated is so great that the concept of recovery is itself hardly meaningful.

Notes

1 A review of historical disaster experiences is provided in J. Hirshleifer, *Disaster and Recovery: A Historical Survey*, RM–3079–PR (Santa Monica, Calif.: RAND Corp., 1963).

2 The most complete analysis of World War II experience is Fred C. Ilké, *The Social Impact of Bomb Destruction* (Univ. of Oklahoma Press, 1958).

3 *The Effects of Atomic Bombs on Hiroshima and Nagasaki* (Washington, D.C.: Strategic Bombing Survey, 1946), p. 8.

4 Research Department, Hiroshima Municipal Office, as cited in *Hiroshima* (Hiroshima Publishing, 1949).

5 This was the situation also after the siege of Budapest, related in Chapter 4.

6 This is the key theme of a great pioneering study based on the aftermath of the 1917 Halifax explosion, Samuel H. Prince, *Catastrophe and Social Change* (New York: Columbia University—Longmans, Green, 1920). Compare the cynical remark about the recent Alaskan disaster: "The earthquake was the best thing that ever happened to Anchorage," and see also Charles E. Fritz, "Disaster," *International Encyclopedia of the Social Sciences* (1968).

7 Ilké, pp. 211–24.

8 J. S. Mill, *Principles of Political Economy* (Ashley's New Edition; London: Longmans, Green, 1929), Book I, pp. 74–75.

9 Both of these instances and also the economic decline of Mesopotamia following the Mongol invasions, have been cited by one author as support for a pessimistic evaluation of the prospect for recovery from nuclear war. T. Stonier, *Nuclear Disaster* (Cleveland and New York: Meridian Books, World Publishing, 1964), pp. 152, 159–65.

10 J. Saltmarsh, "Plague and Economic Decline in England in the Later Middle Ages," *Cambridge Historical Journal*, v. 7, 1941, p. 25.

11 Aggregate production declined with the sharp drop in population, but on a per-capita basis the period may have been a prosperous one. Some historians have called it a "golden age" for the common man, because of the high level of wages prevailing in an era of labor scarcity. See W. H. Beveridge, "The Yield and Price of Corn in the Middle Ages," *The Economic Journal*, Economic History Series No. 2, May 1927, pp. 164–65.

12 Saltmarsh, pp. 27–29.

13 Mill, Book I, p. 75.

14 For a quantitative perspective, see Sidney G. Winter, Jr., *Economic Viability After Thermonuclear War*, RM–3436–PR (Santa Monica: RAND Corp., 1963).

15 Calculating in terms of 1960 data, Winter concluded that the inventories were adequate for at least two years (ibid., p. 117). With somewhat lower recent stocks, and somewhat larger population, an eighteen-month reserve is still a conservative estimate.

16 For a graphic description of city life with utilities suspended and food-supply disrupted, see L. Gouré, *The Siege of Leningrad, 1941–43* (Stanford Univ. Press, 1962).

17 Areas are 20-kilometer (12.5 miles) squares (corresponding roughly to the heavy-damage zone of a 10-MT weapon), on a grid overlying the continental United States. For fuller details, see Winter, Appendix C. The figures understate vulnerability somewhat, since an attacker could tailor his weapons to the targets more effectively. Thus, 60.5 percent of the population was contained in 212 standard metropolitan statistical areas, of which percentage just over half were in "central cities."

18 *Survival Industry* refers to a selection of Standard Industrial Classification (SIC) industries judged to be most essential for postattack survival.

19 The tunnel-grid shelter system described in Chapter 9 provides independent power supplies for tunnel-section modules.

12 Recovery of Basic Industries

IRA C. BECHTOLD

¶ Whereas the preceding chapter was concerned, mainly, with the general principles of economic recovery, the present one considers the reactivation of agriculture and of the most basic industries in some detail. It points to the role which stockpiles of food, of certain materials, and of information can play in making the resumption of production faster and easier. In addition to the problems of agriculture, it discusses central power production and distribution, transportation, the basic process industries, as well as petroleum and natural gas industries specifically. It contains many suggestions for measures which could be undertaken now. The chapter ends with an emphasis on the importance of the subject of the last chapter: the maintaining of order, morale, motivation, and the confidence of the citizen in his country's leadership.—E.P.W.

Ira C. Bechtold
Independent Consultant

¶ Mr. Bechtold was born in Pasadena, California, in 1909 and educated in the same state, at the San Bernardino Valley Junior College, at UCLA, and at the California Institute of Technology. He received his B.S. in Chemistry at the last named institution in 1930. He is registered as a professional chemical and metallurgical engineer in California and is a member of seven engineering societies as well as of the Military Affiliate Radio System (MARS), being state director of Southern California. Also he is certified by the Department of Defense

261

as a fallout shelter analyst. ¶ Mr. Bechtold's principal professional interest is in chemical engineering in general, in process design and automation in particular. He has extensive experience in the problems of the
economical aspects of the geology of raw materials and has been associated with the management of development, design, engineering, and
construction organizations serving numerous industries. He has operating experience in some basic industries and served also as executive secretary and as patent officer of his alma mater. ¶ Mr. Bechtold's principal
hobby as a radio amateur has been applied to the problems of MARS
and his activities in this regard have been recognized by the Department
of Defense by the award of the Gold Medal for Distinguished Public
Service. He is the author of numerous technical articles and figures as
inventor in fifteen U.S. and two foreign patents.

No war, no postwar era, has exactly repeated any
previous example. Hence, even serious studies
of the expected situation after a nuclear war are
subject to doubt. We lack sufficient understanding both of the needs
of the population and of the interdependence of the various industries to foresee the postattack situation well enough to formulate
detailed plans for recovery and to judge the effectiveness of these
plans. Nevertheless, there is more reason to trust these studies than
the bland statements one often encounters in the literature. Many
of these statements claim that recovery will be impossible, that the
economy would be permanently destroyed in a nuclear war. The
studies indicate, however, that even though the damage caused
by a nuclear war would exceed the damage caused by the bombing
of Germany in the last war, recovery is possible without starting
from scratch, i.e., without repeating the long development which
led to the present economic and social structure. This is also our
conclusion, and this chapter presents measures which, if taken
ahead of time, would both shorten the recovery period and decrease the suffering during it.

The most likely targets of the enemy in a nuclear war would be military installations. Industrial centers and larger cities would probably be only secondary targets. Whether or not this estimate is correct, certainly large areas, especially those remote from prime targets, will remain free of damage from explosion, fire, or radiation. Thus, preattack plans for economic survival and recovery should be based on the assumption that, although much of our concentrated industrial capacity may be lost, some parts of the country will be available almost immediately for reconstruction. Foresight and long-range planning would contribute toward maintaining and assuring the preservation of resources and add immeasurably to our security and speedy recovery.

Shelters and Shelter Stocking

Preservation of life is our first concern in any preattack planning, and with this in mind, fallout shelter areas have been marked and stocked in many public buildings, particularly in metropolitan areas, and plans for the building of private shelters are available. However, in target areas, only blast shelters can save the vast majority of lives. The Civil Defense Research Project at Oak Ridge National Laboratory has developed a plan consisting of connected underground tunnels with entrances at reasonable intervals, which would be suitable for cities. The mobility possible in such an interconnected system not only would enable families to reunite but would make available through the shelter system such key personnel as repairmen, police, and especially doctors. It would also eliminate the need for duplication of stocking of drugs, repair parts, radiation meters, tools, etc.

The shelters should, of course, be stocked with food and water. These should be replaced as often as necessary and should be of sufficient quantity to last for four weeks. Also included should be a roster of the skills of the men and women likely to be present during the emergency.

Outside target areas fallout shelters will offer sufficient protection. They should be similarly stocked but possibly only with a two weeks' supply because after such an interval the fallout radiation will have decreased sufficiently to enable the shelter occupants to leave the shelter. In most areas it should be safe to leave shelters for short periods after a few days to get emergency supplies, to move to another shelter, or for similar purposes. In fact, it will be safe for the shelter population everywhere to be exposed for a few hours to the radiation outside long before it is safe to live continuously exposed to this same radiation.

The questions of survival and shelters have been discussed in more detail in earlier parts of this book, and the preceding remarks are intended mainly to place the rest of this chapter into context.

Economic Preparations

Basic Industries

Before discussing the essential need for supplying food and other fundamental requirements for the maintenance of health and a reasonable degree of well-being, it is important to point out that certain basic industries must be protected and reestablished as soon as possible. These are the industries without which none of the others can operate and which supply certain basic materials to the rest of our modern industrial complex.

One of these is limestone, which is essential to the production of iron and steel, even in the newest processes which are now in the developmental stage.[1] It is the major ingredient of cement which will be needed in large amounts during reconstruction; it provides a fundamental alkaline reagent (lime) for many chemical industries including water treating.

Another is the one which produces sulfur for manufacturing numerous sulfur compounds, the most important of which is sulfuric acid required in many industries including steel, fertilizer, and numerous others. Elemental sulfur is also essential for insecticides and for curing rubber.

The energy supplying industries, such as petroleum, coal, gas,

and their companion industries including power, must be rehabilitated and expanded as rapidly as possible to supply the required
energy for all industry and the general requirements of the
population.

Salt is a required product, not only in the industrial world, but
also for human consumption because it is an essential part of the
food supply.

The nitrogen fixation industries, especially that which produces
ammonia, is basic to numerous others. It may be the primary emergency source of explosives.

Some experts would include as essential such industries as steel
(which themselves rely upon the basic industries) because of their
importance in supplying construction materials. In this sense the
lumber industry is also basic.

All mining activities, except those associated with gems and
luxuries, are an essential part of the industrial complex and must
be maintained in operation as completely as possible and even expanded. Thus, vast amounts of ores of copper, aluminum, nickel,
manganese, and other metals besides iron will be needed in the
reconstruction program.

Of course, the most basic of all are those industries related to
the maintenance of life and the continuance of human activity. First
among these is food.

Stockpiling of Food

If properly stocked, the shelters would provide the sustenance
of those therein for a period of about four weeks. In rural areas,
where the shelters may contain less food, the damage would be
smaller and food left in the houses, growing in the fields or gardens,
and the animals which could be saved, would provide for an even
longer period. However, this type of supply would be exhausted
after a period of a couple of months at most. It would be important
to provide supplies for a much longer period so that the reconstruction of the economy would not be impeded by constant worry about

tomorrow's bread. Unfortunately, large quantities of surplus grain —at one time a two-year supply—held by the U.S. Government, have greatly decreased, primarily because of distribution to foreign countries in our AID program. Such a reserve, if reestablished as a supply for the postattack food industry, would reduce the time during which only storable food would be available. The present supplies include processed food in wholesale warehouses, which are well distributed throughout the country, and, more important but concentrated in the Midwest, large supplies of grain in the elevators of large processors and farmers' cooperatives, which can be quickly prepared for consumption.

A great deal could be done to protect cattle on farms from radiation by plowing the ground around stables and erecting small earthen dikes around them after the arrival of fallout. No detailed studies of this have been undertaken and the knowledge of our farmers and cattle ranchers concerning radiation is inadequate, to say the least. It is likely that a great number of cattle would have to be slaughtered to prevent their dying as a result of fallout radiation and their meat would have to be consumed in a relatively short period, since cold storage would probably be unavailable for some time. Thus, it is conceivable that a surplus of food might obtain for a while, even if the loss of human life remained at a low level. During the early postattack period the problem of feeding people may be for several months one of transportation rather than supply. This applies also to grains and cereal foods which, if they are mostly in private hands—as they now are—would be difficult to distribute evenly over the country. Since any damaged food stores would have to be replenished promptly, high priority for fuel and energy should be assigned to food-processing plants, to the agricultural community supplying them, and to the necessary transportation.

It would also be desirable to explore the widespread use of "multipurpose" food.[2] This could be produced from vegetable sources, if animal sources of protein such as meat and eggs were not available. Animal protein foods require refrigeration and sometimes sterilization (e.g., milk, for preservation and safety), the provision of which would be an additional strain on industry, and they might not be available in some areas for long periods of time. A balanced protein-carbohydrate food could be produced from the high-lysine corn developed at Purdue University. If the production of this corn meets with success—and the chances are good—this type of corn alone could supply the protein and caloric requirements of our diet.[3] Borsook, on the other hand, has suggested that the universal food could be obtained by combining cereal grains with soybeans, which are at present used largely as animal feed.[4] He has pointed out that both the animal feed plants and cottonseed oil-processing plants could be quickly converted to processing soybeans for human consumption.[5]

In order to establish an industry producing these basic foods and to keep it in steady operation, it could be made standard policy to stock shelters, at least partially, with some multipurpose food. The shelf life of this food is about a year so that it should be disposed of after such a period. It could be consumed then either in this country or be shipped as a part of the AID or other food distribution programs to needy nations.

The basic food must be supplemented with minerals and vitamins, usually supplied from milk, meat, and fresh vegetables. For palatability flavoring is very imporant. Because of their small volume, neither flavoring nor minerals would cause a problem.[6]

Almost more important than food is water. Fallout will deposit on all uncovered water supplies, but studies have shown that the fallout particles sink to the bottom in a relatively short time, leaving the water supply itself free of contamination. This finding is of great importance and should be once more carefully scrutinized.

It seems, therefore, that even during severe emergencies food and water adequate to a healthful, though simple, diet could be supplied until agriculture could again take over. Time necessary for this would probably be controlled to a greater extent by the availability of equipment and fuels for transportation to farmers than the subsidence of radiation. The latter should not impede farm work for more than two or three months.

The two most important measures which could render the transitional period less difficult would be a more even distribution of grain and other storable supplies over the country, together with their safe storage, and a better knowledge on the part of each county agricultural board member, at least, of the problems posed for agriculture by radiation, the magnitude of safe doses, their measurement, etc.

Stockpiles of Raw Materials

The Office of Emergency Planning has recently published a revised list of the size of the stockpiles of raw materials needed for our industrial plants after an all-out nuclear attack. This is based on their conclusion that 130 million people will survive such an attack—with the construction of a blast shelter system, it is hoped this figure will be higher—and that considerable industrial capacity will remain intact. They conclude that the present stockpiles of seventy-seven basic materials, planned for a conventional non-nuclear war, are more than adequate for a nuclear conflict. The list includes mostly metals, but also such commodities as quinine and rubber. Thus insofar as the supply of raw materials is concerned, industrial plants could resume operation soon after an attack.

Storing adequate commodities does little good, however, if they are not easily and quickly available, especially since our transportation system is sensitive to any abnormality and is easily disrupted. Dispersal of warehouses, if possible to locations near the plants, would be a first step in this direction. Some products such as lubricants can be standardized under existing specifications, thus reducing the variety to be stored and increasing their availability. Lastly, substitutes which do not deteriorate with time can sometimes replace those products which do age. Thus, time-consuming rotation and replacement can be eliminated and the usability of the stored commodities can be assured.

Stockpiling of Information

Files, records, and libraries, if suitably "stockpiled," would also greatly contribute to the speed of recovery. In this case, "stockpiling" means storage of these papers in the plant with duplicates placed in a remote, safe, yet available, location other than the plant itself. Included would be plant design data (including drawings), specifications, basic design calculations, maintenance manuals for apparatus, typical operating logs, activation manuals for new plants and for existing plants after shutdowns, and records of fiscal matters and management operations. The records should be kept in clear, simple language and in such detail that they can be used by inexperienced personnel, who would be able to start up plants which have been shut down or cut off from their former management.

Several storage centers for records have already been developed in worked-out limestone and salt mines and similar places. One example is in the Inland Maximum Security Depository near Kansas City; it has vast underground storage facilities with cold storage also available, and there is adequate transportation, including full-scale trains.[7] Similar installations have been proposed for underground laboratories and other important plants.[8] Here again, industry might be induced to do the investing, eliminating the need for federal funds and massive public programs with their attendant cost.

Oskar Morgenstern has proposed the "stockpiling" of brains of older people who are experts in some field of industry.[9] After retirement, these men might be induced to live in areas least likely to be targets and to serve as custodians of the stored records in their special fields. Since their experience would include the more primitive grass-roots stages of plant operation, they could provide a great deal of help in starting and operating industrial plants by the simpler manual procedures, if more modern mechanized and automated systems were inoperable. This group should include specialists of all kinds: scientists, engineers, foremen, technicians, accountants, to name a few.

Since the supply of older men is limited, it is very important to train more young engineers in emergency plant design and operating skills and to develop a reserve of similarly trained technicians.

Decomplexing of Technology

Preattack planning should include preparations for rendering our technology less complex during an emergency.[10] The technological efficiency which has brought success to our industrial plants implies the use of so much specialized equipment that it may impede their operation in a postattack era, even if they themselves suffer no bomb damage. Even our farms are so highly mechanized that inability to procure a spare part for a tractor, or a scarcity of diesel fuel, can delay or perhaps prevent the harvesting of a crop. The plans under consideration for postattack implementation include suggestions for simplification of the physical plant, decentralization so that individual plants can operate independently, use or manufacture of substitutes, and even changes in operation.

Particularly vulnerable are those industries, such as automobile manufacture, in which the different parts are made in plants distant from one another. If a distant plant is damaged or transportation between plants interrupted, the whole complex becomes inoperable. Fortunately, many of the products, the manufacture of which might be most imperiled, are luxury items. Some, however, such as trucks, tractors, and road-building equipment will be sorely needed. In order to keep old vehicles running, stockpiling of spare parts and training of operators to perform emergency repairs should be a part of preattack planning.

Immediately following an attack the supply of power may be limited, and modern plants are much more sensitive to this than older ones. Thus, a modern cement plant must function as a whole; if any major unit operation is damaged, the whole plant must shut down. The production equipment of cement plants is massive, and the newest plants use motors of about 1,000 horsepower, or more. They are provided with special switching equipment and starting apparatus which are critically matched to the entire power system of the plant. Unless these large motors, which operate such things as mills and kilns, can be run, the plant is totally inoperative. Since cement is a necessity for repairing bomb damage, alternate methods of operating these plants more flexibly should be planned.

In earlier days some industrial plants, e.g., cement factories, employed waste-heat boilers which converted heat to steam for driving generators, and the power from these generators, in turn, ran some or most of the plant equipment. The plants used some outside power, but they could operate under adverse conditions with only the in-plant power generated by the waste-heat recovery process. In the interest of national security, a serious study of power generation by waste heat should be encouraged, and this may reveal its potential for incorporation into modern designs.

Simpler methods of manufacture can often be employed to produce substitutes only slightly less satisfactory than those now in use. One example is the manufacture of explosives, at present a highly specialized product of chemical plants often located in target areas. To replace these explosives, ammonium nitrate can be used if it is properly placed and activated by some hydrocarbon, such as diesel oil.[11] Ammonium nitrate is readily produced in any ammonia plant which is integrated with a nitric acid plant. Many fertilizer plants located in remote areas produce ammonium nitrate for agricultural use.

The foregoing examples illustrate but a few of the many possibilities for simplifying industrial facilities to enable industry to operate under conditions of severe damage, lack of transportation, and absence of skilled personnel. Success would then depend on the inventiveness and ingenuity of those in charge during the post-attack period as well as on the extent to which stockpiled materials, brains, and records are available.

An important condition for the validity of the preceding assessments, which are more optimistic than one commonly hears, is that the hostilities terminate completely and reliably after a not-too-long period. Such termination would not only create the necessary physical conditions for implementing the recovery measures, it would also improve the morale of the people and provide the incentive for working hard on the economic restoration of the country. The examples of Germany and Japan show that human industry and inventiveness can accomplish near miracles under such conditions. Establishment of a reliable peace after a nuclear conflict is not a problem of civil defense but one for military and political authorities; however, it is essential that the authorities fully realize the significance of the reliable termination of hostilities for the immediate, and also for the more distant, future of the country.

The Power Industry

Power is the common necessity of all industries. Even though some plants could be operated with power produced on site, restoration of central power remains a prime condition of significant industrial recovery. It requires not only the operation of the generating plants but also the functioning of an intricate distribution system. In 1964, of the 1.1×10^{12} kw hours power consumption of the United States, 54 percent was derived from coal, 28 percent from oil and gas, and 18 percent from water power; of these three, hydroelectric power may be the most reliable in a postattack era, and therefore it may play a disproportionately important role. The plants are located mostly in presumably safe areas, the supply requirements are minor, and except in the case of a direct hit, the hydroelectric plants can continue to operate. Fortunately, three independent studies[12] have concluded that the present capacity of our electric power systems will be adequate to meet, temporarily, the immediate needs. In addition, the recent upsurge in nuclear power plant construction could also help relieve the postattack power shortage; these plants are practically independent of fuel transportation.

Many power plants serving our large cities are located in the neighborhood of these cities and use coal, although coal is being replaced increasingly by oil. The deposits of these fuels are for the most part safely underground, well protected against atomic blasts, but far from the plants. Oil and natural gas can be transported by pipelines, but coal travels by truck or rail, both of which are themselves dependent on diesel fuel to a large extent. Thus, a large stockpile of diesel fuel, or conversion of engines to other fuel, is necessary to keep coal-powered plants supplied.

To eliminate the problem of transporting coal, mine-mouth electric power installations have been suggested as efficient peacetime projects, and they would have the same virtue from the point of view of civil defense as would the hydroelectric plants: the proximity of energy source to plant. On-site production of power also has many advantages in a postattack era, but it requires storage of fuel. The standby generators sometimes use natural gas,[13] but diesel is a more common fuel. For short-term emergency use, as in hospitals or shelters, both have proved their value.[14]

The question has been raised whether it would be possible to incorporate conversion units in the design of power plants so that coal-consuming units could be converted to oil or gas, and vice versa, depending on which fuel were available in an emergency. In small heating units for dwellings this was done in the Second World War when oil was scarcer than coal. The conversion of power-generating plants is more difficult.

The power supply of the United States is furnished by a large number of public utility organizations, both private and governmental. There are crossties between some entities, but this is not universal. From one point of view large, interconnected grids would be a distinct civil defense asset because they would provide many alternatives for power supply to an area of demand. However, our recent blackouts have demonstrated the vulnerability of these gigantic and sensitive systems to minor damage to controls. The northeast power failure of November 1965 and the El Paso failure of December 1965 were caused by the failure of a relay and a fuel-pressure regulator, respectively.[15] Others have followed. The Federal Power Commission has stated the obvious conclusion: "What is required now is an intensive re-examination of the service problem throughout the industry, based upon a realistic appraisal of the susceptibility of the particular supply facilities to interruptions. . . ."[16]

A massive Pacific Northwest–Pacific Southwest Intertie system is now being installed,[17] but its design does not prevent vulnerability. Alternating current (AC) will be generated on the Columbia River, converted to direct current (DC, 2,000 amperes) and transmitted by new high-voltage (800 kilovolts) lines to a conversion station at Los Angeles for use there as AC. The high-voltage DC transmission lines are not intended for intermediate takeoff between conversion stations, and if a conversion station is out of commission the intertie is useless. The vulnerability might be overcome by mobile converters which could be positioned for service at intermediate points along the DC lines. AC lines can be supplied with portable transformers, or substations could be moved along the high voltage line to furnish power of the voltage required at intermediate points.

Russia is reported to be installing a similar DC grid system to cover all of the Soviet Union and expects to complete it in 1971.[18] Several other countries have, or will have, relatively large DC transmission systems[19] for crossing seaways.

The proper functioning of a power supply depends on the regulation of voltage and frequency. Small changes in voltage seldom cause difficulties and, in addition, may be minimized by taking preparatory measures, which could be implemented during the emergency; but frequency control, which is especially important in instrumentation systems, presents a more difficult problem. Frequency control can be achieved only at the power-generating station and involves systems and methods of operation easily disrupted by nuclear attack.[20]

Transportation

The outlook for the maintenance of transportation by truck and rail in a postattack era is more promising. Studies by the Office of Civil Defense have concluded that even a large nuclear attack would leave enough locomotives and rolling stock in unaffected locations between metropolitan centers to transport coal and other vital necessities by rail.[21] Another OCD study concludes that there will be adequate diesel fuel for this in the early postattack period.[22] The same conditions exist for the trucking industry, for which equipment and supplies will similarly be available.[23] Thus, maintaining transportation where rails and roads are intact depends mostly on adequate diesel fuel, widely distributed throughout transportation centers, or quick conversion of engines to other fuels, and prompt rehabilitation of plants which produce all fuels.

Interestingly enough, liquefied petroleum gas (LPG) is emerging as a versatile fuel to replace gasoline or even diesel fuel for transportation purposes, especially in emergencies. Even now, many trucks have been converted to use this fuel, and others can possibly be modified through the addition of ignition systems and suitable carburetors. This suggests the stockpiling of carburetor kits with instructions for such conversions of gasoline or diesel engines. Diesel locomotives can also be designed so that conversion to LPG would not be difficult; tank cars can be used as tenders and only flexible hose connections would be necessary to carry the fuel to the engine. The main advantage of conversion to the use of LPG is that this fuel does not deteriorate with time as does gasoline and diesel oil. Thus it can be stored for long periods in numerous tanks, large and small, throughout the country. The common practice of storing excess supplies of LPG in underground reservoirs, such as exhausted oil fields, may be of great help.[24]

Petroleum Industry

Civil defense preattack planning should extend to most industries, but few of them share the importance of the petroleum industry. The power supply and transportation facilities both depend on an adequate supply of fuel, mostly diesel, and very little else is independent of this. The deposits of oil are underground; many are so deep that they will not be damaged even by a direct hit. The surface installations of the oil fields can be damaged, but on the whole they are not located in likely target areas. In addition, they can be moved from one location to another if necessity demands. These field installations also are among the very few of our industrial plants which could be independent of outside sources of power because they could use the very oil and gas that they produce. On the other hand, most refineries are located in vulnerable metropolitan areas, and use commercial power, and for these reasons reliance in a postattack period will have to be placed to a greater extent on plants in outlying districts or those remotely located along pipelines which connect the fields to the prime target areas.

The remote facilities are, in many cases, natural gasoline plants, which receive the material directly from the oil wells; extract several hydrocarbons such as propane and butane, which are liquefied under pressure; and supply the resulting natural gasoline to the refining centers. The remote facilities described could be converted to the production of diesel fuel in an emergency if plans and equipment are available. They are independent of outside power sources and would probably survive a nuclear attack. It is possible that a damaged or isolated plant might find its automated system out of commission, and plans should include "decomplexing," or preparations for more elementary control.

A possible simplification in the petroleum industry, should its highly complicated refining operations become impossible, is the old-time pot still for the fractionation of crude oils to produce petroleum products. These stills are merely large vessels containing the crude oil, which are directly heated by fires. Sometimes these have primitive fractionating columns, which deliver the distilled products to primitive condensers. Until recently, some refineries kept such stills in operation mainly because they were economical to use. Of course, this type of equipment would supply only a small portion of the normal flow of petroleum products, but it could contribute greatly to the production of essential fuels when other means are not available. This is another example of reversion to less complex plant operations.

The extensive pipeline system which is part of the petroleum industry is a very distinct civil defense asset. The pipes which inherently provide some storage are underground, although on the whole not very deep, but they are interconnected and self-powered, and different commodities can be transported through the pipes in succession: oil, gasoline, diesel, etc.

Lubricants, another product of the petroleum industry, are essential to the operation of transportation systems and industry in general. Most important of these is lubricating oil for engines, but there are many other vital lubricants without which industry cannot operate for long periods. Fortunately, there are large stocks of lubricants in normal commerce. On the other hand, most lubricants are produced by refineries of advanced design and located in key target areas. Design and construction of the plants necessary to reestablish lubricant production of the type now in use would take several months to a year, and much modern equipment in other industries could not operate long on crude substitutes produced by simple plants. Thus, unless lubricant stockpiles are increased, the supply of lubricants would have to be assured in a postattack situation either by duplication of plants, by provision for rapid reconstruction of old plants, or the construction of new ones. The deficiency in lubricants played a large adverse role in wartime Germany.

The conclusion of the report prepared for OCD on the petroleum industry states: "No nationwide shortage of gasoline is anticipated . . . certain states would have a shortage of gasoline."

Natural Gas

Natural gas is one of the most advantageous fuels for both industry and domestic users. It requires very little processing to place it in use, and in emergency conditions can be used as it comes from the wells, except that hydrogen sulfide and carbon dioxide must be removed from some sources.

Many chemical industries are associated with the natural gas industry and are located near large gas supplies. These industries are almost self-sufficient in that they use the products of the gas fields for raw material and that a large part of their energy can be derived from natural gas if they are provided with electric power generators.

Natural gas has a considerable advantage over fuel oils for heating because no trucking system is needed for its distribution. Also, its use would alleviate the shortage of gasoline and of diesel oil, which may be urgently needed for transportation.

The gas industry, like the petroleum industry, has established many interconnected networks of pipelines which cover a large portion of the United States. Where connections have not already been made, it would be relatively simply to establish them because the various lines cross, or at least closely approach one another. The pipelines have an inherent storage feature and are self-powered in the sense that the compressor stations use the gas for developing the pressure (800 psi or more) needed to assure the flow of the gas. They also could provide fuel and perhaps some raw materials for the areas between the wells and the final destination of the gas, usually in metropolitan areas.

Natural gas frequently is stored underground in reservoirs such as old oil or gas fields. Techniques already exist for the storage of large amounts of natural gas under high pressure in well-protected underground facilities. Some of these are deep under metropolitan areas (e.g., Los Angeles) where they could serve as fuel supplies after an attack.

There is an increasing trend—given impetus by the improvement of equipment—toward the use of natural gas as a fuel for on-site power generation in those instances where it is both economical and desirable.[25] Plants so equipped show promise for maintaining operations through the early postattack period because they are independent of the more vulnerable electrical facilities. This method of power generation should be encouraged for civil defense planning.

Other Industries

When basic needs for raw materials, power, fuel, and transportation have been met, the rehabilitation and resumption of operation for other industries can follow. Priorities must be assigned to these, for there is little hope that our present extravagant demands on power, for instance, can soon be satisfied. Most reliance must first be placed on industrial plants in unaffected areas, and many of these are expected to survive a nuclear war undamaged. Unfortunately, many other major problems still need further study and planning, especially sociological problems such as preservation of order, evacuation, and resettling. No amount of stockpiling or economic planning will succeed in rehabilitating our industries if social and organizational problems are neglected. Establishment of order is a prime requisite. The speed of rehabilitation will then depend on the ingenuity, determination and devotion of industrial leaders, and the loyalties of their co-workers.

The primary aim of preattack plans is the introduction of order into chaos, of determining how best to employ the available material and personnel, and of assuring that essential materials have been stockpiled as much as possible and are available. The accompanying effect on the general morale of the population, although a by-product, may make a very great contribution to national recovery. The knowledge that stockpiles and plans exist brings hope and confidence. Men and women will throw themselves into the most pressing jobs with vigor and spirit; tension and depression will be

lessened in bodies that are tired, minds that are busy, and hearts
that have hope.

Notes

1 "Continuous Iron Process Nears Pilot Plant," *Chemical and Engineering News,* Aug. 7, 1967.

2 Henry Borsook, "We Could Feed the World," address given at California Institute of Technology, Pasadena, California; available from Meals for Millions Foundation, 1800 Olympic Blvd., Santa Monica, Calif. 90406.

3 Edwin T. Mertz and Oliver E. Nelson, eds., *Proceedings of the High Lysine Corn Conference,* June 21–22, 1966, at Purdue University, Lafayette, Ind. (Washington, D.C.: Corn Industries Research Foundation, 1966).

4 Henry Borsook, "Plain Talk About Nutrition," *Engineering and Science,* Vol. XXVI, No. 1 (Oct. 1962).

5 Henry Borsook, private communication, California Institute of Technology, Pasadena, Calif., Sept. 8, 1965.

6 Joseph Merry, *Food Flavorings—Composition, Manufacture and Use* (Westport, Conn.: AVI Publishing, 1960).

7 Advertising bulletin 1960–61, Inland Maximum Security Depository, 6400 Inland Drive, Kansas City, Kan., and "A Unique Freezer Warehouse," advertising bulletin, Inland Cold Storage Company, 6500 Inland Drive, Kansas City, Kan.

8 "Building Underground: Factories and Offices in a Cave," *Engineering News-Record,* May 18, 1961, pp. 58–59.

9 Oskar Morgenstern, "Civil Defense: Economic Problems," *Scientist and Citizen,* Feb.–Mar. 1966, pp. 1–5.

10 *The National Plan for Emergency Preparedness* (Washington, D.C.: Office of Emergency Planning, 1964).

11 "Ammonium Nitrate and Its Use as a Blasting Agent," *Coal Age,* November 1958, pp. 104–106.

12 *National Power Survey—Part I: Direct Current Transmission* and *Part II: High Voltage Direct Current Transmission* (Washington, D.C.: Federal Power Commission, 1964); *Vulnerability of Electric Power Systems to Nuclear Weapons* (Washington, D.C.: Defense Electric Power Administration, U.S. Department of Interior, 1964); R. H. Powley and O. H. Fernald, *Critical Industry Repair Analysis:*

Electric Power, OCD–OS–62–257, Final Report to Office of Civil Defense (Wellesley Hills, Mass.: Advance Research, 1962).

13 "No-Fail Power—A New Dimension in Uninterrupted Power," advertising brochure Dynamics Corporation of America, Fermont Division, 141 North Ave., Bridgeport, Connecticut 06606.

14 Roger W. Benedict, "A Hedge Against Darkness: On-Site 'Total Energy' Plants Supplant Purchased Electricity at Some Projects," *Wall Street Journal*, Nov. 11, 1965, p. 24, and "Keeping the Lights from Going Out Again," *Business Week*, Nov. 5, 1966, pp. 136–38.

15 *Northeast Power Failure—November 9 and 10, 1965* (Washington, D.C.: Federal Power Commission, 1965), p. 1; Lee C. White, *El Paso Power Failure December 2, 1965* (a report to United States Senate Committee on Commerce; Washington, D.C.: Federal Power Commission, 1966); and Gordon D. Friedlander, "The Northeast Power Failure—A Blanket of Darkness," *IEEE Spectrum* (Institute of Electrical and Electronic Engineers), Feb. 1966, pp. 54–73.

16 *Northeast Power Failure . . .*, ibid.

17 Everett J. Harrington and Edward F. Weitzel, *H-V D-C Transmission—Background and Present Status* (Portland, Ore.: Division of Engineering, Bonneville Power Administration, 1965); Wayne H. Aspinall, "Electricity in the Pacific Northwest" (88th Cong., 2nd sess., House of Representatives Report No. 1822, 1964); and Lawrence Lessing, "DC Power's Big Comeback," *Fortune*, Sept. 1965, pp. 174–76, 192, 194, 197.

18 Colin Adamson and N. C. Hingorani, "USSR Progress in Power," *Energy International*, June 1965, pp. 20–22.

19 Daniel T. Braymer, ed., "DC Transmission Around the World," *Electrical World*, Aug. 13, 1962, pp. 41–54, and E. M. Hunter, G. D. Breuer, and C. C. Kerskind, "EHV DC Transmission," *Transmission and Distribution*, Sept. 1965.

20 "FPC Releases Report on April 26 Power Disturbance in Four Western States and British Columbia," Press Release No. 14529 (Washington, D.C.: Federal Power Commission, Aug. 4, 1966).

21 Harvey L. Dixon, Dan G. Haney, and Paul S. Jones, *A System Analysis of the Effects of Nuclear Attack on Railroad Transportation in the Continental U.S.*, Project IU–3084 (Menlo Park, Calif.: Stanford Research Institute, 1960).

22 Sanford B. Thayer and Willis W. Shaner, *The Effects of Nuclear Attacks on the Petroleum Industry*, Project IU–3084 (Menlo Park, Calif.: Stanford Research Institute, 1960).

23 Charles D. Bigelow and Harvey L. Dixon, *The Effects of Nuclear Attack on Motor Truck Transportation in the Continental United States,* Project No. 3711–4000 (Menlo Park, Calif.: Stanford Research Institute, 1963).

24 *Major Natural Gas Pipelines as of December 31, 1965* (Washington, D.C.: Federal Power Commission, 1966), Map FPC M–79.

25 Benton F. Massell and Charles Wolf, Jr., Economic Development and Postwar Recuperation, Memo RM 2952–PR (Santa Monica, Calif.: RAND Corp., 1962).

13 Societal Recovery

PETER G. NORDLIE

¶ This last chapter deals with the human, emotional, and organizational problems of recovery. It is written in a confident tone but does emphasize the primitive nature of our knowledge of human behavior under conditions of hardship and our lack of ability to foresee events under conditions as different from present ones as would prevail after a nuclear war. There are some remarks in earlier chapters—Chapters 3, 4, and 11— which supplement the general condsiderations of the present one by examples from the histories of past disasters.—E.P.W.

Peter G. Nordlie

Research Director, Human Sciences Research, Inc.

¶ Dr. Nordlie received his B.A. in psychology from the University of Maryland in 1952 and his M.A. in 1954. He received his Ph.D. in social psychology at the University of Michigan in 1958. In 1956–57 he was a Junior Fellow at the Center for Advanced Studies in the Behavioral Sciences at Palo Alto, California. Before receiving his Ph.D., Dr. Nordlie worked for both the Institute for Research in Human Relations and Psychological Research Associated. He was one of the founders, and is now vice-president and research director of Human Sciences Research, Inc. ¶ Dr. Nordlie has conducted and directed research in a variety of areas including the methodology of systems research, mass transportation, tactical performance measures for infantry groups, training methods for infantry tactics, psychological operations in the Navy, performance criteria for practicing physicians, performance evaluation of survival school training, community leadership in redevelopment, aerial observer training, helicopter and spacecraft cockpit and control design, and teleconferencing research. ¶ His field of special interest is the functioning of social systems under stress and conditions of rapid change. His principal area of research over the past six years has been the study of society in disaster. This research has involved a number of studies of the likely social and psychological effects of nuclear attack and the vulnerabilities and recovery problems of American society.

After a massive nuclear attack on the United States, what would the survivors do? Could the social order be maintained? Would it be possible to preserve the long-held, fundamental values of American society? Would social, political, religious, legal, economic, and familial institutions survive? In what ways might they be changed? Would the size of the surviving population decline, remain constant, or increase? Would it be possible for the production and distribution systems to continue to utilize the technology in use before the attack? These questions are all parts of the general question of society's capability for surviving and recovering from a major nuclear attack.

Can we afford to ignore the question of societal recovery? The fact is that we can hardly avoid answering it, and, much more to the point, it is already being answered and in quite different ways for different people. The legislature and the administration assume some answer to it when they decide that there will be a national civil defense effort. Civil defense policy-makers assume some answer to it when they propose civil defense policies and specific programs. Opponents of civil defense assume some answer to it when they condemn civil defense or some particular program in it. Any of these actions implies assumptions about the effects of the action in the postattack situation. Proponents of civil defense programs must argue that they would make a positive contribution to enhancing the probability of recovery. Opponents must argue that civil defense measures would not enhance the probability of recovery either because they would not work or because destruction would be so complete that preparations for recovery would be futile.[1] In both cases, the validity of the argument rests on the accuracy of the presumed effects in a postattack situation. But also in both cases, given our present state of knowledge, neither assumption rests on very substantial evidence. Nevertheless, since what we do or do not do as a response to the possibility of a nuclear war depends in large measure on what answers we give to the societal recovery question, we cannot avoid considering it.

To discuss recovery of society, we need first to say a word about what we understand a society to be. As used in this chapter, a society is understood to be an organized population that interacts with its environment, extracting from it the energy to maintain and perpetuate itself. Societies are organized in patterned ways and act in patterned ways in accomplishing the basic functions of production, distribution, and consumption. Members of a society are interrelated through kinship, formal and informal organizations, and through their relationships to a polity. Within a society, identifiable patterns of behavior evolve reflecting basic values and ideologies of the members. When we speak of the survival and recovery of a society, we refer not just to people, but to their interrelationships, organizations, institutions, values, and ideology as well. Mere continued survival of a population, therefore, does not necessarily imply recovery of the society.

In this chapter, we will attempt to break down the complex question of societal recovery into the elements upon which predictions of recovery depend, to review some of what is known about these elements, and to delineate the questions which must be answered. Our objective is not to predict recovery but rather to determine what it would mean and on what it would depend.

A Perspective from Which to View Recovery Questions

In considering the questions of societal recovery, there is a need to adopt some consistent frame of reference, or perspective, from which to address the problems involved. We offer the concept of a recovery management system as providing an especially relevant perspective from which to consider societal recovery. By recovery management system, we refer to an organization having the responsibility for directing and managing recovery activities within the society. We want a term which conveys the idea of directing and controlling functions but does not pre-judge the characteristics of the organization responsible for carrying them out—as might be the case if we referred instead to a specific existing agency, such as the Office of Civil Defense or the Office of Emergency Planning.

By adopting the perspective of a recovery management system, attention is immediately focused on the need for specifying its goals or objectives, because what would be required for recovery cannot be determined until the desired recovery state is specified. By first delineating specific objectives of recovery management, we can more meaningfully consider what would have to be true before, during, and after an attack in order that those objectives be achieved. In the remainder of the chapter recovery goals are postulated and requisites for achieving those goals are delineated and discussed.

Recovery Goals

Postulating a set of societal recovery goals is as much a statement of values as it is a statement of "requirements." That there must be survivors is an obvious requirement for recovery, but who they should be and how many is more a matter of what is most highly valued. Within limits, therefore, recovery goals are what we decide we want them to be. The set of recovery goals described below is an attempt to identify characteristics of the society which would have to exist before we would be willing to consider it "recovered." No claim is made that this set is definitive or that it includes all the elements one may ultimately want to include. Hopefully, however, it will illuminate the recovery question and provide a suitable point of departure for its analysis.

1. *Maximum Viability.* By viability, we refer to the balance between the resources required by a population for maintenance and growth and the resources available to satisfy those requirements. Where the available resources are insufficient to satisfy requirements, the population will decline and, in the extreme case, die off completely. Continued survival of the population and the capacity for growth can be achieved only to the extent that available resources meet and *exceed* daily requirements of the population.* Hence, maximum viability is identified as a key goal of a recovery management system.

2. *Maximum Acceptability.* The concept of acceptability is more difficult to define precisely, and ultimately it is definable only in terms of some consensus. While its specific content is debatable, this crucial aspect cannot be ignored in attempting to define recovery goals. Presumably, a society would only risk incurring a nuclear war in order to defend and preserve what it values. Therefore, we need to confront the difficult task of specifying its highly valued characteristics. For present purposes we will assume acceptability to include an acceptable polity, minimum alteration of the preattack social system, and the preservation of basic values, ideology, and institutions. From the standpoint of a recovery management system, a critical goal is to achieve viability by means that are maximally acceptable to the society as a whole.

3. *Continued Use of Preattack Technology.* A society's technology is related not only to its productive capacity, but also to its forms of social organization. For a modern, industrialized society, failure to reinstitute preattack technology, especially with respect to communication, transportation, and production capabilities,

---

* EDITOR's NOTE—This problem was, of course, dealt with in the preceding two chapters.

would result in decreased likelihood of achieving maximum viability on the one hand and preserving valued institutions and forms of social organization on the other. Sometimes the image of a collection of relatively isolated and self-sufficient rural enclaves of population is invoked in discussions of recovery. It is argued here not only that such a situation is unlikely, but that it is not an appropriate goal for the recovery management system. The more appropriate goal is reconstitution of an urban-based, pluralistic, highly interdependent, and productive social system. Recovery efforts should aim, *ultimately,* not toward a return to older technologies, but toward the preservation and reconstitution of modern technology, even if return to a simple technology should prove necessary as an intermediate short-term step.

4. *Preservation of the Maximum Number of Lives.* The goal of preserving lives places a high premium on the provision of protection for the population against the blast, heat, and fallout effects of an attack. Perhaps more important, though less obvious, is the emphasis it places on requirements for keeping the survivors alive *after* the initial effects of the attack have subsided, and on provisions for the continued maintenance and growth of the surviving population. A program of extensive shelter facilities alone would tend to exacerbate the problem to the extent that it results in a greater number of survivors relative to the surviving resources. This fact illuminates the requirement that recovery must be dealt with as an integrated, long-range, comprehensive program or it cannot hope to come to terms with the problems it faces.

5. *Minimum Threat to Legitimate Authority.* A desirable characteristic of the recovered society is a stable polity not threatened by coup or other takeover from either inside or outside the society. Taken together with the acceptability goal, this means a government both acceptable and strong.

6. *Maximum Ability to Cope with Emergent Situations.* While preplanning and contingency planning are obvious prerequisites of successful recovery management, we can be relatively certain that,

no matter how much prior planning is undertaken, in the event itself the situation will differ from the one assumed by the plan, and there will be need for rapid adaptation. There is little to argue against the proposition that the postattack society will be confronted repeatedly by unforeseen situations, and survival will depend on its capability for rapid adaptive response.

If this tentative set of goals can be accepted as descriptive of a desired societal recovery end-state, we can proceed to identify propositions—which must be true if the goals are to be achieved. Such propositions we call recovery requisites.

Recovery Requisites

In Table 13.1 the basic elements of the overall societal recovery question, as formulated here, are arrayed. The essential questions are: Given the initial characteristics of the postattack system, is it possible for the desired characteristics of the system to be achieved at some later time? If so, how likely would it be? How long would it take? What would impede the process? What would facilitate it?

Six recovery requisites will be identified in the following sections; certain significant questions implied by each are raised and discussed.

Population   Requisite: *A surviving population of sufficient size and appropriate composition to permit reproduction and growth.*

The size and composition of the surviving population are important to the recovery question because they will determine, in part, the adequacy of the surviving natural and capital resources, the availability of skills, the immediate and future labor force, the future growth rate, the existence of critical social problems such as a large number of orphans, and the magnitude and nature of recovery management tasks. Perhaps the most crucial aspect of the societal recovery problem is the ratio between the requirements of the surviving population and the surviving natural and capital resources. If the requirements of the surviving population cannot be

Table 13.1. Elements of the Societal Recovery Problem

Requisites For Societal Recovery

	POPULATION	ORGANIZATIONAL CAPABILITIES	RESOURCES
POPULATION	sufficient size and composition to permit reproduction and increase	sufficient to permit concerted coordinated implementation of recovery activities	sufficient to support surviving population during recovery period
INDIVIDUALS	sufficient number of survivors motivated and capable of undertaking required recovery activities	RECOVERY MANAGEMENT CAPABILITIES adequate and appropriate for assessing postattack situation, determining required activities and ensuring their performance	

Societal Recovery Goals

	POPULATION	ORGANIZATIONAL CAPABILITIES	RESOURCES
	maximum viability	continued use of preattack technology	sufficient to support maximum possible population
	preservation of maximum number of lives	minimum alteration of social system	
	preservation of basic values and ideology	preservation of highly valued institutions	
		SYSTEM MANAGEMENT	
		acceptable polity	
		preservation of basic values and ideology	
		minimum threat to legitimate authority	
		maximum ability to cope with emergent situations	

met for a sufficient period of time, a new set of disaster conditions would confront the survivors, resulting in additional deaths until resources balanced requirements.

The initial size and composition of the surviving population would depend upon its preattack size and composition, the characteristics of the attack, and the effectiveness of defensive countermeasures. Great variation has been characteristic of the casualty estimates available in the literature. Estimates anywhere between negligible and total destruction can be found. Among the estimates from systematic and objective casualty estimation techniques, most of the variance is attributable to differences in explicit assumptions. In general, it would appear appropriate to consider the societal recovery problem within a range of casualty possibilities of between 15 and 40 percent of the preattack population. Outside of these limits the recovery question is considerably different from that considered in this chapter.

The effects of an attack on population composition have not yet been the subject of extensive research. Two demographic analyses of postattack population have been published, one by Heer and one by Dentler and Cutright.[2] Heer undertook a pilot study in which he generated estimates of the demographic characteristics of surviving U.S. populations following two different hypothetical attacks under a number of assumed conditions. For the attacks and conditions Heer analyzed (which resulted in 30 and 18 percent casualties respectively), with one exception, he did not find differences between pre- and postattack population composition to be as large as might have been expected. Generally, the pre- to postattack change was less than 4 percent on all variables analyzed, except for marital and family status, which was much higher. Concerning this point, he found that up to 17 percent of surviving husbands and wives would be widowed and as high as 26 percent of all children would lose one or both parents.[3]

Heer summarized some of the implications of the general pattern of his findings as follows:

First, as a result of attack, we can expect some changes in age composition. These may be caused directly by attack, or by changes in age-specific mortality following attack, or by a reduction in the number of births immediately following attack. These changes in age composition will have various consequences, both beneficial and adverse, over a period of time lasting up to 80 years. Second, during the first few years immediately following an all-out attack, we may expect a sharp reduction in the proportion of persons currently married and for a period up to twenty years following attack a sharp increase in the proportion of orphaned children, many of whom will require care in an extra-family setting. Third, there will be a decline in the nation's educational and occupational skill level, caused directly by attack and by the strong possibility that educational facilities could not be restored to the pre-attack level until several years thereafter. This decline in skill level might endure for at least 55 years. Finally, there will be an increase in the proportion of disabled persons, continuing up to 80 years following attack.[4]

Dentler and Cutright present results and conclusions differing markedly from those of Heer. The attacks they analyzed were different, but the differences appear minor in comparison with the difference in results. For example, although they defined religious affiliation in slightly different ways, and the base populations they used were not for the same year, they report substantially different results for the effect of an attack on the religious composition of the surviving population. Whereas Heer finds only minor differences in religious composition, Dentler and Cutright find dramatic changes. This difference underlines the sensitivity of the results of such analyses to differences in assumption and method. Dentler and Cutright, in determining their casualty assessments, assumed that everyone in the seventy target areas would be killed and no one outside of them.[5] Heer, on the other hand, used the fatality data computed by the National Resources Evaluation Center for the two attacks on each of 44,000 areas in the United States.[6] The NREC blast and thermal casualty estimates are computed as a function of distance from ground zero and employ assumptions about shielding. While the factors utilized to generate such estimates may be in error and are subject to modification on the basis of future research, they would appear to be part of a more useful approach than that of Dentler and Cutright, based as it is on such gross generalizations. ("We assume that a thermonuclear war is a war with no holds barred. Thus it is realistic to assume that everyone within each of these 70 areas would be killed by blast, firestorms or radiation."[7])

This comparative example, which can be repeated for a whole set of variables, emphasizes the importance of developing sound methodology for postattack demographic analyses before placing much confidence in the conclusions based on the results available to date.

The specific findings of Heer's pilot study might best be considered heuristic because of the limited number and range of attacks considered, the questionableness of some of the assumptions he found it necessary to use, and the grossness of the units of analysis.[8] He has shown, however, the feasibility of systematic and quantitative projections of the demographic characteristics of postattack populations. A much sharper outline of one significant, and heretofore only vaguely conceived element in the societal recovery problem, therefore, has begun to emerge. In addition, Heer's work clearly illuminates the impossibility of making meaningful projections of societal recovery possibilities without rather precise inputs reflecting population composition. Variations in postattack population composition would clearly affect the ability of society to achieve maximum viability, maintain preattack technology, minimize alteration of the preattack social system, and preserve highly valued institutions.

Resources **Requisite:** *Resources sufficient to support the surviving population during the recovery period.*

Under the general term resources, we include agricultural lands, the raw materials of production, factories, housing, schools, hospitals, and transport and communication equipment. We also include raw and processed materials which may be in long-term or temporary storage, in transit, or so situated that they can be conceived as constituting inventory.

The recovery of society would depend first on the contined survival of its members, which, in turn, first depends on the continued satisfaction of the biological requirements of the individual members. This basic fact offers a point of departure for considering the role of resources in the recovery process. In view of the fact that this subject has been covered in previous chapters, we will point only to the primary issue involved.

The effect of a nationwide attack would be to stop production and distribution processes for some period of time. Consumption of a specifiable minimum amount per capita, however, must continue virtually uninterrupted. Ignoring for the moment that the total inventory would not be equally available to all survivors, two time constraints can be seen to have crucial implications for almost all recovery activities.

1. Distribution must be restarted before available inventory is exhausted.

2. Production must be restarted before total inventory is exhausted.[9]

The failure to restart production and distribution at levels sufficient to satisfy these time constraints would result in further reduction of the population by starvation and would decrease the likelihood of achieving maximum viability.

Individuals Requisite: *A sufficient number of survivors motivated and capable of undertaking required recovery activities.*

If we can assume a postattack situation in which the surviving population and resources meet the minimum conditions required for societal recovery, the problems of the survivors as individuals can then be considered. For recovery to occur, there must be a sufficient number of survivors physically able, motivated, and capable of undertaking required recovery activities. This is simply to say that recovery would depend on the actions of people, and we are interested here in the possibilities of the survivors being physically and mentally capable of performing required actions. The number of physically disabled survivors and the nature of their disabilities are technical matters of damage and casualty assessment. They involve translating the physical effects of an attack into the physical consequences for the people exposed to those effects. Determining the psychological state of survivors, on the other hand, cannot be approached in the same way, simply because we do not know enough to perform the translation.

The question can be approached by examining the behavior of people in past disaster situations and trying to identify the similarities and differences between these situations and the hypothetical postattack situation. The shaky step is extrapolating from behavior in nonnuclear disaster situations to postattack situations. But if this step is taken by explicit specification of the similarities and differences of the situations involved and explicit statement of the evidence and the rules by which any given inference is drawn, we are then in a position to evaluate the probable validity of the inference; our alternative is simply to assume that a nuclear attack would create a unique situation in man's experience to which inferences based on his past experience could not possibly apply. By following the former alternative, debate can center on specific questions of similarities between situations, the validity of the evidence used, and errors in the logic of drawing the inference.[10]

What can be learned from the studies of man's behavior in past disaster situations? There has developed over the past three decades a growing body of literature concerned with behavior of individuals and organizations under conditions of violent disruption of normal situations. The Disaster Research Group of the National Academy of Sciences sponsored a number of studies and assembled the literature on many more studies of behavior in floods, fires, earthquakes, bombings, explosions, etc.[11] The U.S. Strategic Bombing Survey undertook on-site surveys in Germany and Japan at the end of World War II.[12] More recently, a number of studies with the specific aim of reviewing the disaster literature have been done for the purpose of assessing its relevance to the postnuclear attack situation. Nordlie and Popper in 1961 made one of the early attempts to examine the implications of the disaster literature for postattack situations.[13] One research program, under the direction of the writer and sponsored by the Office of Civil Defense for the past five years, has focused on the study of social and psychological effects of nuclear attack and their implications for societal recovery and civil defense.[14] People in conditions of captivity, isolation, and stress have been studied.[15] The literature on social organization under stress has been brought together and reviewed by Barton.[16] Eyewitness and historical studies of major disasters have been published.[17]

A detailed review of all these studies cannot be presented here, but we will attempt to outline the picture of man's response to disaster that begins to emerge from them.

In much of the early public dialogue concerning the behavior of survivors in a postattack situation, two opposing images defined the range of views expressed. One is the Hobbsian "war of all against all,"[18] where social norms collapse and individuals suddenly become brutish, amoral, lawless, savage, and totally selfish, killing each other in competition for scarce resources. The opposing image is curiously devoid of reference to effects on individual motivations, perceptions, and behavior.[19] It merely assumes man is rational, will remain rational after an attack, and will satisfactorily resolve the problems he faces. Neither image appears supported by citable evidence and neither contributes to our understanding of postattack behavioral phenomena. The general picture that can be developed from the studies mentioned above lies between these extremes, is far less clear-cut, and leaves many questions yet unanswered. Still, it leads to quite different implications for recovery management than either of the more definitively stated extremes.

In constructing this picture, the statements we make are necessarily generalizations of what would appear to be true for most of the survivors. That the opposite would be true in specific instances for every generalization we make would undoubtedly be the case. Not only would situations differ across survivors; one would also expect variation among responses of individuals exposed to the same situation. Therefore, one is unable to deny the possibility that some individuals would shoot their neighbors. Some undoubtedly would (it occurs every day now); but it is difficult to construct the situation in which the shooting of neighbors on a grand scale could be reasonably anticipated on the basis of what is known about human behavior. Our generalizations, therefore, must be understood as attempts to characterize what appears to be generally likely to happen and not as statements of what is or is not possible.

There seems to be no evidence to suggest that the effects of an attack on the survivors would deprive them of their abilities to function mentally within normal ranges. There is little evidence that survivors would lack the motivation to continue to survive in the postattack environment. Nor does it appear that the social norms by which people govern their relationships with other people would be suddenly abandoned. Past experience does not support the hypothesis that an attacked population would display widespread mass panic. The available evidence does not suggest that cooperative and adaptive behavior would not be prevalent among survivors.

The evidence from past experiences in disaster situations supports the expectations that survivors would endeavor to adapt to living in their altered environment, that extreme fear is likely to characterize their emotional state over a long period of time, and that their psychological state in the immediate aftermath of the attack would be passive, quiet, docile, and responsive to positive direction. This state is likely to persist until the initial shock of the disaster wears off and objective conditions improve. Only later is a more active state expected, in which hostility toward authorities may appear.

We can expect a survivor's motivation to be dominated by extreme fear and concern for the safety of both himself and his family, from the time he believes an attack is imminent until he understands the attack to be over. As the extreme fear produced by the attack subsides to a lower level, there are likely to appear strong motivations to learn the fate of separated family members and others who are important to him. Continuing fear of new disasters and feelings of general anxiety can be expected, together with grief over known personal losses. Within a short time everyday biological demands will reassert themselves, and will be accompanied by an increasingly strong concern for the continued safety and well-being of his family and others important to him.

Associated with this sequence of motivational states would be certain characteristic behavior patterns. With the acceptance of the likely imminence of an attack, people would tend to act so as to provide protection for themselves and their families. Assuming there are meaningful protective actions for people to take, three factors may inhibit their taking them. First, warning may not be received, or may not be believed if received. Second, appropriate behavior may not be known to the individual. Third, protective action may be delayed in order to locate other family members. The significance of each of these three factors would depend upon the preattack training and experience of the public as well as on the character of the sheltering system.[20]

After the attack is over, survivors would try to seek information about the fate of family members from whom they are separated and information about national and local conditions. This behavior would continue until the information is received. After the immediate effects of the attack have subsided, and biological needs for food and water become prominent again, one can expect most behavior to focus on the problem of supplying these needs for one's self and family. During the shelter period, this behavior would be constrained by what is available within the shelter and how its allocation and distribution are managed. Once the requirement for shelter passes, the availability of food and water would become the principal concern. Unless this appears assured, people will try to accumulate the largest possible stores of food for themselves and their families. The preoccupation with the problem of food could very seriously interfere with activities designed to restore production, and has so interfered in several past emergencies. This reemphasizes the importance of secure and accessible supplies of food for all people.

If we designate as *maintenance* activties those activities which serve the function of meeting basic needs from immediately available resources, we are saying that after initial responses to the attack itself, one can expect survivors to engage primarily in maintenance activities. Maintenance activities consume available resources and do not contribute to bringing about future resupply. To the extent that the surviving population engages in maintenance activities to the exclusion of activities which lead to regeneration of the damaged social system, it is doomed to future starvation. For societal recovery to occur within the time constraints discussed earlier, a considerable proportion of the survivors' activities must be devoted to system regenerative activities to an extent sufficient to establish the resupply capabilities of the total system.

The general problem this picture creates for recovery management is the discrepancy between what people will be inclined to do and what they must do if recovery is to occur. Societal recovery requires that they do not restrict their efforts to maintenance activities only, but engage in necessary regenerative activities. A significant implication for the recovery management system is that means must be found for satisfying maintenance needs while at the same time motivating and directing the efforts of survivors in recovery activities.

How, it is sometimes asked, could survivors possibly adjust to the shock of the event, to the sight of the dead and injured, to the loss of loved ones, to the knowledge of the staggering loss of human life, to the idea of the awesome barbarity man has perpetrated against man, and to the drastically altered conditions of life? How could they possibly attempt to pick up the pieces and go on? By arraying such questions, the answer is often implied that they could not or would not do so. I think, however, that history suggests that they would. Across all of recorded history, people, individually and collectively, have displayed a tenacious grasp on life and continued living. There is little evidence to support the hypothesis that in the event itself survivors would prefer death to continuation of the struggle.

For a society as a whole, the impact of a major nuclear attack is without close parallel in human history. For the individual, however, it is difficult to show the ways that situations and events produced by an attack would create any greater hardship and horror than individuals have frequently faced, endured, and adapted to in the past.

In summary, we can conclude that survivors would be psychologically capable of performing required recovery activities. Whether or the extent to which they would perform them can be seen to depend in large measure on the nature and effectiveness of the education and training experienced before the attack, the particular postattack conditions existing locally, and the means employed to motivate recovery activities. Varying assumptions about any of these factors would result in different estimates of the survivors' ability to achieve recovery goals.

Organizational Capabilities   Requisite: *Sufficient organizational capabilities to permit concerted coordinated implementation of recovery activities.*

The survival of sufficient manpower and resources in itself would not provide recovery capabilities. An appropriate division of labor and the proper organization of available manpower must be added.[21] The need for efficiency in organizational functioning is heightened by the time constraints on restarting production and distribution.

Organizational capabilities include:

1. The capacity to motivate individuals to participate in organizational roles through rewards and sanctions

2. The division of labor and a shared understanding of organizational role relationships

3. A decision-making capability at various loci within the organization

4. The capability for translating decisions into actions

5. A feedback capability whereby decision-makers are kept aware of the progress of implementation

6. The ability to recruit needed new members

7. The ability to adapt to unpredictable events both internal and external to the organization

8. The capability for communicating among all elements of the organization

9. The capacity to move goods and people as organizational tasks require.

Such capabilities are required by any task-performing organization, be it a local well-drilling company or the U.S. Government. And clearly, the effects of a nuclear attack would severely impair such capabilities in a number of ways. In particular, any reduction in communication and transport ability would have pervasive influence in reducing the possibilities of coordinating activities. To the extent that the traditional bases which give meaning to work are undercut, the ability of organizations to motivate members to participate will be impaired. The preattack division of labor will not only be disrupted by the removal of a significant portion of the population through casualties, but it is not likely to be appropriate for postattack work requirements. In short, we can expect significant difficulties in creating sufficient organizational capabilities in the postattack world.

The accomplishment of complex tasks, the coordination of widespread and diverse activities, the mobilization and concentration of effort on critical tasks, the adaptive response of organizations to changing situations, and the implementation of a society-wide recovery plan all emphasize the critical requirement for the existence of organizational capabilities throughout all levels of the society. In considering means to reduce the vulnerability of society to nuclear attack and to enhance the ability of society to recover, it is as important to find ways of ensuring the existence of sufficient organizational capabilities as it is to provide for the protection of people and material resources.

Recovery Management Capabilities **Requisite:** *Recovery management capabilities adequate and appropriate for assessing postattack situations, determining required recovery activities, and ensuring their performance.*

Given sufficient human, organizational, and material resources to accomplish recovery activities, the requirement exists for assessing the postattack situation, determining the appropriate recovery activities and ensuring their performance on a nationwide basis. To do this, an organization is implied which (a) has all the organizational capabilities discussed in the previous section, (b) can exercise these capabilities nationwide, and (c) can articulate and coordinate the activities of all other organizations. Under the circumstances of a nuclear attack, it can be assumed that the national government is the only organization that could conceivably fill the recovery management role.

The special capabilities and characteristics the recovery management must have in order to fulfill its function include:

1. A nationwide damage assessment capability
2. Means for evaluating, and selecting from, alternative action plans
3. Means for obtaining compliance with the action by all other organizations

4. Means for obtaining feedback information on the status of implementation

5. Means for evaluating performance and adapting subsequent actions

6. Acceptance by other organizations and the public as a credible source of information

7. Acceptance by other organizations and the public as the legitimate ultimate authority

8. Security against coups

9. Orderly means for temporarily suspending and guaranteeing return to normal democratic procedures.*

The total set of capabilities required of the recovery management system has obvious far-reaching implications for civil defense planning and preattack preparations. In addition to the technical questions of how such capabilities can be created before the event, there is at least one which is a most sensitive and difficult question for American society to address. The capabilities of the recovery management system which have been indicated lead to the requirement for a highly centralized system with the ability to exercise its authority at all levels of the society. But this requirement conflicts with the division of responsibilities and authority built into our federal form of government and embodied in existing civil defense legislation. A thorough reexamination of the organizational bases for recovery management in a postattack situation would appear in order.

Concluding Comment

We have tried to ask the questions which need answering before meaningful predictions of societal recovery can be made. The answers to all are variable, depending upon attack and preattack

* EDITOR's NOTE—The reader will note that the requirements here enumerated are similar to those postulated in earlier chapters but not identical with them.

assumptions; the answers to some are as yet unknown; and the answers to most are inadequate. Some of the requirements for societal recovery have become more clear, and the obstacles in the way of determining whether the requirements are likely to be met in any hypothetical instance have become more evident. Societal recovery would depend upon successfully meeting a whole set of requirements, and different preattack and attack assumptions would lead to different estimates of the likelihood of any given requirement being met. It is easy to imagine preattack and attack conditions under which the likelihood of meeting the requirements is very low and others where it is high. Societal recovery appears possible under some conditions, but difficult to achieve under all of them.

There are many ways for society to fail to achieve recovery goals, and only a few for it to succeed. It is problematical that it could succeed even with extensive prior preparations; it is unlikely that it could succeed without them.

Consideration of most, if not all, of the requisites for societal recovery revealed that prior preparations could make a substantial difference in the probability of their occurrence. Prior preparations could not guarantee but could increase the probability of the requisites being satisfied and increase the range of conditions over which the requisites could be established. The provision of shelter and other means for reducing the magnitude of attack effects on people and property can be assumed to be of first importance. No less important is the preservation of organizational capabilities throughout society and the establishment of society-wide recovery management capabilities. For a range of attacks, there is a reasonable likelihood that the "raw material" of societal recovery—people, resources, and environment—would exist in the immediate post-attack period. The existence of sufficient organizational and recovery management capabilities is far more problematical and even more dependent on the particular prior preparations made. If this is true, we would expect that if societal recovery should fail, it would be most likely because of the inability of the system to utilize the surviving people and resources to accomplish the tasks on which recovery depends.

Notes

1 It is possible to grant the possible postattack efficacy of civil defense and still oppose it on the grounds that any serious preparations would be provocative, leading to a greater probability of war occurring, or that it diverts effort that could otherwise be expended to reduce the probability of war.

2 David M. Heer, *After Nuclear Attack: A Demographic Inquiry* (New York: Praeger, 1965); R. A. Dentler and P. Cutright, "Social Effects of Nuclear War," *Nuclear Information* (St. Louis Citizens' Committee for Nuclear Information), July 1963.

3 Heer, p. 392.

4 David M. Heer, "Demographic Aspects of Vulnerability and Recuperation from Nuclear Attack," in S. D. Vestermark, Jr., ed., *Vulnerabilities of Social Structure: Studies of the Social Dimensions of Nuclear Attack.* HSR–RR–66/21–Cr (McLean, Va.: Human Sciences Research, 1966), p. 310.

5 Dentler and Cutright, p. 2.

6 Heer, p. 9.

7 Dentler and Cutright, p. 2.

8 W. W. Pendleton, "The Demography of Nuclear War: Specifying Surviving Populations," prepared in conjunction with OCD Project 3514A (McLean, Va.: Human Sciences Research, 1965).

9 For an extended discussion of the issues involved in restarting production, see Sidney G. Winter, Jr., "Societal Recovery after Nuclear War: The Economic Dimensions," in S. D. Vestermark, Jr., ed. See also, Hirshleifer's chapter on economic recovery in the same work and Chapter 11 in this volume.

10 For a detailed and extended analysis of the problems the researcher faces as he attempts to draw valid inferences about postattack behavioral phenomena from the evidence available, see S. D. Vestermark, Jr., "Social Vulnerability and Recovery as Analytic Problems," in S. D. Vestermark, Jr., ed. See also I. Janis, Chapter 3 in this volume.

11 *Field Studies of Disaster Behavior: An Inventory* (Washington,

D.C.: National Academy of Sciences, 1961); and George W. Baker and Dwight W. Chapman, eds., *Man and Society in Disaster* (New York: Basic Books, 1962).

12 *The Effects of Strategic Bombing on German Morale*, Vols. I & II (Washington, D.C.: Morale Division, U.S. Strategic Bombing Survey, 1947). Also, *The Effects of Strategic Bombing on Japanese Morale* (Washington, D.C.: Morale Division, U.S. Strategic Bombing Survey, 1947).

13 Peter G. Nordlie and Robert D. Popper, *Social Phenomena in a Post-Nuclear Attack Situation: Synopses of Likely Social Effects of the Physical Damage* (Arlington, Va.: Human Sciences Research, 1961).

14 *An Approach to the Study of Social and Psychological Effects of Nuclear Attack* (McLean, Va.: Human Sciences Research, 1963). Also, S. D. Vestermark, Jr., ed.

15 Albert D. Biderman, et al., *Historical Incidents of Extreme Over-Crowding* (Washington, D.C.: Bureau of Social Science Research, 1963). Also, A. D. Biderman, *The Relevance of Studies of Internment for the Problems of Shelter Habitability*, reprinted from Symposium on *Human Problems in the Utilization of Fallout Shelters*, Publication 800 (Washington, D.C.: National Research Council, National Academy of Sciences, n.d.); Saul B. Sells, *Military Small Group Performance under Isolation and Stress: An Annotated Bibliography*, Project 8243–11 (Fort Wainwright, Alaska: Arctic Aeromedical Laboratory, 1961).

16 Allen H. Barton, *Social Organization under Stress*, Disaster Study No. 17 (Washington, D.C.: National Research Council, National Academy of Sciences, 1963).

17 N. F. Busch, *Two Minutes to Noon* (The Story of the Great Tokyo Earthquake and Fire) (New York: Simon & Schuster, 1962); Leon Gouré, *The Siege of Leningrad* (Stanford Univ. Press, 1962); Dmitri V. Pavlov, *Leningrad 1941: The Blockade* (Univ. of Chicago Press, 1965); John Hersey, *Hiroshima* (New York: Alfred A. Knopf, 1958); T. Nagai, *We of Nagasaki* (New York: Duell, Sloan, & Pearce, 1958); Alexander Werth, *Russia at War: 1941–1945* (New York: E. P. Dutton, 1964); and I. L. Janis, *Air War and Emotional Stress; Psychological Studies of Bombing and Civil Defense* (New York: McGraw-Hill, 1951).

18 Otto Klineberg, Department of Social Psychology, Columbia University, "Dangers of the Shelter Psychology" (paper, n.d.).

19 Herman Kahn, *On Thermonuclear War* (Princeton Univ. Press, 1960), p. 84.

20 See in this connection the enumeration of desirable features of shelters in Chapter 9.

21 The distinction drawn here is in part similar to the distinction between organizational and technological considerations discussed by Jack Hirshleifer, *Disaster and Recovery: A Historical Survey* (Santa Monica, Calif.: RAND Corp., 1963) and Sidney G. Winter, "Societal Recovery after Nuclear War: The Economic Dimensions," in S. D. Vestermark, Jr., ed. Both Hirshleifer and Winter use *organizational considerations* to refer to the management of human and material resources and *technological considerations* to refer to the availability of such resources. We divide organizational considerations into two categories: (a) those considerations that apply to any organization within the society and (b) those that apply to the organization whose function it is to guide the activities of all other organizations. This latter category applies to what we have labeled the *recovery management system* and whose characteristics will be discussed separately in the next section.